The Renaissance III

History of Art

Illustration on title-page:

Hans Holbein the Younger
Augsburg 1497/1498-London 1543
Henry VIII
Oil on canvas 34″ × 29″
Palazzo Barberini, Rome

Illustration on cover·

Lucas Cranach the Elder
Jesus and the Little Children
Oil on wood
Winterthur Museum

History of Painting

Prehistoric Painting
Egyptian Painting and the Ancient East
Greek and Etruscan Painting
Roman and Palaeochristian Painting
Byzantine and Russian Painting
Romanesque Painting
Gothic Painting I
Gothic Painting II
The Renaissance I
The Renaissance II
The Renaissance III
The XVIIth Century I
The XVIIth Century II
The XVIIIth Century
Romanticism
Impressionism
Expressionism
Post-Impressionism
Cubism
Futurism and Dadaism
Surrealism
The Great Masters of Modern Painting
Abstract Painting
Chinese Painting
Japanese Painting
Islamic and Indian Painting
American Painting

History of Sculpture

Primitive Art: Africa, Oceania,
Pre-Columbian American
Egypt and the Near East
India and Southern Asia: Khmer, Bali
Greece, Etruscan Art, Roman Art
Romanesque Art, Gothic Art
The Renaissance
The XVIIth and XVIIIth Centuries
The XIXth and XXth Centuries
The Far East

The Renaissance III

lie-Charles Flamand

Heron Books, London

Series edited by Claude Schaeffner
Artistic adviser:
Jean-Clarence Lambert
Illustrations chosen by André Held
Assistant: Martine Caputo
Translated by J. B. Donne

The colour illustrations in the first part were provided by:
Giraudon, Paris: pages 6, 9, 17, 28, 33, 34, 36, 37, 39, 40, 43, 44, 47, 49, 50, 58, 61, 65, 66, 76, 79, 81, 82, 85, 87, 91, 94
André Held, Lausanne: jacket, and pages 3, 10, 13, 14, 15, 16, 18, 21, 23, 24, 26, 35, 45, 52, 55, 56, 70, 74, 88
Bulloz, Paris: pages 22, 27, 62, 69, 73, 86

The black-and-white illustrations in the Dictionary were provided by:
Giraudon, Paris: pages 146, 150, 151, 152, 153, 154, 157, 161, 166, 168, 169, 174, 180, 181, 182, 188, 189, 192, 194, 195, 197, 201;
André Held, Lausanne: pages 148, 155, 159, 175, 186, 187;
Anderson-Giraudon, Paris: page 191;
Anderson-Viollet, Paris: page 190;
ND Viollet, Paris: page 170.

Table of Contents

Grünewald
Virgin in the Garden
Musée de l'Œuvre, Strasbourg

Introduction

There are some words that have become separated from their simple, natural meaning and, thanks to the aura that surrounds them and the echoes that have borne them down the centuries, have acquired such a power of suggestion and a fascination that they have almost become spells. Thus for the majority of people, however remote may be their enjoyment of the arts, despite the respect for culture to which modern man is almost completely enslaved, the Renaissance means Italy, and in particular painting. This denotes a general familiarity with the term, but also a broadening of its significance. The majority of people are here in the right for, in fact, the Renaissance is as essential in Italy as it is incidental elsewhere, and its principal representatives, as well as its chief chroniclers, were indeed painters. Nor is it wrong to regard the art of the Renaissance as a return to the aesthetic ideals of Antiquity (provided that one realizes that the Latin influence is dominant, while that of Hellenism is weak), but it is a short-sighted attitude which does not long survive a close study of two and a half centuries of the history of painting. In actual fact, the Renaissance (which finds expression in the world of science, literature and the arts, and especially in painting) marks the beginning of that great development in man which terminate in the French Revolution, and out of which modern man is born. In the history of this development, Italy can no more lay claim to the heritage of the Renaissance than France can to that of the French Revolution itself. The fact that painters, as can here so clearly be seen, were the prime movers, may cause astonishment to some. But painting is a sign of the times: paintings are like bright meteors in the heavens which reflect the destiny of civilizations.

Time and again over the years it has been remarked that the Renaissance brought to a close the Middle Ages, and that thereafter the artist became an individual. Historically, it has been the custom to extend the Middle Ages down to the Fall of Constantinople to the Turks, on 29th May 1453, and to state that by this fatal date such magnificent artists whose names have been preserved from anonymity as the Van Eyck brothers in Flanders, and Masolino and Masaccio in Italy, had already disappeared from the scene... Without going into too much detail, one can say that this attitude is not completely wrong. Indeed it serves to clarify the problem, which consists, basically, in determining a limit in time, and it is, after all, as difficult to trace the frontier between two periods or two schools of painting as it is between two human communities. On the other hand, it is well known that only since the Renaissance have we developed the custom of appreciating or even of under-appreciating the work and personality of painters as individuals, a custom that has grown stronger than ever in recent times. In contrast to the Middle Ages then, let us accept the idea of regarding the artist of the Renaissance as a man apart from the masses, as much through his style as his ideas, as an undermining influence who contradicts and even denies the past. But, let me repeat, there are several kinds of Renaissance.

In Italy, doubtless on account of the long period of civil war, the painters from the fifteenth century onwards are violent, and the upheaval which they introduce into art is almost an insurrection. In Germany the situation is more or less the same, but it arises half-a-century later, and under the undoubted influence of the Italian example. France first underwent a sort of slow crystallization of the individuality of the artist in the Romanist and Gothic schools, and then an invasion of Italian painting as a repercussion of the invasion of Italy

Bruegel the Elder
Landscape with the Fall of Icarus (detail)
Musée des Beaux-Arts, Brussels

by the French armies. Thereupon the revolution in Italian art became established from the Loire to Fontainebleau and Paris, and the country was conquered. In Flanders, on the other hand, tradition remained almost intact, at least during the early period of reawakening.

Though it did not have such a spectacular beginning, the Flemish Renaissance is as old as that of Italy. Hubert and Jan Van Eyck were contemporaries of Filippo Brunelleschi, the architect of the Duomo in Florence, and Roger Van der Weyden comes only slightly later. The invention of wood engraving and, especially, that of oil-painting are Flemish and date from the beginning of the fifteenth century. Thereafter, through the identification of painters and the development of technical processes, the Renaissance progresses in the wealthy cities of the Netherlands. Gothic painting does not disappear, indeed it persists, and it is within its rather outworm frame that the new tendencies make their appearance, attaining the height of their achievement in Memlinc in the second half of the fifteenth century. Later, painting leaves the Gothic behind and, in Patinir and above all Hieronymus Bosch, becomes the supreme expression of poetic lyricism and the sense of wonder. The Flemish Renaissance is brought to a superb end by Bruegel the Elder who, helped and followed by his sons, prepares the way for the great masters of the seventeenth century.

So rich are these almost two hundred years of Flemish painting that, in comparison, the French Renaissance looks rather slight. Its beginnings were the same, however, and the painters of the school of Avignon and Jean Fouquet arose out of mediaeval art in the same way as the earliest Flemish painters. Then, the flow from across the Alps became so great that today one has to make an effort to see anything more in the school of Fontainebleau than an Italian off-shoot, though this in no way diminishes our appreciation of the mannerism, eroticism and dream-like qualities which the painters of the day made fashionable, and which continued in vogue for most of the reign of Louis XIII.

As to Germany, her Renaissance comes somewhat later than the Flemish and Italian, but it is so magnificent when it does arise that it is dazzling to contemplate. Furthermore, unlike other countries Germany has produced painters worthy of the name only—with the exception of the Romantic landscape painter Caspar David Frierich—during the Gothic age, the Renaissance and in this century before Hitler's rise to power. The period from the last third of the fifteenth century to the end of the first half of the sixteenth is brief indeed, but what a magnificent group of artists it produced along the banks of the Rhine! Hans Baldung, Nicolas Manuel, Urs Graf, Dürer, Grünewald, Altdorfer, Cranach, Holbein—such a profusion of genius that it is quite amazing that German painting should afterwards have fallen into so pitiful a state of mediocrity, and have remained there for so long. The mysterious power of Dürer alone is in itself devastating. As much a poet and a philosopher as a painter, he casts a dark light around us, and one has the impression that if one could understand him totally and completely, one would understand the universe.

From Northern Europe down to the far South, the painters of the Renaissance changed and broadened man's outlook on the world. Far from considering it as a reaction, we are justified in saying today that the Renaissance constituted a revolution. Its painters are heroes whom we regard with admiration and love.

André Pieyre de Mandiargues

School of Fontainebleau
End of 16th century
Lady at her Toilet
Oil on wood 38″ × 29″
Museum, Dijon

France

It is with the accession of Francis I in 1515 that the Renaissance really begins to take place in France. The young king—he was only twenty-one when he came to the throne—was intelligent, widely read, and extravagant, and he enjoyed a life of luxury. He did everything in his power to encourage the new movement, whose aims he appreciated, and which was to make his reign a brilliant one. During the French wars with Italy he had travelled from Milan as far south as Naples when the Italian Renaissance was at its height, and as a result he hoped to see the arts similarly reborn in his own country. Furthermore, his natural rivalry with the German Emperor, Charles V, himself a great patron of the arts, extended also to the artistic field. At great expense he bought the works of such Italian masters as Leonardo da Vinci, Raphael, Titian, Fra Bartolommeo and Sebastiano del Piombo. He invited Leonardo to France, and granted him the Château de Cloux near Amboise. But Leonardo was reaching the end of his life, and he died three years later without having founded a school. Subsequently, Francis I persuaded Andrea del Sarto to visit France, but after he had painted a few pictures at the court, including his *Charity*, he was entrusted on a mission to Florence to collect works of art. However, he squandered the money which the king had advanced him, and never returned to France. Finally, the king engaged first Giovanni Battista Rosso and then Francesco Primaticcio, who in turn persuaded Niccolo dell'Abbate to join him. Together they succeeded in training a large number of young French artists and thus founded the First School of Fontainebleau.

The School of Fontainebleau

Giovanni Battista Rosso*, sometimes known as 'Rosso Fiorentino', arrived at the French court in 1530. He was the first person to work on the Palais de Fontainebleau, which Francis I had just started to build. On several occasions the king had tried to induce Michelangelo to undertake the work, but the latter had finally decided to remain in Italy. However, Rosso was on excellent terms with Michelangelo and it is assumed that the king turned to him on Michelangelo's recommendation.

Rosso began his career in Florence, but then moved to Rome, where he led a life of pleasure and dissipation in the company of a merry group of friends, which included the famous Florentine, Benvenuto Cellini. Nevertheless, he found time to carry out a great deal of work, but none of it has survived apart from two very mediocre frescoes, *The Creation of Eve* and *Original Sin* in the Cesi Chapel of Santa Maria della Pace, and a charming little piece, *The Challenge of the Muses*, now in the Louvre. When the troops of the Constable of Bourbon entered Rome, 'poor Rosso,' Vasari tells us, 'was taken prisoner by the Germans, who treated him barbarously: they stripped him from head to foot, and made him bear loads on his back and clear out almost the entire contents of a butcher's shop. Eventually he succeeded in fleeing to Perugia, where he was kindly given shelter by a painter named Domenico da Parigi, who supplied him with clothes'. Thereafter for a period of three years, Rosso wandered from place to place. From this period

*An asterisk after a name or word refers the reader to the Dictionary at the end of the volume for further details.

dates an extremely violent work, *Christ Mourned by His People*, which adorns the altar of the Orfanelle in Borgo San Sepolcro. He received the invitation of Francis I in the autumn of 1530 while he was staying in Venice with his friend Aretino, the famous satirist.

His first production in France was a *Leda and the Swan*, now in the National Gallery. For a long time this was thought to be by Michelangelo, but it is now known to be a copy of one of the latter's works. Immediately after this, Rosso began the most important work of his life, the decoration of the Francis I Gallery* in the Palais de Fontainebleau, in which his astonishing imagination was given free rein, and which had such a profound influence on French art. The painted figures appear in large panels, variously adorned with modelled vases, garlands, shells, masks, rams' skulls, fruit, fantastic animals, and so forth. It appears that it was the king himself who inspired this completely novel arrangement, which involves the use of woodwork, stucco and fresco. In the words of Pierre Francastel, 'In the Francis I Gallery one sees the beginnings of that alliance of art, craft and design which is the unchallenged glory of classical France'. A whole team of painters and workers in stucco, whose names have been preserved in 'the king's building accounts', assisted Rosso in this task, which was to keep him employed for eight whole years, up to the time of his death. The frescoes consist of a series of thirteen main subjects, drawn for the most part from ancient history and mythology, as follows: a *Sacrificial Scene*, *The Elephant with Fleurs de Lis*, *Amphonimus and Anapicus Bearing their Parents out of Catana Destroyed by an Eruption of Etna*, *The Nymph of Fontainebleau*, *The Shipwreck of Ajax*, *Achilles being Taught by the Centaur Chiron*, *Love Chastized by his Mother Venus for having Loved Psyche*, *The Fight of the Lapithae and the Centaurs*, *The Fountain of Youth*, *Venus Weeping for Adonis* and *Cleobis and Biton Drawing their Mother's Chariot to the Temple of Juno*, and finally two compositions showing Francis I himself in Roman dress, *The Unity of the State* and *Ignorance Driven Forth*. Moreover, it seems that all these subjects bear allegorical interpretations referring to the great king's powers of intellect and his love affairs, as well as the main events in his life and reign. Thus the *Elephant with Fleurs de Lis* represents the king's power; *The Fight of the Lapithae and the Centaurs* his valour in war; *The Shipwreck of Ajax* is an allusion to the disastrous Battle of Pavia, in which the king was taken prisoner; *Venus Weeping for Adonis* recalls the death of the dauphin.

Rosso is a Florentine Mannerist who was considerably influenced by the work of Michelangelo, and who had an extraordinary gift as an ornamentalist. His fertile imagination continually developed fresh ideas. His drawing is skilful, his compositions are full of spirited movement. He is not lacking in elegance, but he strives after vigorousness, and a use of high lights or deep shadow. His influence in France was enormous, and spread as far afield as Flanders and Germany. According to Vasari, Rosso's death resulted from a tragic error. He had been robbed, and his suspicions fell on his friend and assistant, Francesco Pellegrino, whom he accused and had put to the torture. But the latter was found innocent, and Rosso, in a fit of remorse, poisoned himself. He died on 14th November 1540.

Francesco di Bologna, called Primaticcio
1505-70
Alexander Taming Bucephalus
Fresco in the Duchesse d'Etampes' bedchamber
Château de Fontainebleau

Primaticcio
Alexander Offering a Crown to Campaspe
Fresco in the Duchesse d'Etampes' bedchamber
Château de Fontainebleau

After Rosso's death, Francesco Primaticcio* was entrusted with completing the work at Fontainebleau, where he arrived when he was only twenty-seven years old. Primaticcio was first employed on decorating the King's Chamber*. These decorations have all since disappeared, but it is possible to reconstruct them from old engravings and pencil studies. They consisted of paintings and stucco-work, whose general arrangement followed that used by Rosso in the Francis I Gallery. Primaticcio helped Rosso to decorate Pomona's Pavilion in the gardens of Fontainebleau, and they also worked together on the paintings in the Canopy Pavilion, built on the edge of the lake, which was where Charles V stayed when he visited Francis I. (These buildings have since been destroyed.) Tradition says that the two painters loathed each other, but this seems highly exaggerated. It is quite possible that there existed a feeling of rivalry between them, but the fact that they carried out all this work in common shows that there must have been a certain amount of agreement between them.

At the beginning of 1540, the king employed Primaticcio to go to Italy to collect ancient works of art with which he wished to embellish his living-quarters and gardens. Primaticcio succeeded in finding one hundred and twenty-five statues and busts. He also took mouldings of famous ancient sculptures, including the *Laocoon* of the Tiber, the *Commodus Hercules*, and the Cnidos *Venus*, from which bronze casts were made in France. It was during this period of absence that Rosso died, and on his return in 1542, Primaticcio was put completely in charge of the work at Fontainebleau. First he completed the

Antoine Caron
Massacres under the Triumvirs
Canvas 46″ × 77″
Louvre, Paris

Francis I Gallery, which Rosso had been unable to finish, by including two paintings, a *Danaë* and a *Semele*. He then turned his attention to the bedchamber of the king's favourite, the Duchesse d'Etampes. This room, which became part of a stairwell under Louis XV, was decorated in the same style as the Francis I Gallery. The subject of the series of paintings was the history of Alexander the Great.

The two greatest undertakings that Primaticcio then worked on were the paintings for the bathing chamber and those for the Ulysses Gallery. The sumptuous bathing chamber was decorated with the *History of Jupiter and Callisto*, which contained a beautiful composition of mythological figures executed with startling vigour. These buildings were destroyed in 1697. The Ulysses Gallery*, pulled down in the reign of Louis XV, was over 150 yards long and contained 161 paintings covering the walls and vaulted ceiling. Those on the ceiling were divided into a series of fifteen panels, which was reminiscent of the Loggie painted by Raphael in the Vatican. Primaticcio represented the *The Hours* and various scenes from the *History of the Gods*, whose arrangement was partly due to astrological symbolism. One of his very rare easel-paintings has survived, *Ulysses and Penelope*, which was repeated in one of the frescoes. It enables us to gain some idea of the highly poetic and charming way in which Primaticcio handled the 58 episodes from the *Odyssey* which were the subjects for the murals. This enormous work, which took seven years to complete, was carried out with the assistance of Niccolo dell'Abbate, the third of the important Italian artists to work at Fontainebleau. Only

three quarters of the work were finished when Francis I died in 1547. In the reign of Henry II, Primaticcio undertook the decoration of the Ballroom*. In the eight pendentives between the windows there are large scenes full of lively figures. Unfortunately, nothing of the original work actually survives, since it was all repainted by poor artists under Louis-Philippe. Once again, it is only from Primaticcio's designs that one can form any opinion of the quality of the expression and technique of the originals. On Henry II's death in 1559, Catharine de Medici, who held the reins of power, appointed Primaticcio director of the king's buildings in place of Philibert Delorme*. Thereafter, he confined himself almost entirely to architecture and the arrangement of works of sculpture. He died at the age of sixty-five, at the height of his fame, in 1570. He had spent almost forty years of his life in the service of the kings of France.

Jean-Louis Vaudoyer has written of him: 'This Italian from Bologna long breathed the air of the French Gâtinais; he became permeated with it, and in spite of himself he placed some of it around his figures. His adopted country eventually triumphed over his country of birth. The School of Fontainebleau is a grafted school; but through the roots of the tree, the graft was nourished from French earth; and it is to French blood that it owes its growth, health and life.'

Niccolo dell'Abbate

In 1552 Niccolo dell'Abbate arrived in France. He had been invited by Henry II at the suggestion of Primaticcio, who, during his official travels in Italy, had recognized his excellence. At the outset, Niccolo was granted the signal honour of painting the portraits of Henry II and Catharine de Medici. Primaticcio quickly came to rely on him, and for

Antoine Caron
1521-99
The Sibyl of Tibur
Canvas 49″ × 67″
Louvre, Paris

eighteen years the two artists worked together continuously. This close association, unparalleled in the history of art, of a man of ideas on the one hand, and on the other of a man capable of putting them into practice, and at the same time capable of inventing poetic ideas with the same fertile variety and elegance, the same freedom and versatility, gave birth in particular to the Ulysses Gallery and the Ballroom. Certainly, Primaticcio's glory was increased by the fame of the painter, and the day that he succeeded in bringing Niccolo to Fontainebleau, he did a magnificent service to his own reputation as well as the body of his work.

'In contrast with Primaticcio and his ideal of pure decoration, Niccolo appears singularly natural and more of a colourist; beneath his brush, mythology always takes on an air of amorous and romantic enchantment. For him, nature means a landscape out of a fable: he introduces marvels and wanders into the School of Fontainebleau; at the same time his sensuality causes him to be more realistic in his treatment of his subjects.[1] He has been more fortunate than Primaticcio in the number of his easel-paintings that have survived, despite the story recorded by the old historian Sauval, according to whom, 'Queen Anne of Austria, on becoming regent in 1643, had paintings to the value of more than one hundred thousand crowns burnt at Fontainebleau, since she considered them too free in their treatment of pagan subjects'.

Niccolo dell'Abbate had three sons, Giulio-Camillo, Cristoforo and Camillo, all of whom accompanied him to France and helped him in his work. The first became his principal assistant and, after his father's death in 1571, he was appointed 'painter and superintendent of paintings at Fontainebleau'. One of the last of Niccolo's undertakings

[1] Sylvie Béguin: *L'Ecole de Fontainebleau*, Paris, 1963.

School of Fontainebleau
Birth of St John the Baptist
Louvre, Paris

Anonymous master of the 16th century
Sabina Poppaea
Oil on wood 32″ × 24″
Musée d'Art et d'Histoire, Geneva

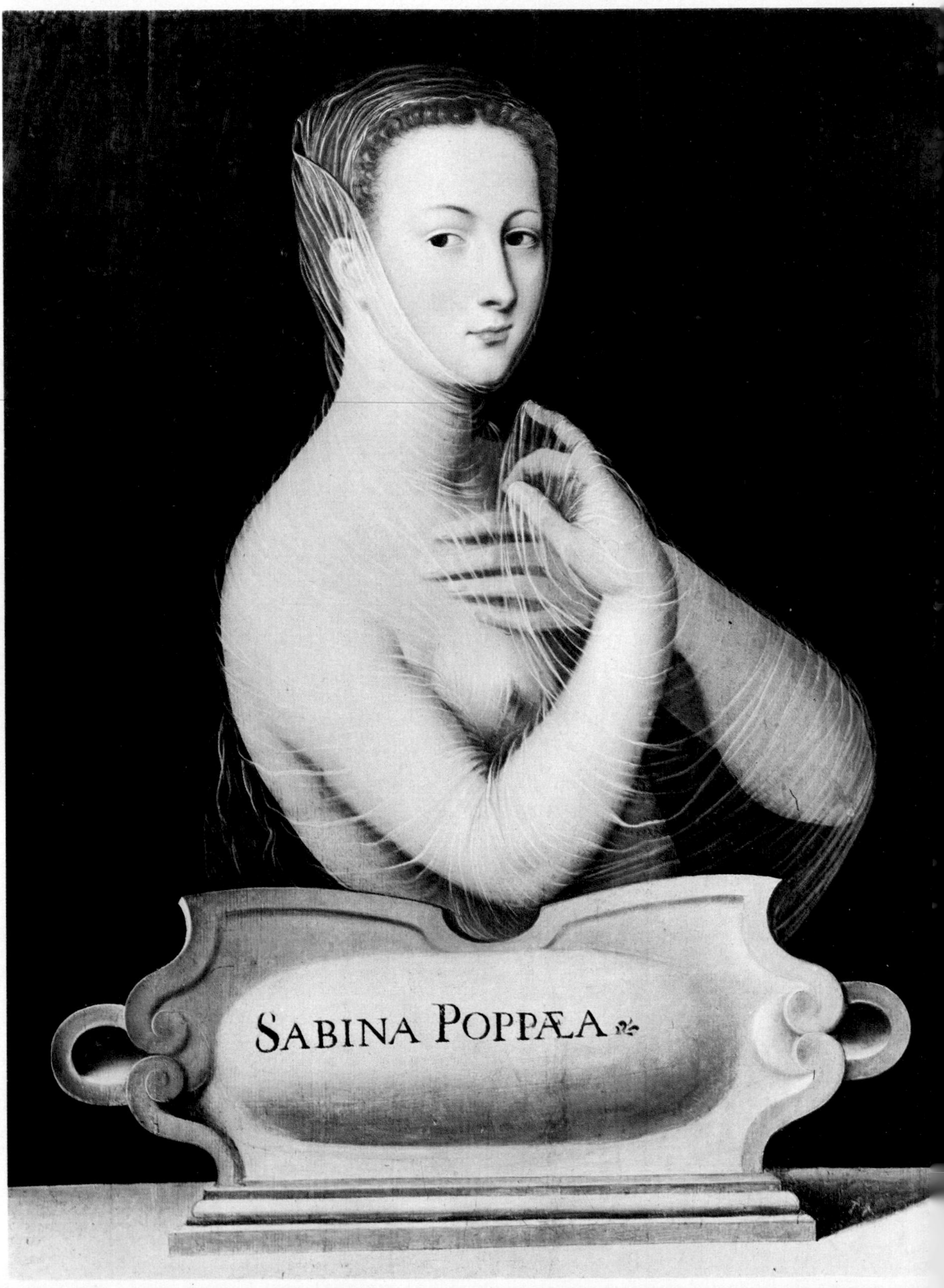

was the ornamentation, carried out with the assistance of Giulio-Camillo, of five triumphal arches for the solemn entry of Charles IX and Elizabeth of Austria into Paris. On this occasion he also decorated the hall of the Bishop's Palace, for which, again with the aid of his son, he painted sixteen historical and allegorical scenes, whose subjects were taken from the works of Ronsard and Daurat. Finally, it should be mentioned that he supplied Léonard Limosin* with the designs for the celebrated enamels in the Sainte-Chapelle.

Jean Cousin, Father and Son

The first of the French painters to come under the influence of the Italian style was Jean Cousin of Sens. He was not a court artist, he received no pension from the king, nor did he form part of the Fontainebleau group. He was a provincial painter who settled in Paris in middle life and worked on his own and not under the immediate supervision of the Italians. But he was also a man with a strong personality, comparable to a certain degree with a Leonardo da Vinci or an Albrecht Dürer. In fact, he was not only an artist in stained glass, a painter, sculptor, engraver and architect, but also a remarkable theoretician. We know relatively little about his life, which is largely shrouded in mystery.

For a long time, scholars confused him with his son of the same name. Jean Cousin the Elder* was born in 1490 at Soucy, just outside Sens. His family were humble vine-growers. Between 1512 and 1515 he served his apprenticeship under two artists in stained glass, Jacques Hympe and Tassin Gassot, who were employed on the stained-glass windows of Sens Cathedral. After 1526 he is recorded in deeds as being a qualified painter and expert surveyor. He was officially employed in this capacity for the whole bailliage of Sens. Nevertheless, he continued his work as an artist, and in the chronicle of the monastery of Vauluisant we find that, in about 1530, the head of this community 'commisioned the tabernacle of the main altar of the church, consisting of woodwork, carving and painting... the paintings [being carried out] by a certain Jehan Cousin'. According to an old tradition, he was responsible for two of the beautiful stained-glass windows of Sens Cathedral, that in the chapel of St Eutropius depicting *Scenes from the Life of the Saint and his Martyrdom* (this masterpiece was completed in 1530, the date being inscribed on Herod's chair), and that in the chapel of Our Lady of Loretto, showing *The Sibyl of Tibur being Consulted by the Emperor Augustus*, dated 1542. As his fame increased, so did his fortune, and in about 1540 Jean Cousin decided to settle in Paris. 'In his huge mansion in the Rue des Marais,' wrote Maurice Roy, 'were workrooms and a study which the master hardly ever left, for since he had made his reputation and his wealth increased day by day, there was little need for him himself to work outside, and he generally contented himself with supplying the plans or designs of the work he was asked to undertake, and this was then carried out by professional contractors.'[1] Thus he produced patterns for copes and pieces of embroidery, the design for an organ-chest, instructions for raising the famous gold tabernacle onto the main altar of Sens Cathedral, cartoons for tapestries*,

[1] Maurice Roy: *Les deux Jean Cousin*, Sens, 1909.

and numerous stained-glass windows, including those of *The Approach of the Last Judgement according to the Apocalypse* in the Sainte-Chapelle at Vincennes, as well as the *Martyrdom of St Lawrence*, *The Woman of Samaria Talking to Christ*, *St Peter Healing a Paralytic* and *King Solomon's Reception for the Queen of Sheba* (these are known only from Félibrien's description, since they were destroyed in 1775). Jean Cousin also produced a large number of wood-engravings*. He would undertake work which today is carried out only by the poorest artists. Booksellers found his assistance invaluable whenever they wished to embellish a work with large blocks, or even when they simply required a colophon, lettering, fleurons or tail-pieces. As a sculptor, he is attributed with the notable monument in memory of Admiral Chabot, now in the Louvre. When the Emperor Charles V visited Paris in 1540, Jean Cousin collaborated in the decoration of the two impressive triumphal arches in the Rue Saint-Antoine. Nine years later, when Henry II entered his capital, he was again commissioned, this time with Jean Goujon, to carry out the decorations. He was the first French painter to write about his art. He produced two theoretical works*, a *Book of Perspective* (1560) and a *Book of Portraiture* (1571), published only after his death.

As one can see, Jean Cousin had a many-sided and engaging personality. The first of the French Renaissance painters, he still looked back to an earlier age in the crafts and minor arts, yet his mathematical speculations and his universal curiosity are typical of his time. The only known painting by him, his *Eva Prima Pandora*, clearly reflects his character, while at the same time providing an excellent example of his aesthetic ideals. This allegorical composition, in which the sacred is combined with the profane, is completely within the spirit of the times. It can be compared with the painting of the nymph on the triumphal arch erected on the occasion of Henry II's entry into Paris. Jean Cousin is the first French painter to have taken the nude as a subject for his art. The naked body was certainly not completely absent from paintings before the time of Cousin, but it was usually confined to popular religious art, and was most often used to depict the tortures of the damned. The nude had previously been depicted as extremely ugly, for painters intended to inspire a feeling of repulsion in the viewer, as for example in the numerous representations of *The Dance of Death*. In this case, however, Jean Cousin was clearly inspired by the Venuses of Giorgione and Titian. But his style is still somewhat naïve and severe, his treatment harsh, gaunt and stiff, unlike that of the great Venetian painters, which is much more spontaneous and natural. There is also a sense of affectation in this work.

Jean Cousin the Elder died in Paris *ca* 1561. His son, Jean Cousin the Younger*, followed the style of his father so closely that, combined with the fact that he bore the same name, the two were long presumed to be one and the same person. His greatest work is the famous *Last Judgement*, which long adorned the sacristy of the Franciscans at Vincennes. It earned him the title of 'the French Michelangelo'. It is comparatively small in size, being barely 4′ 6″ high and a little less in width, and yet its landscape of ruin and destruction teems with hundreds of figures, while in heaven above the prophets, saints and cherubim grouped round the Christ passively regard the end of the world. The

Jean Clouet
Brussels *ca* 1468-Paris 1540
Portrait of Francis I, King of France
Oil on wood 38″ × 29″
Louvre, Paris

painter has completely assimilated the new technical developments imported from Italy, and enters into the problems of geometric and bird's-eye perspective, while at the same time demonstrating his complete mastery of anatomy. The treatment is less crude than that of his father. This is the only work that can be attributed to him with certainty.

Antoine Caron

Among the early followers of the School of Fontainebleau, one of the most extraordinary was Antoine Caron. It is only recently, and thanks to the work of two scholars, Gustave Lebel and Jean Ehrmann, that this most important figure has emerged from the mists of oblivion of over three hundred years, though a great deal remains to be known about him. We know that he died in 1599, from an engraving of him by his son-in-law, Thomas de Lau*. As the inscription there states that he had lived seventy-eight years, he must have been born in 1521. He was born in Beauvais, but we do not know who were his first masters. We know only that he worked at first at Beauvais and that he prepared designs

François Clouet
Diana Bathing
Museum, Rouen

François Clouet
Elizabeth of Austria, Queen of France
Ca 1571
Oil on wood 14″ × 11″
Louvre, Paris

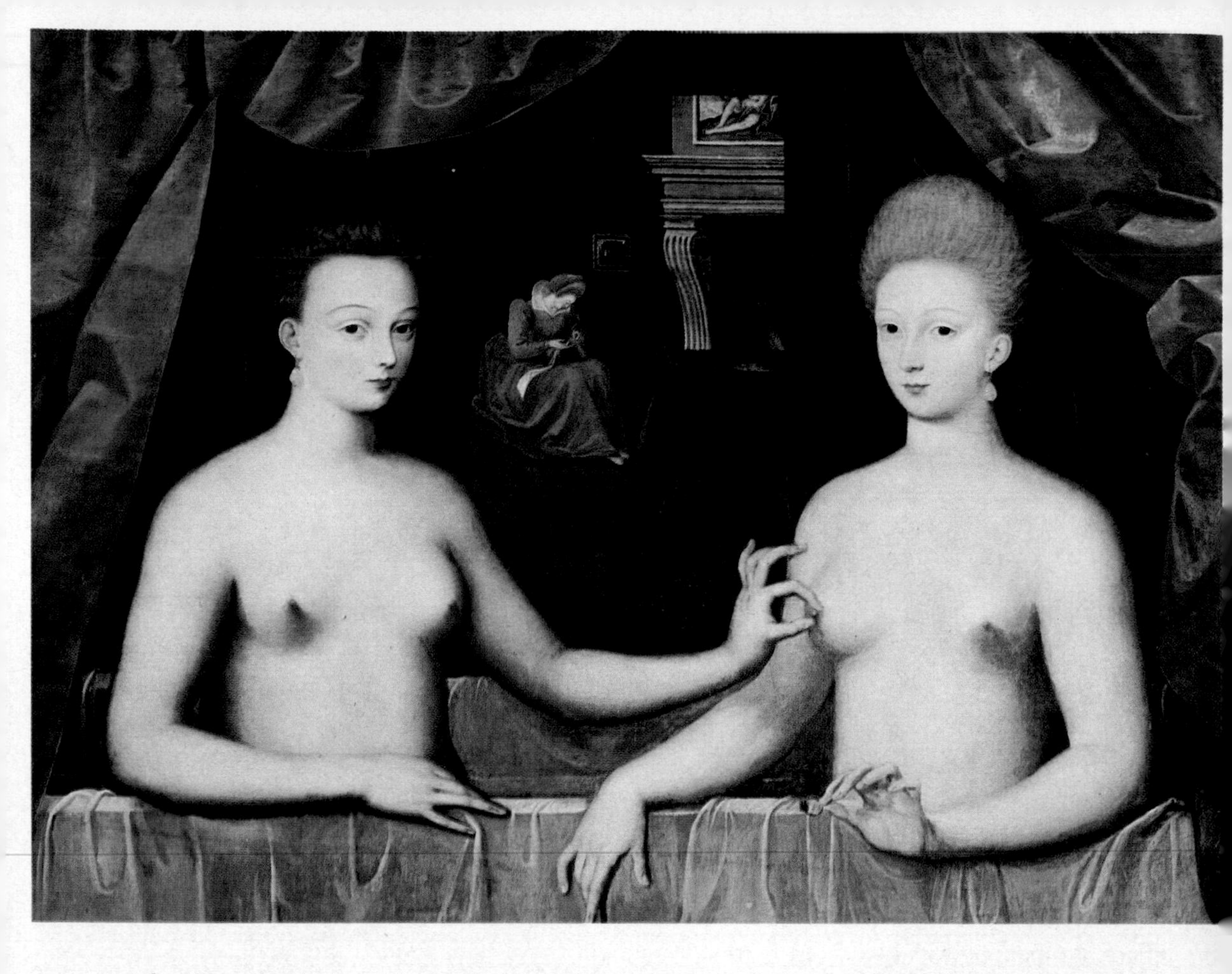

for the stained-glass windows of churches as well as painting religious pictures. According to the chronicler Denis Simon, Caron began his official artistic career in the service of Francis I. He was employed on restoration work under Primaticcio, and so it was among the decorators of Fontainebleau that he received his training in the Italian style. But Niccolo dell'Abbate had an even greater influence on him than Primaticcio. In 1560, he gained favour with Catharine de Medici and became court painter. He was employed in organizing royal occasions and was also expected to record them in drawings and paintings. At court he became a member of a small group of poets and artists which included Ronsard, Daurat and Germain Pilon*, with whom he often had to work on the arrangements for these lavish entertainments.

Caron's pictures consist of a curious mixture of erudite learning expressed with the imagination of a poet, and scenes of court life. Historical allusions are often found to contain the typical flattery of the courtier. In his series of *Triumphs** he takes up one of the classic themes of Italian painting, but he employs it to represent one of those brilliant displays which he excelled in organizing for the court, and disguises it under a subtle mythological allegory. *Augustus and the Sibyl of Tibur** merely records a theatrical performance in the Tuileries given by people wearing ancient costume. Antoine Caron continually referred to contemporary events. For example, he took from Niccolo dell' Abbate the theme of the *Massacres of the Triumvirate*, but gave it a new interpretation in terms of the religious wars of the second half of the sixteenth century. *The Meeting of Abraham and Melchizedek* shows once more the influence of Niccolo, not only in the elegance of the figures themselves, but also in beauty of the landscape. According to Jean Ehrmann, this painting symbolizes the harmonious agreement of spiritual and temporal power, an agreement reached in France after Henry IV's renunciation of

French School of the 16th century
Gabrielle d'Estrée and her Sister
Oil on wood 38″ × 49″
Louvre, Paris

Protestantism (1593), his absolution granted by Pope Clement VIII (1595), and the Treaty of Vervins (1598).

Though Antoine Caron appears first to have been influenced by Flemish masters, his work was soon dominated by the Italian style. But nevertheless, the rather bald, logical arrangement of his compositions, his feeling for clarity which makes even his most complex scenes immediately intelligible, as well as his restrained elegance, are typically French characteristics. One of the most original features of his work is his completely personal interest in the fantastic and flights of the imagination. In fact, he must undoubtedly be considered one of the earliest forerunners of the surrealists.

Unknown Artists

A large number of French paintings of the School of Fontainebleau are by unknown artists. Though in one case it has been possible to group together a number of works which can definitely be attributed to a single painter, nevertheless his identity remains uncertain. He is known as the Master of Flora*, since one of his most attractive productions is his *Triumph of Flora*. It has not even been possible to discover whether he was of French or Italian origin.

Nor have we any knowledge of the authors of a number of paintings portraying mythological subjects, which had been made fashionable by the Italians at Fontainebleau, or else depicting familiar scenes or allegories. The treatment of these works is extremely detailed, rather in the manner of the Flemish School, but one also finds in them that elongation of the figures so dear to Primaticcio. Furthermore, they all reveal a highly erotic content. Among the allegories mention may be made of *Night*, which shows a naked woman asleep, while beside her are a mask, an owl (both symbols evoking the terrors of darkness), and a table on which burns a light; a *Woman between Age and Youth*, depicting a young and an old man both paying court to a beautiful woman who appears to be hesitating in her choice; and *The Allegory of Peace*, showing a nude youth of classic form against the background of a landscape with ruins.

The mythological subjects are always chosen for the opportunities they offer of exalting the female form, for example *Diana the Huntress*, now in the Louvre and thought to be a portrait of Diane de Poitiers, and several paintings of *Diana and Actaeon*, *Venus*, *Ceres*, and so forth. The genre scenes often depict a lady at her toilet, and one of the finest examples of this subject is *The Courtesan* in Dijon Museum. Her nakedness is heightened by the jewellery she is wearing and the intangible veil which is draped over her. The *Tepidarium*, which shows a group of indoor bathers, is a curious reflection on the manners of a period when the bathing-apartments in the Palais de Fontainebleau and in the Palazzo of Ferrara were famous for their luxurious style. This painting, or another in the same vein, probably inspired Ingres' *Turkish Bath* and Chassériau's *Odalisques Bathing*. Many noble ladies had their portraits painted in the bath by artists of the School of Fontainebleau, as can be seen in the picture of *Gabrielle d'Estrées and her Sister*, *the Duchesse de Villars*. This painting, now in the Louvre, shows the two young women

Toussaint Dubreuil
Lady Rising (detail)
Louvre, Paris

out of the picture with a look that is at once provocative and pure-minded. She is the perfect representation of those delicious young girls who gathered at the French court, and who shone as much on account of their superb beauty and uninhibited morals as for their love of art and letters.

The Second School of Fontainebleau

After Henry IV had achieved a peaceful solution to France's problems at the end of the sixteenth century, there followed a period of stability which favoured further development in the arts. The king assembled around him a new group of painters, formed this time of Italianate French and Flemish artists, now known as the Second School of Fontainebleau*. This had only an ephemeral existence, for the art it produced was transitional, preparing the way for the French classicism of the seventeenth century.

Toussaint Dubreuil

Little is known about the life of Toussaint Dubreuil*, though he was one of the three leading figures of the Second School of Fontainebleau. All that is certain is that he was born in Paris in 1561, that he served his apprenticeship under an obscure artist named Médéric Fréminet, the father of Martin Fréminet, and that he died in 1602, at the age of forty-one. Nearly all his works have been destroyed. For the Canopy Pavilion at Fontainebleau he painted *Mars and Venus* above one of the fireplaces and fourteen frescoes depicting the *Story of Hercules*, but the building was pulled down in 1703. He was also employed in restoring the paintings in the Ulysses Gallery. At the Château de Saint-Germain-en-Laye he executed no less than seventy-eight pictures, of which only two survive, an *Ancient Sacrifice* and a *Woman Greeted by a Warrior*. The Kings' Gallery in the Louvre, which he had decorated with the assistance of Jacob Bunel and the Flemish artist Thierry Aertsen, was burnt down in 1661. Dubreuil preferred to draw rather than paint, and he left it to his assistants to translate his designs into paintings. A magnificent collection of his drawings has come down to us, and they reveal a delicacy and precision of workmanship which herald the art of the seventeenth century.

Ambroise Dubois

On Dubreuil's death, Ambroise Dubois* became the leader of the new school. He had settled in France at the age of twenty-five, but it was only after Henri IV's entry into Paris, that is to say, after 1593, that he received the royal summons to Fontainebleau. A few of his works have survived, such as the decorations in the oval Queen's Chamber, in which Louis XII was born. The subjects are drawn from Heliodorus' romance of *Theagenes and Charicleia*, which had become fashionable through a translation by Jacques Amyot. Here Dubois shows his originality in his restrained manner and deep sense of pathos.

His composition is capable, but somewhat static. The Queen's Gallery*, sometimes known as Diana's Gallery, which was considered his masterpiece, has unfortunately been entirely destroyed. One can, however, gain some idea of what it was like from the water-colour paintings that Percier, the famous architect of the time of the Empire, did of it, which reveal its complicated arrangement and magnificent groupings.

Martin Fréminet

Martin Fréminet* is the last representative of the Second School of Fontainebleau, and also the last French painter whom one can consider to belong to the Renaissance. Martin began work in Paris while he was still very young, and executed in particular a *St Sebastian* for the church of Saint-Josse, which we now know only from a contemporary engraving. But Martin was attracted to Italy, and at the age of twenty-five he left for Rome, where among his friends were the poet Mathurin Régnier, who dedicated one of his satires to him, and the engraver Philippe Thomassin*, who engraved several of his works. After working in Rome for six years, Fréminet visited Venice, then stayed for some time in Lombardy, and, before returning to France, painted two pictures in Turin, one of them, a *St Martin*, for Duke Charles-Emmanuel I. By 1603 he was back in Paris, and a little later, on the strength of his growing reputation, he was appointed painter in ordinary and groom to Henry IV, 'in place of and through the death of Dumoustier the Elder', as the 'Statement of Domestic Officers of the King' records. In 1608 he began work on the decoration of the Chapel of the Trinity* at Fontainebleau, which was carried out in oil on plaster. The vaulted ceiling, which is the main part of this vast undertaking and Fréminet's masterpiece, consists of five rectangular panels connected by four ovals. The exuberance of this work, whose subjects are taken from the Old and New Testaments, shows that the artist was endowed with a talent bordering on genius. With astonishing virtuosity Fréminet here tackles the most difficult technical problems of ceiling painting: foreshortening, the depiction of musculation, and the transposition of a complicated decorative design. He has a wonderful sense of grandeur, and his draftsmanship is bold and vigorous. In this he differs considerably from Dubreuil and Dubois. His Roman training predominates in his work, and he was little inclined to soften it under the influence of the more graceful style of Fontainebleau. Furthermore, he rather too flagrantly imitates Michelangelo. Henry IV did not live to see the completion of this particular work, on which the artist was engaged until 1615. When he had finished it, Marie de Medici made him a Knight of the Order of St Michael. Thereafter, Fréminet worked for individual patrons. In particular, he executed eight compositions depicting the *Evangelists* and the *Fathers of the Church* for the square drawing-room in the Château de Richelieu. Here the powerful sculptural figures are treated with a strong contrast of light and shade.

After Fréminet's death the School of Fontainebleau came to an end. It had succeeded in achieving a remarkable balance between Italian virtuosity, northern realism, and French moderation, and its formulations served as a basis for the classical ideal. During the reign of Louis XIII, the sons of Dubois, Fréminet and their contemporaries continued the tradition of palace paintings, but their work was mediocre. It was now Simon Vouet who received the approbation of patrons of art. But for a long time young artists were to make their pilgrimage to Fontainebleau, and Poussin himself acknowledged his enormous debt to the paintings of the royal palace.

Portrait-Painting

During the rule of the Valois kings of France, there existed an extraordinary passion for portraits. Princes and courtiers evinced a desire to amass likenesses of themselves in the most varied costumes. Thus, the fascinating Diane de Poitiers assembled in her bedchamber in the Château d'Anet a curious collection of portraits which showed her in various poses wearing all kinds of dresses which showed off her astonishing beauty to its greatest advantage. Whilst travelling, Catharine de Medici wrote to her children's governess: 'Do not fail to get the painter that you have with you to do portraits from life of all my children, both boys and girls, together with Mary, Queen of Scots [who was affianced to the Dauphin], without omitting anything from their features; but it will suffice if they are drawn in pencil so that they shall be done more quickly, and send them to me as soon as you can.' These sketches, made directly with black-lead crayons and red chalk with some of the highlights painted, clearly played the part occupied by photographs to-day. Moreover, copies were made of them, as nowadays we order prints from a negative. These sketches also served in the marriages of royal children by proxy.

Jean Clouet

Though we do not know when Jean Clouet* was born, it is agreed that he was of Flemish origin. Some scholars maintain, and this is quite probable, that his father was a certain Jehan Cloët, a pupil of Van Orley, who was painting in Brussels in 1475, and carried out work for the Duke of Burgundy. It is unknown when Jean Clouet decided to settle in France, nor why he did so. The 'Statements of the King's Household' show that at the death of Louis XII he was already an official court painter, as were two other famous artists, Jean Bourdichon and Jean Perréal, and two subordinates, Nicolas Belin of Modena and Barthélémy Guéty. Francis I made no changes in this group of royal painters. Thereafter, the accounts of the royal household show the stages of Clouet's promotion. In 1523 he succeeded Bourdichon, who had just died, and became Master of the Robes Extraordinary. Five years later, in 1528, after the death of Perréal, he was appointed to the senior position with the titles of Painter and Master of the King's Bedchamber, and received a salary of two hundred and forty francs a year. In the official records he is referred to by the name of Janet or Jehannet.

Jean Clouet settled in Tours, where he married Jeanne Boucault, the daughter of a goldsmith, some time before 1521. A number of documents exist which record the French king sending a messenger in haste to Tours to collect portraits executed by the

Hieronymus Bosch
The Temptation of St Antony
Central panel
Museum of Ancient Art, Lisbon

court painter. On one occasion, it is Clouet's wife herself who is sent on such a mission. This gives us some idea of the way in which Clouet worked. From time to time he would go to Paris and visit those persons whose portraits were to be painted. He would make a pencil drawing of each from life, and then return to his workshop where he would carry out the paintings on the basis of his sketches. Clouet did not move to Paris until 1529, when he settled in the parish of Saint-Innocent.

The majority of the works by Jean Clouet that have come down to us are drawings. The Musée Condé at Chantilly possesses a remarkable collection of over three hundred which were bought in England by the Duc d'Aumale, and came originally from Catharine de Medici's collection. These crayon portraits were not regarded merely as artist's roughs, but had a value of their own. Those from the hand of Jean Clouet show a marvellous spontaneity: his eye could immediately seize the main features of his models and express them in a few fine bold strokes. These sketches, with their simplicity of line and deliberate objectivity, transport the viewer into the very midst of this witty, refined and well-read society, with all its elegance and its vices, its strange mixture of devotion and debauchery, of bravery on the battlefield and wily scheming, and its cruelty and its politeness. The few paintings known to be from the hand of Jean Clouet show him following in the tradition of the primitives. In the small illustrations representing the *Champions of Marignano* in a manuscript entitled the *Gallic War* in the Bibliothèque Nationale in Paris, and now attributed to Clouet, one finds that he has developed little beyond the highly detailed manner of the miniaturists. With his portraits of *Charlotte of France*, painted *ca* 1521, and *The French Dauphin*, his style becomes more expansive. The subjects are treated on a large scale, and the flesh is bathed in a warm light which also heightens the colouration. In about 1521, Jean Clouet was employed to paint the official portraits of the new monarch, Francis I. Two examples have come down to us. The larger uses the same range of light colours that was so dear to the Flemish artists, with a contrast not only of soft delicate greys but also of violently bright colours. No concession is here made to Italian ideas. Little attention is paid to distance: the subject appears to be laid flat on top of the background. But the details of the decoration and embroidery are treated with minute attention and an astonishingly careful brushwork. Here again, the style is archaic. However, it is curious to note that the artist consciously employs distortion to heighten expression. The second portrait is in a completely different manner. It shows that Clouet had at last perfectly assimilated the chiaroscuro technique. Also attributed to Clouet are two portraits of *William of Montmorency* which are both highly expressive and employ a subtle blend of colours within a rather restricted range. From the point of view of technique they approach the works of Holbein, with whom indeed Clouet has often been compared. The mysterious *Person Holding a Volume of Petrarch* was painted *ca* 1535 according to Louis Dimier. In this picture the artist is once again concerned mainly with light effects. The shadows are heavy and warm, the figure bathed in soft light. One of Clouet's most curious portraits is that of *Guillaume Budé*, discovered in England in 1923. This great French humanist and Greek scholar, who founded the Collège de France, is here shown as an old man of seventy-three. The sitter refers to the portrait in one of his

own works, the *Adversaria*. In one of his last paintings, the *Equestrian Portrait of Francis I*, Clouet returns once again to the careful technique of the miniaturists. This work, with its astonishing virtuosity and its remarkably mannered style, recalls the portraits of the *Champions of Marignano* in the *Manuscript of the Gallic War*. A letter of Francis I's dated November 1541 mentions that Jean Clouet had died at the end of the previous year. Since he was a foreigner who had never taken up French nationality, and so had no right to make a will, all his goods reverted to the Crown. But Francis I wrote to François Clouet, the artist's son, stating that he would surrender to him all his father's personal estate and property which had been seized at his death.

François Clouet

The precise date of François Clouet's birth is unknown. On the death of his father he was immediately appointed painter in ordinary and groom of the bedchamber. When Francis I died in 1547, Clouet was entrusted with the funeral arrangements*. In the sixteenth century the king's chief painter was also a sort of superintendent of fine arts and organizer of entertainments. He carried out both tasks with equal enthusiasm, and did

Hieronymus Bosch
The Conjuror
Municipal Museum, Saint-Germain-en-Laye

not consider that he was demeaning himself by working on 'consecrations and coronations, mummeries and mascarades, ceremonies and tourneys' for the Court.

Henry II, the successor of Francis I, confirmed Clouet in his official positions, and in due course showed his esteem for the artist by granting him the lucrative post of commissioner for the Châtelet area. Francis II showed the same confidence in him as his father had done. Laden with honours and fame, Clouet now lived in fine style, but worked hard up to the last. He died on 22nd September 1572, having made his will the previous evening in the presence of his local parish priest. This document reveals that he never married but that he had two natural daughters, Diane and Lucrèce, to whom he left an income of twelve hundred francs per year.

François Clouet began his career in his father's workshop, and the earliest of the drawings attributed to him show a very similar technique to that of Jean Clouet. But his

Brunswick Monogrammist
Abraham's Sacrifice
Oil on wood 16″ × 13″
Louvre, Paris

Van Orley
Portrait of Charles V
Louvre, Paris

Van Orley
Portrait of Margaret of Austria
Musée des Beaux-Arts, Brussels

own personality soon shone through. While Jean Clouet's drawings consist of hasty sketches crisscrossed with hatchings, in which the few essential outlines reveal the artist's impatience during the act of creation, François' art, while still full of a lively intensity, has a much more charming and delicate air about it. His more delicate and detailed drawings are extremely evocative, due to their fluidity of line which resembles that of Ingres. His use of hatching is always accompanied by stumping.

In his portraits in oils, François Clouet paid meticulous attention to building up the various planes and was also most careful in his blending of tones. His figures do not reveal the same vitality or full-bloodedness as Holbein's, but they are perhaps more straightforward and more clearly present the viewer with the pleasurable feeling that he is in actual contact with a real model. François Clouet is an artist with a completely lucid form of expression, who employs his brush with artless precision. One of his first important works is his portrait of *Henry II*, now in the Uffizi, which he painted in 1559, the year of the king's death, and of which there exists a copy on a small panel in the Louvre. It is a masterpiece of psychological insight. The king is shown life-size, standing in an attitude that suggests great nobility. The treatment is remarkably finished, and despite the picture's size its technique reminds one of the miniaturists, whom Clouet, like his father before him, was never able to get fully away from. Moreover, he treated the portraits of *Catharine de Medici* and *Charles X* in exactly the same manner in two oval medallions placed back to back and fixed in a small golden frame. These miniatures had been commissioned by the Queen of Spain. The half-length portrait of the *Apothecary Pierre Quthe*, a friend and neighbour of the painter, shows a man of science with a beautifully grave and serious face who has about him an aura of wisdom and calm. The green curtain which hangs in one corner of the picture and the dignity of the subject's pose recall the Venitian painters, and this painting has been compared with the works of Moroni and Bronzino. It is just possible that Clouet was inspired by the work of Paris Bordone, who was staying at the French court at the time this picture was painted. Clouet was also influenced by the Italian style of the decorators of Fontainebleau, as can be seen in his *Lady Bathing*. This figure of a nude, shown half-length in her bath, surrounded by two children, one of whom seems to be playing beside her while the other is being suckled by a nurse, was long thought to be Diane de Poitiers, but may be Marie Touchet, mistress of Charles X. Also in the Fontainebleau style is the *Diana Bathing* in Rouen Museum, which has recently been ascribed to Clouet.

A year before his death François Clouet painted a picture which is considered one of his masterpieces—the portrait of *Elizabeth of Austria**, daughter of Maximilian II and granddaughter of the Emperor Charles V, who became Queen of France on her marriage to Charles IX. There is a slight note of melancholy about this figure, as if the young princess already foresaw the unhappiness that lay before her. The technique revealed in this portrait achieves an astonishing standard of perfection. The drawing is delicate, and done with an exquisite lightness of touch; the magnificent finery is rendered with studied detail which in no way detracts from the admirably graceful composition.

It would be impossible to push further than the Clouets did the art of observation,

Van Reymerswaele
Two Tax-Gatherers
National Gallery, London

Lucas Van Leyden
Lot and his Daughters
Oil on wood 23″ × 13″
Louvre, Paris

the careful attention to detail, the analytical approach to realism. This special talent of the Clouets is so typical of French art that, though both painters were of Flemish origin, they have a clear claim to being considered the founders of the French school of portrait-painting.

Corneille de Lyon

One of the very few references to the mysterious artist known as Corneille de Lyon* is to be found in Brantôme, who mentions that Catharine de Medici paid a visit to his workshop in 1665. His family name is unknown, and the space for it is left blank in the records of taxpayers. All that is certain is that he was at The Hague, probably in 1500, but why and when he moved to Lyons is unknown. He had already settled there by 1534, however, for Johannes Secundus, the celebrated author of Latin love-poems, records visiting him in that year. On 7th January 1540, when Francis I was on the throne, he was granted letters patent appointing him painter in ordinary to the Dauphin, who in due course was to reign as Henry II. In 1547 he received his naturalization papers. Four years later he was appointed official painter to Henry II. Subsequently, Francis II and Charles IX confirmed him in these honours and privileges. The last mention of him is in an act of 13th March 1574, which contains a decision on the part of the consulate of Lyons confirming his 'enjoyment of the privileges, exemptions and rights such as those enjoyed by other grooms of the bedchamber and officers of His Majesty's Household'. He presumably died shortly after this.

It is strange to note that the persons painted by Corneille were nearly all lords and ladies of the court, who thus lived far from where he had settled. He must therefore have painted them partly during their visits to Lyons and partly from the sketches of other painters. His own output, which was rediscovered in the noble houses around Lyons in the seventeenth century by the collector Roger de Gaignières, is mixed with a large number of copies which were mass-produced by his numerous assistants. Thus he was able to offer his clients portraits of the celebrities of the day in his famous gallery. It is therefore very difficult to decide which are authentic paintings in the artist's own hand.

Corneille de Lyon's method of work was quite different from that of the Clouets. Like the Clouets, he did not paint his portraits from life but, unlike them, neither did he prepare his own sketches of his sitters. It is assumed that he first drew an outline of his subject on his panel, and then painted directly onto that. These portraits, which are always on a small scale, are very delicately executed and have a certain malicious gaiety about them. The facial expression is always delightful, and the drawing is light and vivacious, despite a certain awkwardness in depicting the body and a certain repetitiousness in the arrangement of the figure. One of their distinguishing features is the background in sea-green or light blue. The clear, glazed colours, which are astonishingly fresh, add to their charm, which in turn has the simplicity associated with the primitives.

The very considerable number of small portraits that have survived from the sixteenth century (despite the inevitable losses, they can be counted in thousands) and the fact that they were the most common form of painting, proves the existence of a multitude of lesser artists. But this enormous quantity of works whose manner is very similar, makes their attribution both difficult and uncertain. The majority are anonymous, since it is only relatively recently that the practice of signing pictures has become widespread. The words of the great expert Etienne Moreau-Nélaton written at the beginning of the century are still true to-day: 'From Perréal and Jean Clouet to Corneille and François Clouet is only a short step, and yet it is impossible to map the path. We walk in complete darkness. Let us admit then that we are powerless to issue forth from this night which from time to time is barely penetrated by a faint gleam.'

Among the main portrait-painters of whom we have some information are Germain Le Mannier*, whom Catharine de Medici engaged for years to make several drawings a month of her children, and to whom Henry II became so attached; Nicolas Denisot, known as the 'Comte d'Alsinois', an anagram based on his real name, painter, poet and friend of Ronsard, who did a portrait of the latter's mistress and lived for a long time in England where he was employed as tutor to Lord Seymour's daughters; Jean de Court*, who was born into a family of enamellers in Limoges and succeeded François Clouet as court painter in 1574, and subsequently became painter to Henry III; Geoffroy Dumoustier*, and especially his sons Etienne and Pierre, who have left us only multi-coloured sketches, the fashion for which they exploited and debased, at the same time paving the way for the introduction of pastel drawing; and François Quesnel*, who came from an old Scottish family and was a very talented pupil of François Clouet. The demand was so great that even Dutch painters were called upon to satisfy it, such as Josse Van Cleef, Nicolas Fenestraux, and particularly François Pourbus, who became official painter to Henry IV.

This brilliant group of sixteenth-century portrait painters prepared the way for the great developments in this field in the following century, begun by Philippe de Champaigne and continued by Pierre and Nicolas Mignard, Lebrun and Robert Nanteuil.

The Netherlands

The end of the fifteenth century in the Netherlands is dominated by the great solitary figure of Hieronymus Bosch*, an artist of unprecedented originality. Of the man himself we know only that his family came from Aix-la-Chapelle and that he worked in Bois-le-Duc, the place where he was born, in northern Brabant, from 1480 to 1516, in which year he died. The chronological order of his work—consisting of only some forty panels that are definitely authentic and some drawings—is difficult to establish. However, recent studies have enabled us to reconstruct his spiritual development and the probable sequence of the paintings that record it. Among the group of early works, painted *ca* 1475 to 1480, religious subjects, such as *The Epiphany*, *The Marriage at Cana*, the *Crucifixion* and *Ecce Homo*, alternate with genre scenes such as *The Deadly Sins* and *The Conjuror*. The main features of these works are an extraordinary enjoyment of cruel

Hieronymus Bosch
Adoration of the Magi
Ca 1495
Wood 54″ × 28″
Prado, Madrid

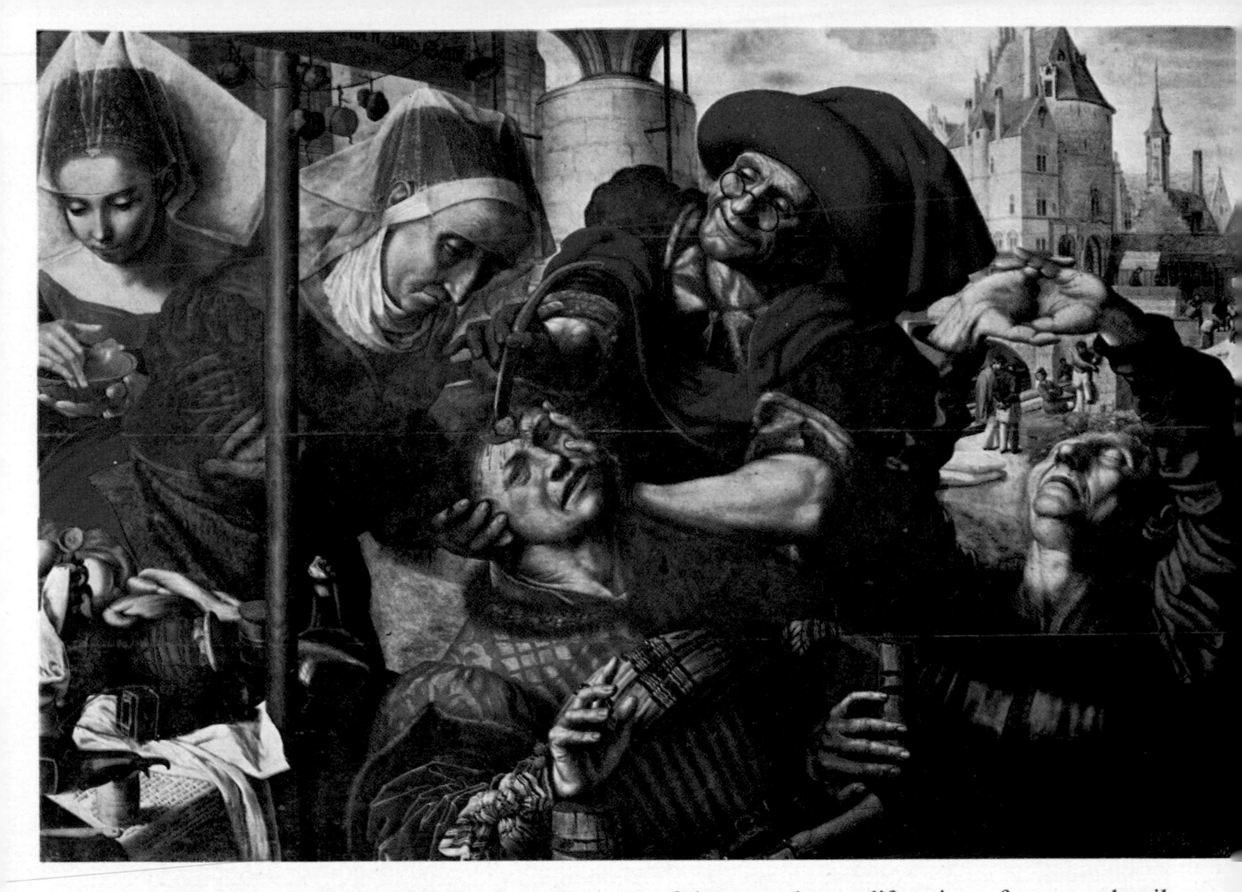

clowning, a bitter satirical vein, a richness of dress, and a proliferation of strange detail, all of which appear in his later work.

As Jean Leymarie has shown, Bosch early on became obsessed (like Erasmus* during the same period) with human folly. *The Ship of Fools* seems to have the whole of mankind embarking on it, while *The Cure of Folly* shows that those treating the patient are suffering from the same disease as he is. *The Hay-Wain*, in which madness has become cosmic, illustrates the Flemish proverb, 'The world is a heap of dry grass and everyone takes what he can'. The panels of this picture depict *The Garden of Eden* and *Hell*. Here for the first time one meets those diabolical monsters that abound in the works of maturity, such as the *Temptation of St Antony*, now in Lisbon, *The Last Judgement* and *The Garden of Delights*. In these later works Bosch achieves an extraordinary degree of power of expression and technical refinement, while at the same time his universe becomes more nightmarish. He is obsessed by the demonologists' stories of the innumerable forms in which the devil can appear. He believes that the Prince of Darkness is capable of transforming himself into the most perverse and unnatural monsters, and that the entire world is crawling with creatures like larvae, which are the result of the continual metamorphosis of demons. In the *Temptation of St Antony* 'the diversity of sensual imaginations conjured up by the wizard's wand reveals the homogeneity of the tacit diabolical world whose expression it is, that invisible world whose aim is to distract our soul from its true vocation: the contemplation of the Deity'.[1] In *The Last Judgement*, only the damned appear before the Sovereign Judge, bearing with them a terrifying train of figures compounded of human and animal forms. *The Garden of Delights*, which is the crowning example of this period of the artist's work, depicts the retrogression of humanity, branded with original sin, from the Garden of Eden to Hell. Here the overriding theme is the sin of lust, and in this microcosm teeming with countless figures naked human beings are

[1] Jacques Combes: *Hieronymus Bosch*, London, 1946, p. 24.

◄ Van Hemessen
The Surgeon
Prado, Madrid

Bruegel the Elder
Brueghel *ca* 1528-Brussels 1569
The Tower of Babel
Oil on copper 12″ × 16″
Musée d'Art et d'Histoire, Geneva
▼

intermixed with fantastic creatures. Bosch took many of his symbols from the field of alchemy—the hollow tree, the crystal egg, the bitter-apple, the three-headed dragon, etc. Indeed, according to this doctrine, the concept of sexuality is extended to minerals and all matter. Between the human couples indulging in erotic revels, the very rocks erupt into fantastic shapes, half mineral and half vegetable. Other symbols Bosch derived from the religious and mystical writings of his day, especially those of Johannes Ruysbroek, such as the dead fish, representing sin; the skate, the impure fish; and the thistle, the symbol of temptation.

While striving to increase awareness of the omnipresence of the spirit of evil, Bosch, who was a Jansenist before his time, appears to be trying to suggest, in his pictures of ascetics, that salvation is still possible for a certain number of privileged persons. In *St John on Patmos* (Berlin), *St Jerome at Prayers* (Ghent), *St Christopher* (Rotterdam) and *St John the Baptist in the Wilderness* (Madrid), the unceasing demoniac fertility of nature abates and sometimes disappears completely. The landscape offers a sense of complete harmony, the distances become a source of divine light. Mortification of the flesh, prayer and grace have, though perhaps only for a short time, brought back a feeling of serenity. However, evil is not far away, as is shown in *The Crowning with Thorns* and *The Carrying of the Cross*. The bestial heads of the human puppets crowd round that of the Man-God who is resigned to his torments. But Bosch's work

terminates on a less pessimistic note. The tondo of *The Prodigal Son* in the guise of a vagabond shows the true searcher after eternal life. He resembles the figure of the Madman in the Tarot Pack. Dressed in rags, rejected by all, pursued by dogs, he appears mad only to a blind humanity—which alone has lost its reason. He is the wise man who has renounced the illusions of the impure world, has reached beyond the unrealities of this world and walks in the path of Perfection.

The genre of the fantastic and the moral painting which Bosch originated were to be taken up again by the artists of the succeeding generation, though they show themselves particularly attentive to the novelties of Italian art. In fact, the immense attraction of the Italian Renaissance which, in the sixteenth century, completely dazzled the whole of the western world, could not fail to have repercussions on the work of various groups of artists living in the Netherlands. (At this time there are still no Dutch and Flemish Schools, which begin to show their distinctive features only at the end of the century.) The period that we are now going to consider falls between two of the greatest epochs of art in the Netherlands, that of the fifteenth-century primitives at one end and of the seventeenth-century Flemish baroque at the other. It is essentially dominated by artists, known as the Romanists, who had made a systematic study of the Italian masters and whose ambition it was to transplant the new developments in painting into their own country. This movement went hand-in-hand with humanism, which had also arrived from Italy and had spread through the Netherlands since the end of the fifteenth century, thanks to Rudolphus Agricola and, a little later, Erasmus. The Netherlands were the home of some of the great printers who played a considerable part in the dissemination of the writings of ancient Greek and Roman authors, as well as those of the humanists themselves. They include Elzevier *, Christophe Plantin (who was of French extraction but had chosen to settle in Antwerp), and the latter's son-in-law Moretus. The Italian Renaissance had already made a timid appearance in the work of Memlinc, who copied Mantegna's * garlands of fruit and flowers, and of Gérard David, who was similarly influenced by the Italian painter, and also imitated his decorative cameos.

Quentin Metsys *, the last of the Gothic artists, was even more markedly inspired by Italian ideas. He possibly travelled in Italy, he often imitates Leonardo, and his work forms a bridge between the old and the new. The composition of his *Virgin and Child*, now in the museum of Poznan, was suggested by Leonardo's *St Anne*, and some of his portraits were even inspired by Leonardo's caricatures. From him he also learnt the art of sfumato. This Italian influence grew stronger in his work over the years, and predominates in the Madonnas painted at the end of his life. The completely human appearance of the Virgin, the representation of the Child as a disobedient naked ' bambino ' and the architectural décor in which they are framed, are all taken directly from Italy.

During the first half of the century these Italian borrowings gave rise to a complete revolution in the arts. The prints of Marcantonio Raimondi * and other engravers, which reproduced the most important works of the Italian masters, were

Mabuse
The Holy Family (detail)
Central panel
Museum of Ancient Art, Lisbon

Bruegel the Elder
The Fall of the Rebel Angels
Musée des Beaux-Arts, Brussels

commonly to be found in the workshops of the artists in the Netherlands, who themselves had usually undertaken the journey to Rome. Those who were unable to do so went to Fontainebleau to study the Italian manner. It was the rather ingenuous ambition of each of these painters to become known as ' the Flemish Raphael ', 'the Michelangelo of the Netherlands', and so on.

This passion for Italian art, and the consequent interest in Antiquity, completely undermined the foundations on which the art of the Netherlands had been based in the fifteenth century. Doubtless artists of little merit became unoriginal imitators, but the truly creative painters, while retaining the essentials of their traditional style, were able to assimilate the Italian influences and reshape them in their own light. This combination of Italianate and early Flemish forms gives their works a certain motley charm, which is sometimes a little bizarre but is nevertheless most enjoyable. Among the leading artists of this style, the local tradition consisting largely of a stark realism, a sense of homeliness in the subjects and a fondness for everyday scenes, can still be recognized. What they took from the Italians was an elegant, passionate and expansive style which is quite different from that of the primitives of the Netherlands, whose technique involves great attention to detail, whose drawing is precise and a little arid, and whose art still looks back to that of the miniaturists from which it sprang. Delighting in the new fashion, these artists also introduced into their country a taste for large compositions, the manifestation of emotions, mythological subjects, anatomical studies, boldly contrasted or carefully blended colours, and a sense of movement that was lacking in the earlier painting of the Netherlands.

Pieter Bruegel the Elder, the heir of Hieronymus Bosch, has sometimes been regarded as the reverse of the Romanists, but in fact he too visited Italy. For a long time the importance of the paintings of the Romanists has been the subject of dispute. ' The long line of Flemish carts was to become bogged down in an enormous rut which another train of carts had formed,' wrote Hippolyte Taine in his *Philosophy of Art in the Low Countries*, and in his *Masters of Former Times* Eugène Fromentin disdainfully treated these painters as 'Italo-Flemish half-breeds'. It is only in the last fifty years that they have begun to be appreciated once more.

Flanders

Mabuse

Though Jan Gossaert was not the first painter in the Netherlands to respond to the new Italian influences, he was the first to wish to reject the traditions of his own country and to try to assimilate completely the lessons of the masters of Tuscany, Lombardy and Venice. He was born in 1478 at Maubeuge, which was then part of Hainault and only later became French. This gave rise to his being called Mabuse* when he went to live in Flanders, Mabeuge being pronounced Mabuse in Ghent, Bruges and Antwerp. He is supposed to have been the son of Simon Gossaert, a bookbinder. In this case, he would from a very early age have had the opportunity of seeing beautiful manuscripts in

his father's workshop, and gazing at the illuminations in them may well have awoken him to his vocation. One can only speculate about the years of his apprenticeship.

Details of Mabuse's life become known to us only from the time that he entered into the service of Philip of Burgundy. This prince, the fifteenth illegitimate child of Philip the Good, was ' High Admiral of the Sea of Zetland and Governor of Gelderland and Zutphen '. Philip of Burgundy was a delightful dilettante with worldly and wanton tastes, an enjoyable companion and a scholarly humanist, who took a great interest in the arts. Moreover, he had himself practised painting and the goldsmith's craft in his youth, and at his court he kept the Italian artist Jacopo de Barbari*. When he went on an embassy to Pope Julius II in 1508, Philip took with him a brilliant entourage of men of letters and painters which included Mabuse. The period that he spent in Rome most certainly had a very strong influence on Mabuse.

While the prince taught him to appreciate the art of the ancients, he at the same time visited the workshops of the great Italian masters, probably guided by Jacopo de Barbari.

By the end of 1509 Mabuse had returned to the Netherlands with his patron. The latter, having discharged his responsibilities, now retired to the castle of Suytberg on the island of Walcheren, where he surrounded himself with men of letters such as Erasmus, Johannes Paludanus and Carlo Bembo (then Venetian ambassador to Charles the Bold), and artists who included Mabuse and Jacopo de Barbari, described by Gerard of Nijmegen as ' the Zeuxis and Apelles of our time '. During this period Mabuse, profiting from his thorough knowledge of Italian art, executed a large number of his most important works. He then accompanied Philip to Utrecht, where the latter had been elected prince-bishop by Charles V's councillors in 1517. Here Mabuse proceeded to decorate the palace of Wyk-te-Duerstede.

After Philip of Burgundy's death in 1524, his nephew Prince Adolphe, Marquis of Veere and Vlissingen, who had succeeded him as Admiral of Zetland, took Mabuse

into his service, the latter having, according to Van Mander *, given one of his Madonnas the features of Adolphe's wife. In the company of his new patron he went to live in Middelburg, where he was to remain for the rest of his life. It was here that he taught his pupil Lambert Lombard of Liège, and struck up a friendship with the young Lucas Van Leyden who at the time was travelling through the Dutch canals by boat. Mabuse died at the end of 1533.

The dating of Mabuse's early works is not established with any certainty. It is however known that the *Adoration of the Magi* was painted for the Abbey of Grammont in eastern Flanders *ca* 1505, and thus before he travelled to Italy. This early work is in the main treated in accordance with the aesthetic ideas of the primitives. The poses of the various figures are stiff and static, the organization of the picture tends towards verticality, the composition is symmetrical, the treatment is highly detailed, and the Virgin is in the tradition of those of Van Eyck, Memlinc and Gérard David. However, the manner in which the architecture is treated shows a departure from the Flemish style of the fifteenth century and reveals a development in taste. From the same period probably dates the excellent *Christ on the Mount of Olives* in Berlin. This night scene is bathed in a chiaroscuro which creates a fantastically confined atmosphere. Mabuse's strong originality succeeds in giving a new interpretation to this scene.

The famous *Malvagna Triptych* * in Palermo probably dates from the artist's residence in Rome. It presents a curious mixture in roughly equal doses of the Flemish and Italian styles, and marks an important step forward in the artist's development. *St Luke Painting the Virgin*, executed for the Painters' Guild in Malines in 1515, and now the great altar-piece of Prague Cathedral, shows the Italian style completely predominating. We are now presented with a work which definitely obeys the canons of the Renaissance. There is something certainly still archaic in the poses of the Virgin and St Luke, and particularly in the treatment of their dress, with stiff, detailed, symmetri-

Bruegel the Elder
Hay-Making (detail)
National Gallery, Prague

cal folds, but the architectural decoration and the subtle effects of perspective which this gives rise to are definitely in the true spirit of the new style. One might almost say that, in his enthusiasm, Mabuse has tried to include within the great palace with its succession of open porticoes, every architectonic, decorative and sculptural feature that had attracted his attention during his Italian wanderings.

Mabuse continued in this style, and his many Madonnas are all extremely human. The profane approach came to replace the idealization and mysticism of the Madonnas of the primitives. Likewise, his devotion to Italian art led to his painting mythological subjects and nudes, the first painter in the Netherlands to do so. His earliest work of this type is his *Neptune and Amphitryon*, which is signed in Latin ' Joannes Malbodius ' and dated 1516. It contains the motto of Philip of Burgundy, *A plus sera*, which shows that it was executed for the palace of Suytberg. Among other works in this genre are *Hercules and Deianira* (1517), *Hercules and Antaeus* (1523), and a series depicting *Adam and Eve:* all show considerable virtuosity and a desire to astonish by means of theatrical effects and a mannered style.

One of Mabuse's last masterpieces is his *Danaë*, dated 1527. Here, within a rotunda of marble columns, we see the mistress of Jupiter, her blue mantle falling from her, receiving the shower of gold. In the spaces between the columns two Renaissance-style buildings and a Gothic monument can be observed. As always in Mabuse's work, the young woman is of the robust Flemish type, and the delicate execution is also Flemish in origin, but in everything else the spirit, style and forms of Italian art predominate. Mabuse was also an excellent portrait-painter, and was meticulous in recording the individuality of his sitters. He was concerned with rendering volume, and underscored the features and details of the flesh with high lights, and attached particular importance to the treatment of the hands, which had not previously received such attention among the portrait-painters of the Netherlands. The three portraits of the *Chancellor Jan Carondelet* and the group of *The Children of Christian II of Denmark* are his greatest achievements in this field.

Mabuse was the first painter from the Netherlands to become enthralled by the Italian masters. Not only did he introduce the new style into his own country, but he also set the fashion for travelling beyond the Alps to study art. His role was that of an innovator, who enabled painting in the Netherlands to assimilate the manner of the Renaissance. The entire school of the Romanists springs from him.

Bernard Van Orley

Bernard Van Orley * is chronologically the second in the series of artists of the new style. He was born in Brussels, probably in 1488. His father, Valentin, was an illegitimate child of the great house of the lords of Orley, who were the legal officers of Luxembourg, but being deprived by his birth of the advantages which his family would otherwise have offered him, he chose to become a painter. It was probably he himself who first taught his son Bernard, for no document has been found referring to the latter's serving his apprenticeship. According to tradition, Bernard Van Orley made two

Bruegel the Elder
The Parable of the Blind
1568
Tempera on canvas 34″ × 61″
Capodimonte, Naples

journeys to Italy as a young man and was the pupil of Raphael. At least it is known that in 1516 he was employed in the Brussels mills to supervise the weaving of Raphael's tapestries illustrating the *Act of the Apostles* which had been commissioned by Leo X for the Sistine Chapel.

Among the artist's earliest works is probably the *Altar-piece of the Apostles Thomas and Matthew*, executed for the chapel of the Charpentiers in Brussels. The central panel, which is signed, is now in the Vienna Museum. The volets, now in the Brussels Museum, depict *St Thomas's Unbelief and Death* and *St Matthew's Election and Martyrdom*. The figures are drawn in the style of the preceding century, but the desire to be modern can be seen in the treatment of the architecture, which consists of a mixture of flamboyant Gothic and rather fantastic Renaissance features. In the *Hanneton Altar-piece*, which dates from 1508-12, the Italian influences are much more marked, especially in the central panel depicting a *Lament for the Dead Christ*.

In 1518 Van Orley became official painter to Margaret of Austria, Regent of the Netherlands. In this capacity he earned only one *sou* per day, but he received special payments for each of the pictures commissioned from him, which included numerous portraits of Margaret herself. As a portrait-painter Van Orley is inferior to Mabuse and has not his sense of volumes. His excellence lies in the simplicity and veracity of his style, which is that of the fifteenth-century masters of Bruges. Moreover, he was good at choosing the best pose and setting for revealing the personality of his sitters. His masterpiece in this genre is his portrait of his friend *Dr George Zelle*, physician to Charles V. In 1521 Margaret of Austria commissioned him to paint a triptych, known

as *Virtue and Patience*, as a gift for one of her favourite ministers, Antoine de Lalaing. It was inspired by one of Margaret's own poems. The principal panel depicts the *Destruction of the Children of Job*, who are seen fleeing in terror from the house in which they have been eating and drinking, and which is about to collapse on top of them. This appalling catastrophe is made to take place in a Renaissance building supported by columns overloaded with medallions, panels and sculptures in high relief. Here Van Orley is clearly intent to display the knowledge that he has gained from the Italians, and to demonstrate that the technical achievements of his art hold no secret for him. Everything in this work calls up memories of Raphael's *Expulsion of Heliodorus from the Temple* and *Fire in the Borgo*, as well as Signorelli's frescoes at Orvieto. One can in fact criticize this painting for its heaviness and over-emphasis in its effects. In about 1525 Van Orley completed his large *Triptych for the Almoners' Chapel* * in Antwerp. The central panel is a *Last Judgement*, in which the Italian manner has become completely assimilated.

In his Madonnas Van Orley imitates Raphael's style, as for example in the *Holy Family*, in which the gesture of the Child throwing himself into the Virgin's arms and the idealized beauty of the angels are both borrowed from the Italian master.

On account of his leanings towards Protestantism, Van Orley and his entire family in 1527 found themselves involved in a trial for heresy, but nevertheless he succeeded in retaining the favour of Margaret of Austria. When she died in 1530, he entered the service of her successor, Maria of Hungary. By the end of his life Van Orley was running a huge workshop with a number of assistants working under his orders. He confined himself to painting the main parts of the pictures which were commissioned from him. He died in Brussels in 1542, laden with honours. During his last years he had turned his attention to the decorative arts, and in particular to high-warp tapestry and stained glass. His cartoons were used in weaving the magnificent series of the *Hunts of Maximilian*, set in the countryside around Brussels. He designed some magnificent stained-glass windows for the collegiate church of St Michael and St Gudula. They no longer recall the mystical ideas of the previous century; on the contrary, buildings in the Renaissance style are introduced and the place of honour is given to the figures of princes.

Marinus Van Reymerswaele

Marinus Van Reymerswaele * had the signal honour of being regarded as one of the finest Flemish painters of the sixteenth century by Guichardin *, Vasari and Van Mander. Thereafter he was quickly forgotten, and the interest in him to-day is largely due to the fact that his harsh expressionism appears to us completely modern. Little is known about the painter's life. He was born *ca* 1495, and came from Reymerswaele, a town in Zeeland which was submerged beneath the sea in the seventeenth century. His father, Nicholas Van Zierickzee, was also a painter. In 1509, ' Marinus Claeszoon (son of Nicholas) of Zeeland ' was registered at Antwerp as being the apprentice of the

Bruegel the Elder
The Misanthrope
1568
Tempera on canvas 35″ diam.
Capodimonte, Naples

stained-glass painter, Simon Van Daele. It has been thought that he then studied under Quentin Metsys, but this is unlikely. However, he borrowed all his subjects from Metsys. The first known picture by him, dated 1521, is a *St Jerome in his Cell*, which is based on a painting by Metsys now in the Vienna Museum. As in in the case of his other works, Marinus produced a number of copies which differ only in detail. He never tires of the theme of the *Money-Changers* and the *Tax-Gatherers*, which Metsys had handled in 1514. But here Marinus diverges completely from his model, both in the composition and in the interpretation of the figures, and in this he shows considerable originality. He depicts these officials and merchants as ferocious diabolical characters, employing an exacerbated—one might almost say convulsive—style which sometimes approaches caricature and which is heightened by the use of acid colours which often clash violently.

Marinus has a vigorous style, his clear-cut shapes stand out sharply. His biting realism reflects his own bitter pessimism. In fact, he took an active part in the excesses of the iconoclasts—a completely contradictory act for a painter. On 23rd June 1576, Marinus Claeszoon Van Reymerswaele was condemned at Middelburg to pay penance in public, that is to say to take his place in a procession wearing only a shift and bearing a lighted candle; thereafter to be banished from the town for a period of six years for having taken part in destroying the images in the Westmunsterkerk the previous month. Marinus had arrived at old age, which probably saved him from the gallows. This is the last record we have of his life.

Lancelot Blondeel

Lancelot Blondeel* was born in Poperinghe *ca* 1498, but later settled in Bruges. In his youth he was a mason, which led him to include a trowel in the monogram with which he signed his works. He was subsequently received into the Painters' Guild of Bruges as a master painter in 1519, and quickly made a considerable reputation. He died in Bruges in 1561. As in the case of the Italian masters, Blondeel was not only a painter but also a sculptor, architect, engraver, engineer, town-planner, picture restorer and organizer of entertainments. He drew up a plan for a new port at Bruges, and though it was not used at the time it served as a basis for the work undertaken in the nineteenth century. He was also responsible for the 'patrons' on the celebrated chimney-piece in the House of the Franc.

The oldest of Blondeel's known works is his *History of St Cosmas and St Damian*, which was painted in 1523 for the Surgeons' Guild in Bruges. The artist here reduces the role of the human figures to an extreme degree in order to give room for the prolific and highly involved architectural ornamentation. He was clearly inspired by the Italian painters of grotesques, which he highly exaggerates. The same occurs in his *St Luke Painting the Virgin* (1545), in which an immense gilded construction almost envelops the canvas, leaving a tiny oval space for the figures. The *Virgin Between St Luke and St Eloi* (1545), executed for the Painters' and Saddlers' Brotherhood in

Bruges, and the *Scenes from the Life of the Virgin* (also 1545), are in the same vein, though there is more balance in them between the figures and the decoration. The *Saint's Martyrdom* (1588) is conceived in a completely different way. The architectural decoration gives place to a Lombardy landscape out of which rise ancient ruins reminiscent of the Coliseum. This picture supports Van Mander's remark that Blondeel has as much talent for painting ruins as for architectural subjects.

Lancelot Blondeel was the first of the Bruges painters to develop such a passion for the Italian Renaissance as to abandon the traditions of the old Netherlands School. But it is difficult to reach a definitive opinion about him, since so few of his works are known.

Lambert Lombard

Lambert Lombard * was born in 1505 in Liège, where his father was a citizen and by trade a butcher. After serving his apprenticeship, the young Lombard travelled in Germany, and then went to Middelburg to complete his training under Mabuse, whose faithful follower he became. On his return to Liège he entered into the service of the prince-bishop of the town, Evrard de la Marck, a humanist and most generous patron who wanted to see a new development in the arts. In 1537, thanks to the munificence of his patron, Lambert Lombard was enabled to achieve what was surely one of his greatest ambitions—to visit Italy, where he stayed two years.

Albrecht Dürer
Nuremberg 1471-1528
Self-portrait
1493
Vellum mounted on canvas 22″ × 18″
Louvre, Paris

Lambert Lombard was a true representative of his time, interested in everything and in touch with the latest ideas as well as the developments in the field of art. Vasari, with whom he corresponded, described him as a ' great man of letters, a discerning painter and a most excellent architect '. Moreover, he had a passion for archaeology. In Germany he sought out Frankish antiquities, and brought back not only a great number of drawings based on them, but also a large collection of medallions and engraved stones. On his return to Liège he founded an academy which for several years gave the town the reputation of being one of the leading art centres in Flanders. He gathered together a crowd of pupils from all over the country and even from abroad. He died in Liège in 1566.

It is hardly possible to reach a true estimate of the work of Lambert Lombard since so few of his paintings can be ascribed to him with any certainty. Essentially all that has survived are the panels, dispersed in the eighteenth century, which accompanied a large sculptured altar-piece from the church of Saint-Denis in Liège. One half of these compositions is devoted to illustrating the *Life of Christ* * and the other to the *Legend of St Denis*.

As a painter-cum-archaeologist with a passion for antiquities, and as a follower of Raphael and Parmigianino, Lambert Lombard was doubtless a second-rate artist, but historically he is of importance as one of those who introduced the conventions of the Italian Renaissance into the Netherlands.

Jan Van Hemessen

The name under which this artist appears in the records of the Painters' Guild in Antwerp is ' Jan Sanders ', but he signed his pictures ' Van Hemessen ' * after his native village of Hemixen, near Antwerp. He was born in 1504, and completed his apprenticeship under Henry Van Cleve in 1523. It is thought that he visited Italy briefly in about 1531. In 1548 he was made Dean of the Painters' Guild. A reversal of fortune obliged him to sell his house in Antwerp and, according to Van Mander, he settled in Haarlem, where he became known as the Dutch Raphael. Guichardin records him in 1567 as already being dead.

An important early work by Van Hemessen is his *Prodigal Son*, dated 1536, and now in the Brussels Museum. This lively painting succeeds in reconciling the Italian features (the architecture, and the rhythmical gestures of the courtesans and the young man) with the typically Flemish realism expressed in the horrible faces of the procurers and the wicked boy. The *Vocation of St Matthew* (1536) is a direct descendant of Reymerswaele's *Money-Changers*, and presents a mixture of charming and repulsive figures, as in the preceding picture. The same can be said of *Ecce Homo*, in which the expression of nobility on the face of the Saviour is in direct contrast with the bloated faces of the executioners; this applies as well to the *Dissolute Company* in the Karlsruhe Museum. Van Hemessen also painted a series on *St Jerome* which are in a different style. In general, the saint is shown completely naked, and is then treated in the manner

of the heroic nude. The important *Last Judgement* in the church of Saint-Jacques in Antwerp also exemplifies the artist's feeling for highly modelled nudes. His attraction to popular subjects—combined in this case with a horrifying interest in depicting physical suffering—is to be found in the *Operation for the Stone of Madness*, which is taken from Hieronymus Bosch. *Tobias Healing his Father*, one of Van Hemessen's last important works, displays his pleasure in showing off his Italianate technique. Here he pushes to an extreme his manner of depicting his figures in close-up, thus giving them the maximum effect.

Friedländer wishes to ascribe to Van Hemessen a number of pictures which are at present attributed to an anonymous painter known as the Brunswick Monogrammist, since they all bear the initial J.S.M.V. or J.H.M. The most famous of these is the *Feeding of the Poor* which is painted with a racy realism. In fact these works closely resemble those of Van Hemessen in their combination of Flemish models and Italian conventions. Whoever he may be, the Brunswick Monogrammist is a brilliant popular painter and a true forerunner of Bruegel.

The Flemish Romanists in the middle of the sixteenth century

Frans Floris

Frans de Vriendt, known as Frans Floris * (the surname Floris was adopted by his grandfather and used by all his descendants), was born into a family of artists in Antwerp *ca* 1516. He began by studying sculpture, but his talent as a painter was

Albrecht Dürer
Adoration of the Magi
Oil on wood 39″ × 49″
Uffizi, Florence

revealed early in his life, and he went to work under Lambert Lombard in Liège. In 1540 he was registered as a master painter in Antwerp. Shortly afterwards he left for Italy. It is possible that he attended the unveiling of the *Last Judgement*. In any case, he certainly made a number of drawings in red chalk based on the frescoes in the Sistine Chapel. On his return to Antwerp his work was quickly appreciated and he soon acquired a considerable reputation. The Prince of Orange, the Counts of Egmont and Horn, the Knights of the Golden Fleece and all the nobles of the Netherlands sought out his company and commissioned paintings from him, for which he was very highly paid. He became a wealthy man and built a splendid house whose façade he decorated himself. His workshop was so popular that, according to Van Mander, he had one hundred and twenty pupils. What is certain is that he successfully set up a sort of factory for mass-producing pictures, which were largely executed by his assistants. Frans Floris greatly delighted in eating and drinking bouts, and these probably hastened his end. In fact he died in 1570, when he was still in his early fifties.

In his own day Frans Floris enjoyed a considerable reputation not only in Flanders but also in Italy. He was commonly described as 'the Incomparable', but posterity has not confirmed this estimate and to-day we are better able to see his limitations. What we most appreciate in his work are those pieces which, in spite of their pandering to fashion, their imitativeness and show of learning, still have a certain earthiness about them. His *Fall of the Rebel Angels*, painted in 1554 for the church of Notre-Dame in Antwerp, strikes one as merely a mass of somewhat conventional figures with over-developed muscles. The *Last Judgement* in Brussels (1566) shows Floris once again copying Michelangelo. On the other hand, his mythological pieces are sometimes better. Here he is more influenced by the Venetian than the Roman school. In some of the really sensual female figures, such as those of *Venus and Cupid* or *Mars and Venus Ensnared by Vulcan*, one is immediately reminded of Titian. This is particularly true of the *Banquet of the Two Sailors* in which, despite a certain stolidity in the composition and the habitual greyish tones, the jollification and excesses of a Flemish village fair break through the mask of Italian-style mythology. Floris was also a remarkable painter of portraits, and one can truly say that, though they appealed less to his contemporaries, they are full of charm. His best works in this genre are *The Falconer* and his *Portrait of an Old Woman*.

The Followers of Frans Floris

Marten de Vos *, who was born and died in Antwerp (1532-1603), was one of the best of Frans Floris' many pupils. He was a prolific painter who was continually in demand to decorate churches whose pictures had been destroyed by the protestant iconoclasts. He was gifted with a powerful imagination and feelings that were sometimes less cold than those of his master. He was less interested in exaggerating the treatment of the muscles, but his monumental works are often bombastic and insipid. Among his most famous paintings are *The Incredulity of St Thomas*, *Christ's Triumph* and *The Tribute of*

Albrecht Dürer
The Feast of the Rosary (detail)
National Gallery, Prague

Caesar. He was also a capable portrait-painter who was scrupulous in depicting solid Flemish types, as can be seen in the *Hoffman Couple* and the *Anselm Family*.

Among Frans Floris' other pupils were several members of the Francken family, including three brothers, Jerom Francken the Elder * (1450-1610), Franz Francken the Elder * (1542-1618) and Ambroise Francken the Elder * (1544-1618), who all continued the tradition of their master. Several works by the youngest, and most talented, of the three brothers are to be found in the churches and museums of Antwerp.

Otto Van Veen*, called Vaenius, was born in Leyden in 1558 and died in Brussels in 1629. If he was not in fact a pupil of Frans Floris, he was certainly strongly influenced by him. He studied in Rome under Federigo Zucchero, an artist of the decadence. From the latter he inherited a taste for extravagant poses and loud colours, which were combined with a certain coldness due to his fondness for Classicism and refined allegorical studies. He was also a man of letters, and wrote several historical works as well as moral emblem books.

François Pourbus the Elder* was born in Bruges in 1545, and died at Antwerp in 1581, at the early age of thirty-six. He worked under Frans Floris, whose niece he married. He was a member of a family of artists, which began with his father, Pierre Pourbus the Elder (1524-87), who was a painter of religious pictures and of remarkable portraits, though his ideas were somewhat old-fashioned. One of François' most important religious works is the altar-piece in the Viglius chapel in St Bavo's, Ghent, depicting *Christ among the Doctors* (1572). It is a rather stiffly academic composition, whose principal point of interest is the gallery of contemporary figures that the artist has included. In fact, like his father, François Pourbus is above all a portrait-painter. His portrait of *Viglius Ayta* (the donor of the previous picture), is full of character and employs a wide colour range. In the *Wedding of the Painter Hoefnaegel* (1571), twenty people are gathered together in an interior, and this shows what a party of artists and scholars who loved music and conversation must have been like in those days. François Pourbus' rather austere but still attractive work is more modern than that of his father, since the volumes are strongly modelled, but he retains his father's polished and minutely detailed technique.

The Northern Netherlands

Lucas Van Leyden

The most important of the artists of the Northern Netherlands in the sixteenth century was formerly called Lucas of Holland, but is now known as Lucas Van Leyden *, since he was born, according to Van Mander, in 1494, the same year as Correggio, in the city that was to be Rembrandt's birthplace a century later. He was the son of Hugo Jacobsz, a painter of talent. Lucas, however, was an infant prodigy for, again according to Van Mander, he was engraving copper plates with his own designs in his father's workshop when he was nine years old; and at the age of twelve he astonished the painters of

Leyden by the spirit, powerfulness and assurance of a painting in tempera showing the *History of St Hubert*. In about 1517, he married Lisbeth Van Boschhuyzen, daughter of one of the most powerful and noble families in Leyden, who brought with her a fortune. He himself had become wealthy in his own right through his prints, which he produced in large numbers. He became a universal favourite: wherever he went he was fêted and acclaimed, he received payments on a royal scale and obtained the patronage of the most important people. In 1521 he undertook the first of his travels to Italy, which were to have a profound effect on his artistic ideas. In the same year he went to Antwerp to attend the reception given by the artists of that city in honour of a visit by Albrecht

Dürer. The two painters immediately became firm friends. Later Lucas Van Leyden decided to visit all the celebrated painters of the Netherlands and for this purpose he had equipped at his own expense a luxury barge for sailing through the canals, and enjoyed the pleasure of travelling like a lord. This ostentatious tour, which had been one long party, was the last indulgence that he was to enjoy. He returned to Leyden a sick man, and though he lived on for another six years, it was always in the shadow of death, for he never had another day of good health. Over-work and over-indulgence had ruined his delicate constitution, and he became a consumptive. Nevertheless, he continued to work with enormous energy right up to the last moment. He had an easel and tools specially designed so that he could paint and engrave in bed. Formerly of a sweet and gentle nature, he now became downcast and embittered. He got it into his head that during his last voyage, some Flemish artist, jealous of his fame and fortune, had poisoned him. He died in 1533, at the age of thirty-nine. Mabuse, whom he met on that famous voyage, had instilled into him the pagan ideals of the Romanist Renaissance through his exaltation of the beauty of flesh.

Lucas Van Leyden was as great an engraver as he was a painter. His innumerable prints combine the gentle simplicity of the primitive with the skill of the artists of the Renaissance. Indeed, his fame outside the Netherlands is due more to his engravings than to his pictures. The well-established chronological sequence of the prints has led to a less certain dating of the paintings.

' The paintings which come from his hand, or which one still runs across, ' wrote Van Mander, ' are few in number, but they are quite remarkable; they have a peculiar charm of their own which has something quite captivating about it.' One of the finest

Francken the Elder
The Story of Tobias
Museum, Besançon

is, without a doubt, the *Game of Chess*. This is a work executed under the influence of Cornelius Engelbrechtsz. The technique is somewhat heavy-handed and awkward, the colours are all sombre browns, greens and greys on a black background. But the players and spectators, pressed one against the other in the style of the primitives, are full of a realism that is truly striking. Lucas is one of the creators of 'genre painting', quite devoid of any religious or moral intent, in which his Dutch compatriots were soon to excel.

Susanna before the Elders and *Potiphar's Wife Displaying Joseph's Garment*, both painted *ca* 1511, are technically less stiff and more personal, and the artist has now lightened the tones of his palette. From the same period dates the *Card-Players*, a fine genre painting which is considered one of the artist's masterpieces. A little later comes the *Self-Portrait* in the Brunswick Museum, painted in shades of brown, grey and green. This is a large, powerful picture, with a freedom of expression which is astonishingly modern and foreshadows Frans Hals and Rembrandt. The intensity of the young artist's feelings is completely concentrated in his penetrating gaze, which is in sharp contrast to the strongly marked and rather heavy features of the face. A fascinating little picture of *Lot and his Daughters* * dates from about 1514. Here the disturbing sensuality of the woman is contrasted with the fantastic landscape in the background.

The celebrated *Last Judgement* summarizes the artist's studies at the end of his career. In this great triptych, which was commissioned in 1526 for the main altar of the Church of St Peter and St Paul in Leyden, the Italian style is triumphant. Doubtless Lucas Van Leyden was partly inspired by Van Orley's treatment of the same subject, but a profound knowledge of the Italian models is also revealed. Despite the beauty to be found in many of the details, the picture as a whole gives an impression of showmanship. The *Dance round the Golden Calf* (*ca* 1525), *Moses Smiting the Rock* (*ca* 1527) and the *Healing of the Blind Man* (1531) are among the artist's last works. In them he displays great ability in arranging crowds, giving them a sense of movement and liveliness. He is always a delightful story-teller, and adds a number of amusing anecdotes to his tales.

Lucas Van Leyden had that multiplicity of gifts combined with technical ability that is common to the great humanist artists. The freedom with which he treats his subjects makes him a forerunner of the Dutch masters of the seventeenth century.

Jan Van Scorel

Jan Van Scorel * was the first of the Dutch artists to visit Italy. In Venice he joined a group of pilgrims who were travelling to the Holy Land under the leadership of a Dutch priest. After visiting Crete and Cyprus, he reached Jerusalem where he was received by the superior of the cloister of Sion. Here he made a number of studies which were to form the basis for the landscapes of several pictures painted later. On his way back to

Van Heemskerck
St Luke Painting the Virgin
Museum, Rennes

Venice he stopped off at Rhodes, and then went on to Rome where Adrian Dedel, a native of Utrecht, had just been elected Pope with the name of Hadrian VI. The latter placed his compatriot in charge of the antiquities in the Belvedere. Jan Van Scorel profited from this appointment to indulge his passion for archaeological specimens. He also painted in the manner of Raphael and drew in the manner of Michelangelo. But twenty months later, in 1523, the pope died and the artist had to return to his own country. He settled permanently in Utrecht, where he set up a workshop in which he taught a large number of pupils, describing to them the wonders he had seen and thus introducing into Holland his own understanding of Italian art. In 1528 he was appointed canon of the church of St Mary. He died in December 1562, at the age of sixty-seven. Jan Van Scorel, who was a man of strong personality, was not only a painter but also an architect, engineer, musician, poet and Latin scholar.

The first known work by Van Scorel is a triptych painted in 1520 for Count Cristoforo Frangipani, who lived in the castle of Falkenstein, in Carinthia, where the painter stopped on his way to Italy. The central panel depicts the Madonna and Child adored by the Frangipani family; on the volets are St Christopher and St Apollonia, the patron saints of the count and his wife. In this work Scorel shows remarkable maturity, though he was only twenty-five years old. He is completely free of any Italian influence. On his return to the Netherlands, Van Scorel executed various pictures for Hermann Van Lochorst, ' a courtly lord and great patron of art ', including a triptych named after the patron himself. During the same period (1525-6) he also painted the *Members of the Brotherhood of Jerusalem in Utrecht*, who had gone to visit the Holy Sepulchre. They are shown each bearing a palm-branch in his hand, and the painter has placed himself among them. Ten years later he was to paint another series of members of the brotherhood. These are the ancestors of those group portraits of companies of harquebusiers and regency councils which later flourished in the Netherlands. *Christ's Baptism* in the Frans Hals Municipal Museum, Haarlem, gave the painter an excuse to make an academic study of nudes in complicated attitudes, which shows the influence of the Romanist School. The composition of the *Presentation in the Temple* is in the manner of Raphael. The *Good Samaritan* reveals the influence of Michelangelo in the naked figure of the traveller waylaid by thieves, while the landscape is quite Venetian in its arrangement. But Van Scorel is never a servile imitator, the old Netherlands tradition is still to be found in his sure touch, his elaborate technique and his forceful colours. The main works of Van Scorel's final period are the unfinished *Bathsheba* in the Amsterdam Museum, *The Queen of Sheba Visiting King Solomon* and in particular the *Mary Magdalen.*

Van Scorel also painted a number of portraits *, in which atavistic qualities of observation are combined with powerful modelling taken from the Italians. Certainly Jan Van Scorel lacks the rich inventiveness and the genius of a Lucas Van Leyden, but nevertheless his work is full of charm. He loves graceful lines, delicacy and softness of tones. He paints lovingly landscapes that are alternately calm and fantastic.

Lucas Cranach
Venus
Louvre, Paris

Martin Heemskerk

Maerten Van Veen, known as Martin Heemskerk*, was a farmer's son. He was born at Heemskerk, a little village near Haarlem, in 1498. Van Manden tells a rather picturesque story of how his father at first yielded to Martin's desire to become a painter and allowed him to be apprenticed to Cornelius Willems of Haarlem, but then repented of such indulgence and forced him to come back and work on the farm. But having one day broken a jar of milk, and fearing his father's punishment, Martin fled across the fields and took refuge in Delft, where he worked for a mediocre artist called Jan Lucas. He soon left the latter and became a pupil of Van Scorel. He made such rapid progress that—still according to Van Mander—the master became jealous of him and dismissed him. One of Heemskerk's most important works of this period is his *St Luke Painting the Virgin* *, executed in 1532 for the Painters' Chapel in Haarlem. This painting has a certain air of coldness about it; the outlines are all angular. Its excellence lies in some of the strange detail.

At the age of thirty-four, Heemskerk travelled to Italy and spent three years in Rome, where he studied the antiquities and Michelangelo's frescoes. He became so infused with the latter's work that he was later called ' the Batavian Michelangelo '. On his return to Holland, Heemskerk settled in Haarlem, where for twenty-five years he served as a churchwarden of the parish. In 1572, at the age of seventy-four, he fled from Haarlem, which was about to be besieged, and took refuge in Amsterdam with his pupil Rauwaerts. Two years later he returned to his adopted city and died there in 1574.

Among the works of his second period, mention must be made of the *Crucifixion* painted during 1538-43, now in Linköping Cathedral in Sweden, the *Crucifixion* in the Ghent Museum, the *Annunciation* and *Adoration of the Magi and Shepherds* in the Haarlem Museum, the *Story of Momus* in Berlin, and *Christ's Baptism* in Brunswick. Heemskerk was a very energetic painter who worked with great facility and who used vigorous colour effects. His faults lie in his rather pedantic display of technical skill, which contrasts with the spontaneity and sober elegance of Van Scorel.

The most sensitive of his paintings are without a doubt his portraits, such as his *Family Portrait* in Cassel, and *Pieter Bicker* and his wife *Anna Codde* in Amsterdam, all three dating from before his visit to Italy and showing the influence of Van Scorel. In 1554, in a picture in which the artist appears to be trying to summarize his Romanist aspirations, he portrays himself as a tormented figure with an anxious look, with a view of the ruins of the Coliseum in the background.

Antonio Moro

Van Scorel's studio also produced the most remarkable of the Dutch portrait-painters of the second half of the century—Antonio Moor Van Dashorst. He was in fact Van Scorel's nephew. During his sojourn in Spain and Portugal in the service of Charles V, he called himself Antonio Moro *, and it is under this name that he is most generally known today.

Lucas Cranach
Courtesan with an Old Man
Museum, Besançon

The first known work by Moro is dated 1544. It is a portrait of *Two Canons of the Brotherhood of Jerusalem* and is very similar to the series of members of this brotherhood that Van Scorel painted. However, though the arrangement is the same as that of his master, Moro distinguishes himself by giving more freedom and flexibility to the figures and by using a thicker and firmly worked paint. The *Portrait of Cardinal Granvella* (1549) marks the achievement of a truly personal style. One can clearly note the influence of Titian, who had also painted the cardinal the previous year. It is possible that Moro had accompanied the cardinal when he attended the Diet of Ausburg in 1548, and there came into contact with Titian, whom we know had gone there to visit Charles V. Thereafter Moro remained faithful to a set formula: the subject standing, depicted half-length against a neutral background, and the head shown in three-quarter profile so that one eye appears in the centre of the facial area. This ' Cyclops' eye ', to borrow a phrase from G. Marlier, is one of Moro's characteristics.

Moro's most successful portraits are his *William of Orange*, still very young, headstrong and stubborn; the *Duke of Alba* in armour with a colourless face and a look of determination and cruelty; *Maximilian II*, looking superbly aristocratic; *Mary Tudor*, completely lacking in grace, sitting stiffly upright in a ceremonial armchair, a striking picture of a relentless, fanatical, murderous queen; and the *Portrait of the Artist by Himself*, with a kindly but searching gaze.

Towards the end of his life Moro painted a few intimate portraits of members of the middle classes. They are unaffected and relaxed, but they always retain a certain amount of reservation, while the artist pays more attention to light effects, as for example in *The Musician Jan Lecoq*, *Jan Van Scorel* and *Hubert Goltzius*. Antonio Moro, in the words of Jean Leymarie, was ' the most lucid and most profound biographer of his time '. He remained truly Dutch in the sobriety of his characterization, his close observation of the features, and the steadfastness with which he pursued his subject-matter. What he learnt from Italian art he used to his own advantage, without letting it alter his work much, as so many others had done. He had a profound influence on the Spanish portrait-painters, and one even finds something of his manner in Velasquez. In Holland, he magnificently prepares the way for Frans Hals.

Pieter Aertsen

Pieter Aertsen * is an artist who forms a link between the Netherlands of the north and of the south. He painted numerous pictures for churches which were highly prized in his day, and Van Mander describes several that were destroyed by the iconoclasts. He was also much appreciated as a designer of cartoons for stained-glass windows. But it is above all in genre paintings, and particularly kitchen scenes, that he excels.

The earliest of his works, the *Farmer's Wife*, dated 1543, shows Aertens already exploring this popular vein which he was to exploit so successfully. His *Calvary*, painted three years later, is one of the few altar-pieces by him that survive: they mean little to us to-day for they are so lacking in originality. With the *Butcher's Window* we come to one

Lucas Cranach
Portrait of John-Frederick, Elector of Saxony
1531
Oil on wood 20″ × 15″
Louvre, Paris

of Aertens' earliest masterpieces. It is a pure still-life, treated with astonishing boldness in a chromatic range of reds and yellows. In *The Bearing of the Cross* the painter introduces an innovation by expressing a sacred scene in day-to-day terms: the accent is placed on the crowd of people accompanying the Saviour up Mount Calvary. *The Peasants' Meal* (1556) may well depict the artist's family on a festive occasion. The justly celebrated *Dance of the Eggs* is dated the following year. It shows a lively folklore scene, enhanced by a profusion of delightful details and painted with a touch of affectation. In his *Christ with Martha and Mary*, now in Brussels, Aertsen is plainly turning a sacred subject into a profane genre scene with a plebeian subject: Martha, a solid Dutch matron, ' plants her great brush, with a gesture of defiance, right in the middle of the picture ', wrote R. Genaille. *The Pancake-Makers*, with its combination of bold colours, is remarkable for its use of the ' close-up ' technique borrowed from Hemessen. Among the finest and most characteristic of the artist's works is *The Cooks*. Here the treatment is simple yet forceful, the colour range is fine and delicate, and the red browns, black and white are in perfect harmony. As Van Mander said: ' Pieter Aersten's style was broad and vigorous; he eagerly tackled any subject and earned himself a great reputation through his art. When he set about painting kitchens containing all sorts of provisions, the result was such a perfect still-life that you would have said it was Life itself. By constantly practising this form of his art, he became the most skilful painter there ever was in the use of colours '. Though his style was subject to Italian borrowings and paid tribute to Mannerism *, Pieter Aersten nevertheless remained faithful to the realist and homely traditions of his own country.

Pieter Bruegel the Elder

We have waited till the close of this section before examining the work of Pieter Bruegel *, since this great artist forms the culminating point of the art of the Renaissance in the northern countries.

We do not know with any great precision either the date or the place of birth of Pieter Bruegel. ' Nature, ' wrote Van Mander, ' made a singularly happy choice when, in an obscure village in Brabant, she selected from among the peasants, as the delineator of peasants, the witty Pieter Bruegel. He was born in the neighbourhood of Breda, in a village whose name he took to himself and transmitted to his descendants.' Now there exists no village of this name near Breda. Was he then born in Brueghel, near Eindhoven, in Northern Brabant, or in Brueghel in the Belgian Campine, east of Antwerp ? It is impossible to decide either way. Likewise, the date of his birth is difficult to establish. The epitaph on his tomb in Notre Dame de la Chapelle in Brussels, which was engraved by his great-grandson David Teniers III, mentions the date of his death, but neither the age he reached nor the date of his birth. It is generally thought that this must be placed between 1525 and 1530; probably nearer the earlier year. The evidence for this is to be found in the date on which Pieter Bruegel was admitted as a master to the Painters' Guild, and on his apparent age in two of his engraved self-portraits. He was

Lucas Cranach
Diana Resting
Museum, Besançon

probably apprenticed in 1545 to the painter Pieter Coeck*, a Romanist and a pupil of Bernard Van Orley who had travelled widely in Italy and the Near East. Coeck was the author of theoretical treatises based on the innovations of the Italian painters of the Cinquecento, and these books had a great success in their day. He trained his pupil in the Italian manner. Pieter Bruegel subsequently entered the workshop of Hieronymus Cock*, though at what date is unknown. Hieronymus Cock was an engraver, a printseller and a picture dealer. He had a shop at the sign of the 'Four Winds' which was the meeting-place of the artists and patrons in Antwerp, and his prints were distributed throughout Europe. Pieter Bruegel engraved for him some of his own compositions as well as reproductions of pictures by Hieronymus Bosch.

It was in Hieronymus Cock's shop, therefore, that Bruegel came into contact with the cheerful artists of Brabant, who left a permanent mark on his work, In 1551, he became a free master of the Painters' Guild of Antwerp, and it was probably shortly after this that he departed for Italy. After passing through Burgundy and going down the Rhône valley, he travelled the whole length of Italy, through Naples to Sicily.

In 1553 he was back in Rome, as is proved by some of his drawings of that year which mention the city. His drawings also show that he returned through mountainous regions, perhaps the Apennines and probably the Alps. He made this journey more as an admirer of landscape than as a lover of art or amateur of antiquities. In fact, throughout his travels he was less passionately concerned with works of art, ancient or modern, than with the beauties of nature. He brought back from Rome not a single sketch of Roman monuments or Renaissance masterpieces, but drawings of the countryside through which he passed.

Bruegel was back in Antwerp towards the end of 1553. He once more returned to his work for Hieronymus Cock, not as pupil now, however, but as his chief collaborator, and henceforth a large number of the engravings issued by the shop of the 'Four Winds' bear the words 'Bruegel invenit'. Furthermore, Bruegel entered into the humanist circles: he was therefore a man of considerable culture, and not a peasant, as has sometimes been suggested. It appears that he had some knowledge of Greek, since one of his drawings bears the name ' Roma ' in Greek lettering. At the same time, this did not inhibit him from mixing with the people. He and his friend Frankert enjoyed dressing up in peasant costume and attending fairs and village weddings. Van Mander informs us that he had as mistress a servant-girl whose honesty and sincerity were not beyond reproach. Eventually he married Mayken Coeck, daughter of his first master. She must have been fifteen to twenty years younger than he was. Bruegel then settled in Brussels, possibly in order to terminate completely his previous affair. The marriage was celebrated in the church of Notre Dame de la Chapelle in Brussels in 1563. The painter went to live in the Rue Haute, which was a district then inhabited by people of good social standing. Here he was held in high esteem, although it is thought that he sympathized with the reformers during this period when religious struggles often led to tragedy. Finally, we know that he died prematurely in 1569, leaving three children, a daughter and two sons. The latter both became painters: the elder, Pieter Bruegel II*,

FONTIS NYMPHA SACRI SOMNVM
NE RVMPE QVIESCO ·

known as 'Hell Bruegel', made numerous copies of his father's work, while the younger, Jan Bruegel*, has come down to posterity as 'Velvet Bruegel' on account of his fondness for rich, soft colours. The latter collaborated with Rubens on several canvases. Both had sons who were given their fathers' first names and became painters, and are known as Pieter III and Jan II. The latter's sister, Anne, married David Teniers.

Pieter Bruegel came to painting comparatively late in life. The first picture that can be attributed to him with certainty, the *Proverbs* in Antwerp, is dated 1558. It consists of a panel divided into twelve compartments in which, against a circular red background, are painted tiny scenes, each representing a popular saying. These tiny figures are completely natural and are delightfully observed, although their treatment is somewhat awkward. The following year, the artist took up the same subject again, but here the composition is completely different and the result is a masterpiece. Within the restricted space of a corner of a village, this picture succeeds in depicting a whole host of characters, each of whom is miming a Flemish proverb or saying, such as 'To play when one is being pilloried', 'He makes the world dance on his thumb', and 'To beat one's head against a brick wall'. Some ninety-two sayings have been recognized, but there is something rather tragic in the way that they are represented, for this work is of the same kind as Erasmus' *Praise of Folly*. A similar example of the juxtaposition of a large number of different episodes is to be found in *The Fight between Carnival and Lent*, in which Bruegel once again reveals his extraordinary sense of detail. As so often in Bruegel's works, realism and the world of the imagination are here completely intermingled. *Children's Games*, painted in 1560, which depicts games of all kinds, also contains a seething mass of tiny figures.

During the years 1562-5, Bruegel produced a group of works which are variously inspired but all of which reflect a mental unbalance veering from extreme optimism to extreme pessimism. The *Tower of Babel* (1563) exalts the actions of mankind, but *The Procession to Calvary* (1564), on the other hand, is tinged with melancholy. In *Landscape with the Fall of Icarus* (*ca* 1563) the drowning Icarus is completely unnoticed by the

other figures in the picture. One may well agree with Charles de Tolnay that this painting 'stresses the subordination of human life to Nature's eternal laws'[1], but Bruegel seems also to be remarking, with a touch of sadness, on mankind's disinterestedness in the destruction of the idealist who is haunted by too great a dream. Here the painter shows us the triumph of mediocrity.

This is also the period in which Bruegel painted his astonishingly horrifying pictures, *The Fall of the Rebel Angels*, *The Triumph of Death* and *The 'Dull Griet' (Mad Meg)*. The influence of Hieronymus Bosch is predominant in all three works. Here Bruegel manages to breathe vigorous life into nightmarish creatures which are at once abhorrent and absurd, compounded as they are out of a mixture of animal and plant forms and inanimate objects. *The Triumph of Death* is like a terrifying vision of the Apocalypse. The subject is the old mediaeval theme that there is no distinction of rank in the face of death. Death here comes in the most hallucinatory forms, ranging from natural catastrophes to various methods of torture. Never, perhaps, has the extinction of human life been recorded with such powerful and harrowing eloquence. *Mad Meg* can be considered the climax of Bruegel's career as a satanic painter. Here the influence of Bosch is even more marked. From him Bruegel borrows the motif of the grappling-iron, the fires that light up the background, and the colour effects. Mad Meg personifies the mad fury of Evil, the spiteful woman of whom even the devil himself is afraid. The proverbial shrew, sword in hand and followed by her companions, dashes with ferocious determination towards the Mouth of Hell, which she intends to lay waste. Demons flee in terror before her. It was been suggested, not without reason, that this work, together with the two previous ones, may in addition allude to the reign of terror which the Spanish imposed on the Flemish.

[1] Charles de Tolnay: *Pierre Bruegel l'Ancien*, Brussels, 1935.

◄◄ Hans Holbein the Younger
Augsburg 1497-London 1543
Portrait of Sir Henry Wyatt
1526-8
Oil on wood
Louvre, Paris

◄ Hans Holbein the Younger
Portrait of Dorothea Kannengiesser, Wife of Jacob Meyer, Burgomaster of Basle
1516
Varnished tempera on wood 15″ × 12″
Museum, Basle

During 1565 there occurred what has been called Bruegel's classical period. For several years now he had been living in Brussels, a much quieter city than Antwerp. And here he moved in different surroundings, those of the court and the nobility. Moreover, his anxieties ceased to trouble him, and he produced the most tranquil of his works,the series of *The Months*, which was commissioned by the banker Jonghelinck. Only five of these paintings have survived—*Hunters in the Snow*, *The Gloomy Day*, *Hay Making*, *The Corn Harvest* and *The Return of the Herd.* In these pictures Bruegel closely allies human life with life in nature. Between 1565 and 1567, still peaceful and relaxed, he extended his attempts at achieving a balanced form of expression. The *Sermon of St John the Baptist* is an amusing study of a crowd-scene, and at the same time an experiment in perspective. In *The Suicide of Saul* Bruegel recalls the alpine scenery that he had so much admired. The *Storm at Sea* in Vienna, which is extraordinarily modern in conception, has the raging ocean as its subject, yet the ships are making for a port behind which the sky is lightening.

In 1566, Bruegel produced two pictures which form a pair and are directly descended from the *Hunters in the Snow*. These are *The Numbering at Bethlehem* and *The Massacre of the Innocents*, both of which are snow scenes and magnificently record the atmosphere of winter. The sacred subjects are in fact a pretext which seems to have enabled Bruegel to make his own personal protest against the exploitation and despotism, the violence and cruelty which he saw increasingly around him.

The *Land of Cockaigne* * (1567) is also a work with social undertones. Here Bruegel returns to allegory, showing the fulfilment of the people's pipe-dream—to be able to eat one's fill. This desire was only increased by the arrival in Flanders of the Duke of Alba, and the setting up of the Council of Troubles.

Between 1566 and 1568, Bruegel painted the series of pictures showing the coarse manners of the people which were to earn him the nickname 'Peasant' Bruegel. The most notable of these are *The Peasant Dance*, *The Wedding Dance in the Open Air* and *The Wedding Banquet*. This group had been preceded long before by a number of pen-and-ink drawings taken from life, which have survived. We know that earlier in his life, Bruegel had much enjoyed joining in these village celebrations in the company of his friend Hans Frankert. In these works he becomes the chronicler of the humble pleasures of rustic life, which he recalls for us in vivid, earthy pictures which may be trivial in character and even sometimes comical, but which are full of vitality and which exalt the sensual joy of living.

However, this cheerful interlude was soon to give way to another bout of depression and bitterness. The pictures Bruegel painted in 1568, his last year of work, reveal his feelings of disillusion. *The Misanthrope* * shows a disenchanted philosopher, wearing a homespun cape and cowl, who is following a path set with man-traps, while around him lies a dismal landscape. The small picture of *The Cripples* * depicts an assembly of beggars who have escaped from a Lepers' Procession. Again, in the *Parable of the Blind* *, which is perhaps the most powerful of the works of the final period,

Grünewald
Calvary
Museum, Basle

Bruegel raises his subject beyond the realms of reality and turns it into his conception of the human conflict.

Bruegel had certainly found in the painters of the Netherlands who had preceded him, his subjects, expression and craft, but his excellence lies in his ability to amplify certain set formulas and enlarge on them until they develop into his proper style without in any way allowing them to become conventional. Furthermore, he brought back from his voyage in Italy not a series of stereotyped patterns, but a broadening of vision and a stylization which never let him lose touch with life. As a true humanist, he was able at one and the same time to share the miseries of the peasants of Brabant placed under the Spanish yoke, and to express in his works his elevated philosophical ideas, which led him to say to his friend Ortelius that ' in all his works there was more thought than painting '. His astonishing clarity of mind made him ever conscious of the power and variety of cosmic forces. Bruegel achieved a synthesis of nature and of the human soul. If he is as much at ease with realism as with the world of the imagination, it is because for him the two were complementary facets of the ultimate truth. Bruegel formed his own mode of critical examination of the visible and invisible world, which is one of the most profound aspects of the neoplatonic * metaphysics of the Renaissance.

Germany

In Germany, as in France and Flanders, the end of the fifteenth and the beginning of the sixteenth century is a period of emancipation and optimism. Certainly, during the first quarter of the sixteenth century Germany underwent a religious and social revolution, whose most spectacular results were the Reformation brought about by Luther * and the Peasants' Wars. But these were only the repercussions of this complete reawakening which they could in no way impede in its course. At the same time, trade developed, and Augsburg, Nuremberg and Frankfurt became great commercial centres. They were governed by city fathers with great business experience, liberal in their outlook and well-educated. These towns were also important centres of intellectual and artistic life. This highly fruitful period produced some of the greatest painters in the history of German art. Though their works always retain a strong Gothic streak, nevertheless artists show an ever-increasing interest in Italian art. Michael Pacher, one of the last truly Gothic painters, was probably also one of the first German painters to visit Italy. He was fascinated by architectural studies in perspective, which shows that he tried to absorb the ideas and achieve the technical skill of the Italian masters. Dürer, Holbein and Nicolas Manuel all went to Italy, while others became familiar with Italian art through engravings, collections of drawings and the models of ornamentalists. As has often been remarked, despite its importance in Germany the Renaissance lasted for only a comparatively short period, coming between the late Gothic and the Baroque, which flourished at the end of the Thirty Years' War.

Albrecht Dürer
The Apostles John and Peter
Pinakothek, Munich

Albrecht Dürer

Albrecht Dürer *, who is certainly the most important figure in the German Renaissance, was born on 21st May 1471 in Nuremberg, a city which, at the end of the fifteenth century, could be regarded as the German Florence. Dürer himself has given us details of his origins and his forebears in an invaluable family history which he wrote late in life. His father, ' a kind and patient man ', taught him the goldsmith's art, and Dürer had already become proficient in this when he confessed that he was more attracted to painting. Somewhat reluctantly, for he regretted the time lost in learning to be a goldsmith, the old man acquiesced in his favourite son's wishes and bound him apprentice to Michael Wolgemut, who was then the most famous painter in Nuremberg. The first work that Dürer produced on his own was a portrait of his father. This painting, which is very life-like and is treated conscientiously and lovingly, already reveals an astonishing talent.

In 1490, the young artist, now aged nineteen and having completed his apprenticeship, went on a study tour, as was then the custom. He visited Colmar, Basle and Strasbourg, and travelled through Venetia, improving his art by making landscape drawings and copying the masters. Among the works produced during these travels, the most important is a *Self-Portrait* painted on vellum and dated 1493. As this picture was intended for his fiancée, in his hand he holds a blue sea-holly, which in German is called *Mannstreu*, meaning ' husband's fidelity '.

The face bears a serious expression and is framed with long blond locks which accentuate Dürer's soft, almost feminine features. In May 1494, Dürer returned to Nuremberg and shortly afterwards he married Agnes Frey, the daughter of a highly esteemed and highly talented jeweller and craftsman. He started a workshop in his father's house and, with the help of his apprentices, he followed the local tradition, though in a rather freer manner and under the strong influence of Mantegna. He proceeded to paint altar-pieces and votive pictures, such as the famous *Paumgärtner Triptych*.

This first period was just as productive in portraits, in which Dürer shows himself to be an excellent interpreter of the human face. He sticks to essentials, concentrating his attention on facial structure and the expression of intelligence which he renders with dramatic intensity. These pictures include such memorable portraits as those of *Frederick the Wise*, *Oswolt Krell* and *Jacob Fugger*, and of himself. He also became known for his woodcuts, such as the *Apocalypse*, *The Life of the Virgin* and *Great Passion*, and his copper-engravings, including *The Holy Family*, *The Prodigal Son*, *Great Fortune* and *Adam and Eve*, whose success was so great that they were quickly copied by Italian engravers. It was on the pretext of having to defend his artist's rights, which had been infringed by a forged engraving of *The Life of the Virgin* produced by Marcantonio, that he undertook his journey to Venice in 1505.

Several large canvases painted on his return are evidence of his ever-increasing mastery. In 1507 he produced the two panels representing *Adam and Eve*, in which the

figures reveal a balance and sense of movement which the artists of Northern Europe had never so far succeeded in achieving. The following year saw the *Martyrdom of the Ten Thousand*, an impassioned, descriptive work, treated with mannered perfectionism, in which he shows his skill in the depiction of the nude. Finally, from 1508 to 1511 he worked on his impressive *Trinity and All Saints*. By about 1510, Dürer had become so discouraged by the poor return on his pictures, considering the amount of time their attention to detail cost him, that he decided to give up painting.

In 1513 and 1514, Dürer made copper-engravings of three of his greatest works, *The Knight, Death and the Devil*, *Melencolia* and *St Jerome in his Study*. For the emperor he employed all his ingenuity in making the designs for *The Triumphal Arch of Maximilian*, consisting of 92 blocks which together form a woodcut 11′2″ high by 7′11″ wide. He also collaborated on the series of 134 woodcuts which make up the *Triumphal Procession*. Shortly after Maximilian's death in 1519, Dürer painted a portrait of him.

In this the emperor is draped in a great black mantle and holds in his hand a pomegranate, which Dürer chose as a symbol of the resurrection.

In 1520 the plague came to Nuremberg, and Dürer made this an excuse for visiting the Netherlands. He wished to have the allowance of 100 florins which Maximilian had granted to him confirmed by his successor Charles V, who was going to Aix-la-Chapelle to be crowned emperor. He also was in search of new horizons. He spent a year in Antwerp, and paid brief visits to Brussels, Aix, Cologne, Zeeland, Ghent, Bruges and Malines. He met all the great Flemish painters, such as Quentin Metsys, Joachim Patenier * and Lucas Van Leyden. Wherever he went he was magnificently entertained. But despite the offers of the councillors of Antwerp, he preferred, as he wrote, to go back and live in his native town ' with a moderate income, rather than to be a rich and important person elsewhere '. On his return to Nuremberg he was commissioned to prepare the cartoons for the decoration of the grand chamber of the Town Hall. He left the work of transferring them to the walls to one of his pupils. These frescoes still exist, but they have been restored to such an extent that their original appearance has been completely destroyed. During his last years, Dürer took up painting again, but it was chiefly the human face that engaged his mind. Completely eliminating the pictorial element or any setting that might reveal the subject's social position, Dürer strives to bring out, as a moralist and as an interpreter of human nature, the essential character, to express the inner life of his models, who, for the most part, consist of his friends, for example *Hans Imhoff the Elder*, *Jacob Muffel*, *Hieronymus Holzschuler* and *Johann Kleeberger*.

Dürer's last major work, *The Four Apostles*, is also his spiritual testament. The meditative figures of St John and St Peter, St Mark and St Paul, are gathered together on two panels. With truly classical economy, Dürer here succeeds in presenting the vast diversity of human nature through a powerful contrast of characters, and at the same time he expresses the essential spirit of Christianity. Having completed this work, he turned his attention to revising and seeing through the press his writings on the theory of art—his *Treatise on the Proportions of the Human Body* and *Instruction in the Measurement with the Compass*. Further weakened by a disease from which he had been suffering for many years, he died in his home in Nuremberg in 1528. He was only fifty-eight years old. The house in which he lived has since been turned into a museum devoted to his life and work, and it still retains much of the decoration that it had in his own day.

In his own country, Albrecht Dürer initiated the new movement. His contemporaries turned to him for their example. In him, for the first time, the Italian ideal, which strove after breadth and style, and the Germanic ideal, with its exaltation of the inner life, are at last combined and united in a new synthesis.

Altdorfer
Birth of the Virgin
Alte Pinakothek, Munich

Hans Baldung Grien
Virgin in the Vine-Arbour
1539
Lime-wood 23″ × 17″
Museum, Strasbourg

Mathias Grünewald

There is a great deal of uncertainty about the life of Mathias Grünewald *, the other great painter who, alongside Dürer, dominates the first third of the sixteenth century in Germany. Melanchthon * mentions him in a book published in 1531 and places him between Dürer and Cranach. Much later, Sandrart *, the German Vasari, speaks at length of Grünewald in his *Teutsche Akademie*. After expressing regret that such a great artist should be so soon forgotten, he states that Grünewald, 'commonly called Matthias of Aschaffenburg, lived in the days of Albrecht Dürer, about 1505'. After listing a number of his works, he goes on to say: 'That is all that I know about this fine German artist, except that he settled in Mainz, where he lived a retired, melancholy life due to an unhappy marriage. I know neither where nor when he died, but I imagine it was about 1510.' The reappraisal of Grünewald in the nineteenth century has led to the discovery that his real name was Matthis Nithardt, called Gothart. This explains the monogram formed from the letters MG and N which appears in the *St Lawrence* in the Frankfurt Museum and again on the frame of the *Madonna* at Stuppach. Matthis Nithardt, the son of an engineer, was born in the village of Würzburg in 1455 or 1460 at the latest. He was trained in Colmar by Martin Schongauer *, and later received the patronage of Canon Heinrich Reitzmann of Aschaffenburg, where he settled in 1480.

In 1490 he was working with a sculptor in Worms. In 1501 he became a member of the Guild, and seven years later he was court painter and art adviser to Uriel von Gemmingen, Archbishop of Mainz. Apart from a visit to Alsace which he made on being commissioned to paint the altar-piece for Isenheim, he worked in the region of the middle Rhine and lower Main. When Albert of Brandenburg succeeded Uriel von Gemmingen in 1514, Grünewald was confirmed in his post. A few years later he was present at the coronation of Charles V at Aix-la-Chapelle, where he met Dürer. In 1525, there was an uprising of peasants and artisans in the Aschaffenburg area, which may explain why he lost his post, though this may have been due to his sympathies with Luther. In any case, he had to take refuge in Frankfurt. From there he moved to Halle, which was a protestant city. Here he worked as an engineer concerned with hydraulic projects. He died in Halle in 1528, only a few months before Dürer.

One of Grünewald's earliest paintings is the *Mocking of Christ* in Munich. Here one already finds the painful expression of violence and suffering which was to become a characteristic feature of his work. In this example, Grünewald sharply contrasts Jesus' resignation with the bestiality and sadism of his tormentors. The use of harsh, clashing colours heightens the dramatic element. This picture has such a powerful effect on the viewer that, as careful examination has revealed, someone in the past scraped out the tormentors' eyes, which the artist has made so repulsive and horrible. The small *Crucifixion* in Basle is only an outline of a subject which Grünewald enlarged on later on various occasions. The figures of *St Cyriacus* and *St Lawrence* in the Frankfurt Museum are grisailles, but the depth and variation of tones give them a contrast and intense feeling of life which are lacking in the grisailles of the Flemish primitives.

In 1508, Grünewald began his masterpiece, the *Isenheim Altar-piece* *, which took him five to six years to complete. It had been commissioned by the Sicilian abbot Guido Guersi, superior of the Antonian convent church at Isenheim, a famous abbey on the upper Rhine, in the Vosges, near Colmar. It is a transformation altar-piece, that is to say it consists of three triptychs forming volets which were superimposed one on top of the other and opened in such a way that one could display them to the faithful in turn, following the feasts of the liturgical year. The first triptych, which covered the other two, contains a *Crucifixion* in the centre panel, flanked by two fixed volets depicting, on the right a *St Sebastian*, and on the left a *St Antony*. The second triptych showed *The Virgin Adored by Angels* between two movable volets of *The Annunciation* and *The Resurrection*. The first two sets were thus devoted to the life of Christ. The last was reserved for St Antony, the church's patron saint. In the centre there was a large statue of the saint, accompanied by St Augustine and St Jerome. The painted volets depicted, on the right the *Temptation of St Antony*, and on the left a *Conversation between St Antony and Paul the Hermit*. Beneath the altar-piece the predella contained an *Entombment*.[1]

Grünewald's later works, though admirable in their own way, lack the breadth of vision of the Isenheim polyptych. Of the altar-piece painted in 1519 which once adorned the chapel of St Mary of the Snows in the collegiate church at Aschaffenburg only two fragments remain: a *Virgin* in the church of Stuppach in Bavaria, and a volet depicting the *Foundation of St Mary Major* in the Freiburg Museum. These paintings show a novel delicacy in the treatment of detail, a certain mannerism which one must, no doubt, attribute to Italian influence. The Karlsruhe *Crucifixion* is reminiscent of that of Colmar, but is more restrained. There are now only the Virgin and St John at the foot of the Cross. Furthermore, the artist has heightened the realism of the crucified body and has succeeded in expressing a combination of horror and sympathy. Grünewald's last work is his *Sts Maurice and Erasmus* (*ca* 1525-6), in which the scene is merely another example of the *sacre conversazioni* imported from Italy.

As Huysmans said, Grünewald is indeed ' the most frenzied realist and idealist '. His extremism, his tumultuous genius, enable him to express the most excessive and contradictory emotions. His art is in turn realistic, mystical, expressionist and surrealist. He always tries to endow his subject with the maximum power of suggestion possible. Contrary to Dürer, who lived by measure and reason, Grünewald relied on instinct and his burning imagination. He was not a pioneer as Dürer was, but was bound even more closely than the latter to the German mediaeval tradition, which he succeeded in raising to its highest point of achievement.

Lucas Cranach

The name Cranach *, by which Lucas Sunder is known, is derived from his birthplace, Kronach, near Bamberg, in Upper Franconia. He was born on 4th October 1472, a year

[1] The altar-piece is now in the Unterlinden Museum in Colmar, and has been dismembered so that all the parts may be seen at the same time.

Hans Baldung Grien
Nativity
Museum, Basle

before Dürer. His father was a painter, about whom nothing else is known. It is assumed that Lucas underwent his apprenticeship in his father's workshop, but in fact there exists absolutely no information about his early years. In 1503 we find him in Vienna, and during his stay there he produced the first of the pictures that have come down to us. These include the *Crucifixion* in the Munich Gallery, which is so intensely dramatic and so original in composition; the portraits of *Dr Reuss*, rector of the university, and of the humanist *Johannes Cuspinian and his Wife;* as well as the very famous *Rest of the Virgin during the Flight into Egypt*, dating from the end of his visit, a poetic piece whose charm is somewhat insipid.

In 1504, Cranach settled in Wittenberg, seat of the court of Saxe, and thereafter until his death he remained court painter to three successive Electors. One of his major works painted at the court of Wittenberg is the *St Catharine Altar-piece* (1506). In the following year he completed the great *Venus*, now in the Hermitage, chronologically the first of the female nudes * which were to become one of his specialities. Whether he turned to mythology, the Bible or Roman history, he always sought out subjects that enabled him to depict the nude. As a result he produced a variety of paintings with titles such as *Venus and Cupid*, *Nymphs*, *Diana and Apollo*, *Adam and Eve*, *David and Bathsheba*, *Samson and Delilah*, *Judith and Holofernes*, and *Lucretia*. Whereas Dürer's women have rather heavy, full figures, Cranach preferred slender bodies with sloping shoulders and the head small and round. The tiny breasts are set high, the stomach is gently curved and the legs are long. The artist liked to set off these figures with transparent veils, heavy necklaces and huge hats, which further underline their naked-

Frans Floris
Athena Visits the Muses
Museum, Condé-sur-l'Escaut

ness. These cold, mysterious beings have a simple and perverse charm. Their breasts are virginal, but the look that passes through their slits of eyes is highly provocative, and the smile on their lips is most suggestive.

In 1508 Cranach travelled to the Netherlands. Frederick the Wise had instructed him to ' show his talent ' at the court of the Emperor Maximilian. He painted the portrait of the emperor's grandson, the future Charles V, who was then eight years old. He visited Malines, Brussels, Antwerp, Ghent and Bruges, studying all the time the art of the Flemish Romanists. He met Quentin Metsys and Mabuse, whose influence is to be seen in the altar-piece of *The Holy Family*, now in the Städelsches Kunstinstitut, Frankfurt, which he painted the following year, after his return. Here the Italian manner (marble columns, ancient bas-reliefs, tapestries, and flagstones shown in perspective) is combined with imaginary landscapes which are completely northern European in appearance, with their dense forests surrounding mountains topped by a walled town.

After 1510, pictures in the authentic hand of Lucas Cranach the Elder become more and more rare. He passed the commissions which flowed into his workshop on to his two sons, Hans and Lucas the Younger, who in turn were assisted by numerous apprentices.

Cranach was an intimate friend of Martin Luther. He had been one of the witnesses at Luther's marriage, and the latter stood godfather to one of his sons. It is therefore not surprising that, in his old age, the painter should have been attracted by the Reformation. From his workshop there issued large numbers of pictures on religious

Manuel Deutsch
St Thomas Aquinas at the Table of St Louis
Museum, Basle

Hans Holbein the Younger
Portrait of Anne of Cleves
1539
Vellum mounted on canvas 26″ × 19″
Louvre, Paris

themes with political or doctrinal implications, such as *Jesus Chasing the Merchants from the Temple*, *Jesus and the Woman Taken in Adultery*, *Let the Little Children Come unto Me*, and *Jesus in the Pharisee's House*. They are of little interest except as documents: the religious feeling is weak and the treatment is indifferent. The only pictures of any artistic value are the portraits of *Martin Luther* and of his wife *Catherine Bora*. Indeed, Cranach produced a number of excellent portraits.

In 1519, Cranach was elected a town councillor of Wittenberg, and on two occasions, in 1537 and 1540, he held the office of Burgomaster. In 1521 he acquired a pharmacy, and the Elector conferred on him a special privilege, namely that, 'except on the occasion of a fair, no other than Lucas, whether a townsman or a stranger, shall be permitted to traffic in spices, jams, sugar, treacle, coloured wax, nor any other provision which apothecaries are accustomed to sell'. He also controlled a printing-press which issued his engravings and a large number of Lutheran pamphlets. Though he was now a very wealthy, solid citizen, Cranach was still able to show his humanitarian feelings on occasion. In 1547, the young Elector John Frederick the Magnanimous, who had joined the coalition of protestant princes, was taken prisoner by the Emperor Charles V at Mühlberg, and condemned to death. Cranach, now aged seventy-five, visited the emperor in order to intercede on behalf of his master. He insisted on sharing the latter's two years of captivity in Augsburg and Innsbruck. After John Frederick's release, he continued to serve him in his new residence at Weimar, and died there on 16th October 1553.

Although his enormous output gained him a great reputation, Cranach is inferior to the German artists we have already considered. Caught between the new ideas and the mediaeval tradition, he failed to unify them in his work. He remains an honest craftsman whose inspiration soon became bogged down by the demands made on his workshop. Nevertheless one cannot deny that he had a definite poetic gift, which is revealed in his nudes and in his landscapes, in which the local countryside is transposed into a dream world of crystalline brooks, fearful forests and fantastic mountains. Melancthon, who was a friend of Cranach's, has described him perfectly in the words ' a humble genius '.

Hans Holbein

The greatest of the German portrait-painters of the sixteenth century was Hans Holbein *, known as the Younger to distinguish him from his father. Hans Holbein the Elder * was himself a fine painter from Augsburg, who had assimilated the discoveries of the Renaissance in his work. His art is a very personal one, and shows a love of simple truth and real people portrayed from life, as can be seen in his *St Sebastian Altarpiece* and his *Baptism of St Paul*. He brought up his two sons, Ambrosius and Hans, in a knowledge of his art. The former died in 1518 at the age of twenty-five, too young to have fulfilled the promise which a few beautiful drawings bear witness to. Hans, the younger son, was probably born in 1497, and was just as talented. He settled in Basle with his brother *ca* 1514, and began to do work for the local printers, notably the

Altdorfer
Battle of Alexander (detail)
Pinakothek, Munich

celebrated Hans Froben, for whom he supplied the designs for borders and decorative letters. He also illustrated a copy of Erasmus' *Praise of Folly* with pen-and-ink drawings, as well as Sir Thomas More's *Utopia*. Having been summoned to Lucerne to decorate a house there, it is thought that he took the opportunity, *ca* 1519, to visit Como and Milan, which would explain his profound knowledge of Italian art. Five years later he visited France. Indeed, his procedure is exactly the same as that of the portrait-painters of the French court. In 1516, Holbein painted two pictures, the portraits of *Jacob Meyer, Burgomaster of Basle*, and of his wife, *Dorothea Kannengiesser*, which form the earliest examples of the series of brilliant works he was to produce. Holbein here shows himself already fully-fledged. The composition is simple. The subjects are painted in half-length, beneath an arch whose vault is decorated with gold ornaments. The drawing is firm and quite striking. The painter has paid particular attention to colour: he violently contrasts the azure of the sky with the very bright red of the burgomaster's bonnet and of his wife's dress. *Bonifacius Amerbach* (1519) is even more successful. Holbein's treatment has become bolder and more supple. The colours and powerful expressiveness of this portrait recall those of Antonello da Messina *. The *Erasmus* in the Louvre (1523), an unforgettable portrait of ' the Dutch Voltaire ', is one of Holbein's major works.

During the Basle period, Holbein had not yet restricted himself entirely to portraits. He painted frescoes, which have since disappeared, for the new Town Hall and various houses. He made designs for stained-glass windows, models of ornaments (a field in which he excelled) for goldsmiths and armourers, and series of vignettes intended to be engraved. In particular, his *Dance of Death* series, the woodblocks of which were made by Hans Lützelburger, were immensely popular. He also executed some pictures on religious themes, the most celebrated of which is his *Dead Christ*. In this painting he attained a degree of realism as moving as anything by Grünewald. However, the feeling of tragedy evoked by this predella from a lost altar-piece is unique in his work. Mention should also be made of *The Madonna of the Burgomaster Jacob Meyer*. The donor and his entire family are here portrayed at the feet of a charming and gentle Virgin. The fact that the Burgomaster of Basle commissioned such a picture demonstrated his steadfastness in the Catholic faith and his unshakeable fidelity to the cult of the Virgin, which was reviled by the Reformation. In fact, religious disagreements began to break out throughout the town. In 1525, the iconoclasts destroyed all religious images, the disorders spread, and a financial crisis endangered Basle's food supply. At the same time, the hostility of the radicals of the Reformation to any form of profane art increased in violence. Holbein therefore decided in 1526 to come to England. On his way he passed through Antwerp, and probably there met Quentin Metsys. In London, he was welcomed by Sir Thomas More, to whom he had an introduction from Erasmus. Thereafter Holbein devoted himself entirely to portrait-painting, and he became accepted as the leading artist in court circles.

In the summer of 1528, Holbein returned to Basle. During his stay in that city, which lasted four years, he painted his famous portrait of his wife and two children. But

he was an unremitting devotee of realism, and in no way flattered his family. The baby which his wife is holding on her knees, has pale swollen cheeks and a button nose. As to the mother, she is shown as a heavy, disgruntled middle-class matron. Although the Council of Basle tried to persuade the artist to stay by offering him the contract for decorating some of the rooms in the Town Hall, Holbein, who had become bored with the dull life he was leading, and also perhaps with his colourless spouse, decided in 1552 to return to London, which he never again left. The German merchants of the Steelyard, the wealthy members of the Hanseatic League, invited him to become their corporation painter. They employed him to decorate their hall with *The Triumphs of Wealth and Poverty*, inspired by Mantegna, and also commissioned him to execute various portraits, including that of *Georg Gisze*. Despite the vulgarity of the sitter, this picture is fascinating on account of the accuracy with which every little object in the setting is depicted. This attention to detail, and even to unusual detail, is pushed to its furthest extent in the portrait of *The Ambassadors*, at whose feet is a skull treated in anamorphosis *. In about 1536, Holbein entered the service of Henry VIII and was appointed court painter. He first painted a portrait of the king, fat and puffy with a vacant expression in his eye, and then of his wife *Lady Jane Seymour*. When the latter died in childbirth, the king entrusted Holbein with the confidential mission of reporting to him on the physical appearance of the candidates for her succession. In 1538 he went to Brussels to paint Christina of Denmark, but the marriage did not take place. The following year he visited the castle of Duren, and painted the portrait of *Anne of Cleves*. The king married her, but shortly afterwards had the marriage declared null and void. Holbein then painted the portrait of the new queen, *Catharine Howard*, who was beheaded six months later.

In 1543, London was struck by the plague. On 7th October Holbein dictated his will, in which he asked that all his goods should be sold to pay off his debts and help maintain his mistress, a young English girl, and the two children she had borne him. No reference was made to his family in Basle. In the autumn he died, probably a victim to the plague.

Even Holbein's slightest portraits show that he regarded every sitter as a specimen of humanity who deserved to be studied impartially. He had a capacity for making his subjects reveal their secret emotions, their habits, the many sides of their characters, by surprising something in their eyes, on their lips, or in their bearing. His work contains no anguish, no fantasies of the imagination, nor any leaning towards sentimentality, only a cold objectivity reflected in the technique itself, which is one of the most incisive that have ever been created.

Albrecht Altdorfer

Although too little known, Albrecht Altdorfer * is yet one of the most important painters of the German Renaissance. He was not a pupil of Dürer's, as was for a long time thought, and as his monogram, inspired by that of Dürer, had suggested. He is the most typical representative of the Danubian school, whose manner was derived from that of the miniature, and tended to favour landscapes rather than figure-painting. Altdorfer was born *ca* 1480 at Amberg, a small town in Bavaria. In 1505 he became a citizen of Ratisbon, and thereafter, up to the time of his death in 1538, he hardly ever left the region. He occasionally travelled in Austria when commissions demanded. It is also assumed that he must have visited Italy, and perhaps stayed in Verona and Venice. He was a painter, architect, engraver on wood and copper, and also took an active part in politics. He was a member of the Grand Council and the Privy Council of Ratisbon, and towards the end of his life he became an ardent supporter of Luther.

One of Altdorfer's earliest important works is a *St George*. The mythical fight between the saint and the dragon, symbolizing the forces of evil, is set in the heart of the German forest which is famous for its legends. The two protagonists are almost completely lost in the luxuriance of nature, and the principal features of the picture are the dense greenery of the wood and the small gap in the trees which opens out into the distance. In the *Holy Family at the Fountain*, which dates from the same period, Altdorfer's taste for architecture already makes its appearance. This is a votive painting which the artist dedicated to the Virgin. A truly dream-like atmosphere is created by this fountain with its intricate decoration and by the strange landscape in which a lake, mountains and a half-ruined Gothic town are deliberately shown out of perspective. In the *St Florian Altar-piece*, which depicts a number of scenes from Christ's Passion and the martyrdom of St Sebastian, as well as on the panels, now dispersed, of another altar-piece painted for the same convent church and devoted to the *Legend of St Florian*, the artist sets several of the episodes in actual landscapes to be found in the Danube valley. He also employs bold lighting effects and plays about with the perspective, without any regard for rigid mathematical rules, but using it as means of suggesting mystery. *The Birth of the Virgin* is bizarrely set in the aisle of a Gothic church. St Anne, who has just given birth, is being offered food while sitting up in a large bed with a tester surrounded by railings. A great circle of tiny angels fluttering round the church pillars gives a strong feeling of spaciousness. The treatment of *Susanna at the Bath* is that of a miniaturist, but the sense of space which Altdorfer establishes in this picture confers on it a strange feeling of grandeur. The subject is merely an excuse for the artist to raise up, alongside the trees and lawns of a park, an immense fairy palace, inspired by Italian buildings, with its open vestibules and galleries.

In 1529, Altdorfer completed *The Battle of Alexander*, one of his most impressive major works. It was commissioned by Duke William IV of Bavaria, and depicts the famous battle between Alexander and Darius, between the West and the East. At the top hangs a heavy stone tablet bearing an inscription which explains the subject and names the combatants. Underneath is the representation of a sixteenth-century battle, an immense mêlée of soldiers on foot and on horseback painted in minute detail. In the centre, Alexander, on horseback and wearing beautiful golden armour, charges with lance raised at Darius, whose war chariot is bearing him off in flight. In the sky the

Manuel Deutsch
St James and St Rock Intercede with St Anne to End the Plague
Museum, Basle

moon is disappearing and the sun is rising. The landscape stretches endlessly in the distance, embracing towns, mountains, castles and blazing clouds. On the horizon lies the sea covered with ships and strewn here and there with islands. The subject is in fact treated on a cosmic scale. Altdorfer contrasts the vastness of Nature with the pettiness of man, like Heracleitus, he extends the idea of struggle to the entire universe. Napoleon was so struck by this work that he had it removed from Munich and hung it in his bathing apartments at Saint-Cloud, so that he could meditate on it at leisure.

In his *View of the Region of the Danube*, painted towards the end of his life, Altdorfer had the courage to depict a landscape from which man was excluded and which he considered sufficient unto itself. One sees simply a path winding between pine-trees and coming out on the edge of a lake bordered by bluish mountains.

Albrecht Altdorfer paid little attention to the concept of rational organization with which Dürer was so completely involved. Giving his imagination free rein, he tries to enumerate all the infinite possibilities in the world. Like Paracelsus, his cosmic attitude makes him regard man as merely a part of the great symphony of nature. But his work contains not only poetic qualities: it also has historical importance. Altdorfer cleared the way for the development of such different genres as the architectural picture and the landscape, genres which were to flourish in the following century.

Hans Baldung Grien

Hans Baldung, one of the most typical painters of Southern Germany during the Renaissance, was probably born at Gmünd in Swabia *ca* 1485. He early moved to Strasbourg, where he was apprenticed to a pupil of Schongauer. In about 1503 he moved to Nuremberg, where he was employed in Dürer's workshop. The influence of Dürer remained with him all his life, and indeed he kept on close terms with his master. In 1509 he became a citizen of Strasbourg, and thereafter left it only on the occasion of painting an altar-piece for Freiburg-im-Brisgau. He died in 1545 in his adopted city where he had been official painter to the bishopric and a town councillor. His earliest paintings, the altar-pieces of *St Sebastian* and of the *Adoration of the Magi* (1507), were carried out under the direct influence of Dürer, from whom he got his lively and vigorous skill in drawing, though he here shows himself a better colourist than his teacher. His preference for warm tones of green earned him his surname Grien, which is a dialect form of the German ' grün '.

From 1513 to 1517, Baldung worked on one of his major productions, the altar-piece for Notre-Dame in Freiburg, depicting the *Coronation of the Virgin*, with four scenes from the life of Mary on the volets—the *Annunciation*, the *Visitation*, the *Nativity* and the *Flight into Egypt*. In the *Visitation* Baldung presents us with his ideal of female beauty, inspired by that of Dürer, but more full-blown and sensual. The *Nativity*, and also the *Annunciation*, with their light effects which concentrate on certain predetermined points, reveal the influence of Grünewald, who had a profound effect on Baldung's work. While Baldung was painting this altar-piece at Freiburg, Grünewald was finishing his famous altar-piece at Isenheim in Alsace. The two towns were quite near, and it is certain that Baldung visited Grünewald on several occasions. These meetings were of the greatest importance to Baldung. He resembles Grünewald not only in his use of lighting effects, as we have just mentioned, and in his preference for rich colours, but also in his heightened imagination which tends towards the fantastic. He gives this free rein in his mythological pictures and allegories, which are the side of his work that most interests us today. Taking his inspiration from the mediaeval Dance of Death, Baldung associates Death with Lust, as in *Young Girl and Death* and *Death Dragging a Woman towards the Tomb*.

In the *Seven Ages of Life*, the presence of Death is merely suggested: the series of figures depicts a woman's progressive decline. Baldung was concerned with the powers of evil, and did not fail to treat the subject of witches and the witches' sabbath in many of his paintings, drawings and engravings. The women are always well-built, plump, sensual. In his last pictures, such as *Noli Me Tangere* (1539), the figures are contorted and the poses are somewhat affected. In fact, towards the end of his life Baldung came under the influence of Italian Mannerism.

Nicolas Manuel Deutsch

Hans Baldung had a considerable influence on a Swiss painter, who is famous for his delight in recording the German foot-soldiers of the day. Nicolas Manuel*, surnamed Deutsch, was also an engraver and poet as well as a painter. His output was extraordinarily large when one considers that he died at the age of forty-six and that he was able to devote only part of his adventurous life to the various arts that he cultivated. He was a soldier of fortune who wandered across the Italian countryside sword in hand. In 1522 he was appointed historiographer in the service of Francis I, and crossed the Alps and reached Milan. He was wounded in the left hand before Novara and joined in the Swiss defeat. On returning to Switzerland, he took up politics, was made prefect of Erlach, and was entrusted by the government of Berne with various diplomatic missions on behalf of the Reformation. He was also a member of the Consistory Court, whose jurisdiction extended to all religious matters.

From 1514 to 1526, Nicolas Manuel spent most of his time in Berne, where he painted a fresco in the convent church of the Dominicans depicting a *Dance of Death* *. This was considered by his contemporaries as one of his most important works, but unfortunately we know of it only from a seventeenth-century copy. In the same vein is an easel-painting in grisaille showing *Death Embracing a Prostitute*. Here Death dressed as a German mercenary obscenely clasps a beautiful courtesan in his arms. *The Judgement of Paris* is a somewhat erotic picture painted in the heroic style and is typical of another aspect of Nicolas Manuel's work.

Evidence and Documents

Jean Cousin the Elder

After spending the first part of his life at Sens, where he worked as a surveyor, painter and designer of stained glass, Jean Cousin left in 1540 to settle in Paris, where he was to find a wider field for exercising his talents and where his reputation was to be confirmed. He also decided to go there because his son was then completing his studies at the university.

On his arrival in Paris, Jean Cousin first took lodgings in the old Rue du Temple, and immediately, as a master painter, became a citizen of Paris, as is shown by a contract dated 6th January 1541 for supplying the Brotherhood of Sainte-Geneviève-du-Mont with three tapestry designs ' painted on canvas ', depicting six scenes from the life of their patron saint. A little later he acquired a large plot of land on the corner of the Rue de Seine and the new Rue des Marais just outside the city, in the fief of the Abbey of Saint-Germain-des-Prés, near the gate of Saint-Germain. Here he built a superb mansion consisting of several blocks of buildings with a courtyard and garden enclosed by walls. The plans of Paris drawn up by Truchet (1550) and Cerceau (1560) give one some idea of the extent of this property. One soon realizes that Jean Cousin was extremely well-off, and that as soon as he arrived in Paris he naturally joined the ranks of the burghers. M. A. de Montaiglon was well aware of the painter's social position and put forward the suggestion, since verified, that the reason Jean Cousin kept apart and did not intrigue for court favours or solicit, like so many others, official titles, was that his personal wealth was such that he could afford to be completely independent.

His vast house in the Rue des Marais contained workrooms and a study which Jean Cousin hardly ever left, for since his reputation was made and his fortune increased day by day, he needed to do little work outside, and usually contented himself with supplying plans or designs for work which was then carried out by professional contractors. We have just mentioned the patterns commissioned by the Brotherhood of Sainte-Geneviève. Likewise in the contracts dated 16th July and 29th November 1557 granted by the Corporation of Paris Goldsmiths for the stained glass for the newly restored chapel, it is stipulated that these windows will be put in by Jacques Aubry, master glazier, ' in accordance with and following the portrait (that is to say, the model) to be made by Master Jean Cousin or one of his choosing '. The wealthy Corporation of Paris Goldsmiths, who employed Philibert Delorme as architect and Germain Pilon as sculptor, dealt only with the great artists of the day. This form of contract, drawn up by a contemporary notary, gives the impression that Jean Cousin, whose name is listed before any other, must have been the leading figure in this field. His reputation extended even abroad, as is evidenced by Giorgio Vasari who, in his *Lives of the Most Excellent Painters, Sculptors and Architects*, the first edition of which was dedicated to Cosimo de Medici and published in Florence in 1550, says at the end of his account of Marcantonio Raimondi and other engravers, ' Jacopo Barozzio da Vignola also distinguished himself by putting together a book illustrated with copper-engravings in which he clearly explains the principles of the proportions of the five orders. This has been of use to many artists and has earned its author the same recognition as that accorded to Jean Cousin of Paris for his engravings and treatises on architecture.' In fact Jean Cousin executed numerous compositions which were reproduced by engraving. Mention may be made of the woodcuts of the *Annunciation*, the *Descent from the Cross* and the *Holy Family*, the latter bearing the initials IC and the date 1554, the attractive vignettes of the *Livre des Coutumes de Sens* printed by Gilles Richeboys in 1556, the illustrations of Henry II's entry into Paris on 16th June 1549, published by Jacques Roffet, and those in the *Holomètre* of 1555, as well as a great number of wood-engravings which are attributed to Jean Cousin purely on the grounds of similarity of various details with those found in the genuine works. In painting he is represented by the famous *Last Judgement*[1] and according to Jacques Taveau and Félibien, he is also to be credited with that masterpiece of sculpture, the Tomb of Admiral Chabot.

Nevertheless, despite his wonderful position in Paris and his wide interests, Jean Cousin never forgot his birthplace, and did not fail to return to Sens when his knowledge and experience were needed there. In 1545 he was still surveyor for the bailliage of Sens, and a judge describing his position calls him ' Jean Cousin, painter, domiciled in Paris ', and adds that in cases of absence his functions should devolve onto Bertrand Aubry, painter. In 1550, the Chapter requested him to examine the famous golden tabernacle and give plans and instructions for raising it onto the great altar of the cathedral. He also made designs for orfrays and copes. The following year he also produced designs for ' an organ-chest and further patterns for orfrays and a cope of green damask '. We have also found that, during the fairly long period of his stay in Sens in 1550-1, he appeared as a witness to the marriage contract signed on 18th January 1550 (o.s.), between Simon Herbelin, merchant of Sens, and Philippe Cousin. In this document he is referred to simply as ' Jean Cousin, painter, domiciled in Sens '. He had, in fact, kept on a house in Sens, whose exact position we have long been trying to discover. It must have been situated in the Grande-Rue, near what was once called the Carrefour du Loup, a name applied to the crossroads of the Grande-Rue and the Rue des Trois-Croissants and the Rue du Lion d'Or. While still waiting to find the true location, one can already state that the Renaissance house in the street that now bears the artist's name never belonged to him but to Jean Minagier, esquire, lord of Etigny, king's representative at Sens, who owned it from at least as early as 1540.

One of the last visits that Jean Cousin paid to Sens was on the occasion of the marriage of his wife's niece, Antoinette Thomyn, daughter of Guillaumette Rousseau and Nicole Thomyn, prosecutor in the ecclesiastical courts, who wed Jean Hérardin, king's sergeant. He was present, together with Christine Rousseau, when the marriage contract was signed on 30th January 1558 before Pierre Cellier, king's notary.

At this time, Jean Cousin was completing his *Book of Perspective* and preparing it for publication. In it he wished to hand down to posterity his knowledge of his art

[1] Since Maurice Roy wrote this in 1909, research has proved that this painting is in fact by Jean Cousin the Younger. (Editor's note.)

and his experience of surveying. The only edition known is that of 1560 printed by Jehan le Royer, ' king's printer in the field of mathematics '.

In his preliminary notice to the reader, Jean Cousin gives evidence of his independence, which he hides, it is true, beneath an exaggerated modesty. He begins with the words, ' I would gladly have dedicated and addressed this work to the king or to some prince or great lord, as is customarily done, if I had felt that I had sufficient eloquence and knowledge to dare to do so '. Then, a little later, he clearly states that his work is that of a man who has reached an advanced age, and bears the fruit of his long experience. ' Indeed, ' he says,'I have been even more bold in that it seemed to me that the experience which I have gained over the years must have left me with some judgement and knowledge which allow me to speak for the purpose of instructing and advancing those who are new to and unskilled in the art, and for the pleasure of my friends who have requested me to do so.'

It is interesting to add the opinion of Jacques Taveau, the historian of Sens, who wrote only thirty years after the publication of the *Book of Perspective*. ' He wished to pass on to posterity, ' he wrote, ' whatever was of excellence in his art, and left for this purpose a *Book of Perspective*, printed in Paris in the year MDLX by Jehan Royer. This is a kind of manual showing painters how they can draw geometrically figures of palaces, houses, buildings and all objects that can be found on the ground, whether high or low, by means of foreshortening in accordance with the disappearance of the view in the distance, for which book he drew the figures required for a true understanding, which he engraved with his own hand on blocks of wood.'

This beautiful work appears to have been Jean Cousin's last production, for he died, probably in Paris, in the same year, or at the latest in 1561. This terminal point is fixed by subsequent records which we have been fortunate enough to discover among the minutes of Adrien Arragon, notary at the Châtelet in Paris.

Maurice Roy
Les Deux Jean Cousin
Sens, 1909

Corneille de Lyon

That reminds me that she (Catharine de Medici) went one day to see a painter in Lyons called Corneille, who had painted in a large room all the great lords, princes, knights, and the great queens, princesses, ladies and young women of the court of France. Being then in this room full of paintings, we saw a portrait of the queen painted extremely well in all her beauty and perfection, dressed in the French manner in a hood with large pearls and a dress with great sleeves of silver linen lined with lynx; the whole so well representing the living person with her beautiful face that only the sound of her voice was wanting, her three daughters being with her. Thereupon she took exceedingly great pleasure at the sight, and all the company that was with her vastly enjoyed gazing on it and admiring and praising her beauty above all others'. She herself was delighted to gaze on it, so much so that she could not take her eyes from it, until at last M. de Nemours came and said to her: ' Madame, I consider that you are very well portrayed here, there is no doubt of that; and I think that your daughters do you great honour, for they do not emulate you and they surpass you in nothing.' She replied, 'Cousin, I think you well remember the time when the picture was painted, the age that I then was, and the clothes here depicted. You who saw me like this are better able to judge than any other of these present whether I was esteemed as you say and whether I was as you see me portrayed here. ' And there was not one among the gathering who did not highly praise and admire such beauty, and did not say that the mother was worthy of her daughters and the daughters worthy of their mother. And this beauty lasted throughout her marriage and during her widowhood almost up to the time of her death. Not that she was so fresh as in her heyday, but nevertheless well preserved and most desirable and attractive.

Brantôme
Lives of Illustrious Ladies, 1665

Jan Gossaert, known as Mabuse

The pictorial faculty which germinates at the root of thought or imagination before practice has given its tangible expression perfect form, demands of those who possess it both a calm mind and a regular life in order that they may devote themselves in peace to intellectual work of such a high order. Yet one would hardly imagine this from the cast of mind and the way of life of skilful Little John, or John of Mabuse, who came into this world in a small village in Hainault or Artois called Mabeuge, and who was the contemporary of Lucas Van Leyden and many other eminent persons.

He was a man of dissolute life and nevertheless it is remarkable that there was never a painter more skilful, more painstaking nor more patient in his work. His artistic ability did not come to him in his sleep. In his youth he applied himself fervently to the study of nature in order to arrive at perfection, for it is a rough road that leads thither.

He visited Italy and other countries and was one of the first to bring back to Flanders the fine manner of composing and producing religious works, peopled with naked figures and subjects drawn from Fable, which had not previously been the custom in this country.

Among many other works, the principal and most glorious of his creations was a large altar-piece in Middelburg with double volets, which it was necessary to support on trestles when they were opened.

When the famous Albrecht Dürer was at Antwerp, he made a journey specially to see this picture, and praised it highly. The abbot who had it done was Maximilian of Burgundy, who died in 1524. The work depicted a *Descent from the Cross*, the painting of which cost a great deal of time. It was destroyed along with the church itself in a fire caused by lightning—an immense loss to art.

There still remain at Middelburg several works by Mabuse, notably some beautiful representations of the Virgin. But it is above all in M. Magnus's collection in Delft that one finds one of the most beautiful and excellent examples of his work. This is a *Descent from the Cross*; around the body, which has already been taken down, various people, who stand about one and a half feet high, are grouped together most artfully. The painting is carefully done, the arrangement of the figures is beautiful, as are the draperies, thrown into numerous folds, and the expressions of sorrow are particularly well rendered.

In the collection of the great art-lover Melchior Wijntgis, in the same town, one finds a beautiful *Lucretia*.

In Martin Papenbroeck's house in Waermoerstraat, Amsterdam, there is a delightful vertical painting of *Adam and Eve*, with the figures almost life-size and very carefully executed, a priceless picture for which considerable sums have been offered.

In Jan Nicquet's house in Amsterdam there is a large picture depicting the *Beheading of St James* painted in grisaille and, as it were, colourless. It is a simple scumble, and one can roll and rub the canvas without any fear of damaging it. It is very well done.

Mabuse painted another *Virgin* while he was in the service of the Marquis de la Vere. The Marquise posed for the Madonna, and the Infant Jesus was painted after her child. This picture was so remarkable and so carefully executed that the master's other works appear crude beside it. There was a piece of blue drapery that was so beautiful and so fresh that one would have said it had only just been painted. This painting later found its way into the collection of M. de Froidmond of Ghent.

In London he painted several beautiful portraits. In the Palace of Whitehall there are—or there were—heads of young boys or children from his brush which were painted in an excellent manner.

For several years Mabuse was in the service of the Marquis de la Vere. Now it happened that this lord was to give a splendid reception for Charles V, and for the occasion he had given all his people fine costumes of white damask. The painter, who tried everything possible to obtain the money he required to satisfy his dissolute tastes, succeeded in having his portion of the material delivered to him personally so that he could make it up himself, but he sold it and spent the proceeds. What was to be done? For the time was fast approaching when the festivities were to be held.

In his predicament, Mabuse took some fine white paper and made a robe out of it which he then decorated with damask flowers and other designs.

At the Marquis's court there was a learned philosopher, a poet and the painter. All three had to march past in front of the palace while the Emperor and his host watched from a window. During the parade, the Marquis asked his Majesty which damask pleased him most. The Emperor cast his eye on that of the painter, which was a brilliant white and decorated with far more beautiful flowers than the other costumes. On this account, Mabuse was chosen to serve at their table. When he was summoned by the Marquis, who knew what had happened, to appear before the Emperor, the latter felt the material and discovered the trick.

When he was told of the circumstances the Emperor was immensely amused, so that the Marquis would not have regretted the loss of any amount of damask for the sake of the painter's playing a trick which pleased the sovereign so greatly.

Mabuse, who was rather loose in his behaviour, was for some reason or other imprisoned in Middelburg, and during his incarceration he made several attractive drawings. I have had the opportunity of seeing some of them, which were very well done in black crayon.

I do not know either the date of his birth or that of his death.

Karel Van Mander
Schilderboek, 1604

Lucas Van Leyden

In the Louvre there is a painting by a primitive who may or may not be famous, I do not know, but whose name will never represent an important period in the history of art. He is known as Lucas Van Leyden, and to my feeling he renders null and void the four or five hundred years of painting that have come after him. The canvas to which I refer is entitled *Lot and his Daughters*, a biblical subject much in fashion at that period. Certainly the Bible was not understood in the Middle Ages as we understand it to-day, and this picture is a strange example of the mystical deductions that can be drawn from it. In any case, its pathos can be seen even at a distance, it strikes the mind with a sort of overwhelming visual balance, I mean its keenness of vision acts all at once and is immediately apparent at a first glance. Even before one has been able to see what is happening, one feels that something great is taking place; the ear, one might say, is affected at the same time as the eye. A drama of the utmost intellectual importance appears to have been concentrated here like the sudden gathering of clouds which the wind, or a much more direct act of fate, has brought together so as to test their thunderbolts.

And indeed in the picture the sky is black and overcast, but even before one has realized that the drama originated in the sky, was played out in the sky, the peculiar lighting effects of the canvas, the tangle of forms, the impression produced at a distance, all this underlines a sort of dramatic intensity in nature of which I defy any artist of the great periods of painting to provide the equivalent.

A tent stands by the sea-shore, and in front of it sits Lot in his cuirass and with a most beautiful red beard, watching his daughters behaving as if this were a banquet of whores.

And in fact they strut about, some pretending to be mothers, others warriors, combing their hair or bearing arms, as if they had never had any other aim in life than to charm their father, and act as the toy or instrument of his desires. In this way the painter succeeds in bringing out the deeply incestuous nature of the ancient theme, using the effects of passion. This is proof that he has understood the profoundly sexual character of the subject absolutely as a modern man, that is to say, as we ourselves understand it. Proof, too, that its deeply sexual but poetic nature did not escape him any more than it does us.

On the left of the picture and slightly in the background a black tower rises to prodigious heights, supported at its base by a great conglomeration of rocks, plants, twisting roads bounded by stones, with occasional houses here and there. A happy effect of perspective detaches one of these roads at a certain point from the tumble of rocks through which it has been wandering, and it runs across a bridge and finally receives a ray of the stormy light which breaks through the clouds and occasionally illuminates the countryside. The tide is very high, and in the background the sea is also extremely calm, considering the coils of flame boiling in a corner of the sky.

With the crackling of fireworks, the night is bombarded with stars, rockets and shells, and we suddenly have revealed to our eyes in a hallucinatory light that stands out against the night sky, certain details of the landscape—trees, towers, mountains, houses, whose appearance and illumination remain forever connected in our mind with the idea of explosive noise. One cannot better describe the subjection of the various features of the landscape to the fire in the sky than by saying that though they possess their own lighting, nevertheless they are related to the fire like echoes, like points of reference which originate from it and were placed where they are in order to let the fire exert its destructive force to the full.

Furthermore, the way in which the painter treats this fire is terribly energetic and disturbing, so that it is like an active, moving element in a study of immobility. It matters little how this effect is achieved, it is real. It is sufficient to see the canvas in order to be convinced of it.

However, this fire, with the impression of being both deliberate and wicked which it produces, serves by its very violence to counterbalance in the mind's eye the solid, heavy static features of the rest of the picture.

Between the sea and the sky on the right, and in the same middle distance as the black tower, a thin tongue of land stretches out with a ruined monastery on it.

This strip of land appears so near that it seems at first to form part of the sea-shore where Lot's tent stands, but it gives place to a large bay in which an unprecedented sea disaster occurs. Ships cut in two and yet unable to sink rest on the sea as if on crutches, while their masts and spars point in every direction.

It is difficult to explain why it is that the sense of disaster given by the sight of only one or two ships shattered to pieces should be so complete.

It appears that the painter had a knowledge of some of the secrets of linear balance and of the ways to make it act directly on the brain, producing a physical reaction. In any case, this impression of an intelligence informing nature, and in particular the manner of representing it, is visible in other details of the canvas, such as the bridge as high as an eight-storey building rising over the sea, along which figures pass in single file like the Ideas in Plato's cave.

It would be quite wrong to pretend that the ideas contained in this picture are clear. In any case, they belong to a level of greatness which painting which is merely concerned with paint, that is to say, all the painting for the last several centuries, has made us completely unfamiliar with.

Besides all this, Lot and his daughters contain an attitude to sexuality and reproduction in which Lot appears to be present in order to pester his daughters and abuse them.

This is almost the only social idea that the painting contains.

All the other ideas are metaphysical. I regret having to use this word, but it is their proper name. I shall even go so far as to say that their poetic greatness, their real effect on us, springs from the fact that they are metaphysical, and that their spiritual depth is inseparable from the formal and external balance of the picture.

There is also a sense of development, which the various details of the landscape and the manner in which they are painted—their planes cancel one another out and yet reveal correspondences—plant in our minds in exactly the same way as music would.

There is also a fatalistic attitude which is expressed less by the sudden appearance of the fire than by the solemn manner in which forms are organized or disorganized beneath it, some distorted by a wind of irresistible panic, others motionless and almost ironical, yet all of them submitting to the demands of a powerful intellectual balance which seems the very essence of exteriorized nature.

Once more, there is the idea of chaos, of the marvellous, of harmony, and even of the powerlessness of the word, whose impotence appears to be demonstrated by this supremely materialistic and anarchical painting.

Antonin Artaud
Le Théâtre et son Double
Paris, 1938

Albrecht Dürer

Dürer is one of the most genuinely great figures ever to grace mankind. Though one of the finest representatives of the German race, he is above all a universal genius. He participated heart and soul in the intellectual and religious life of his times, in its anguishes and its achievements. They touched him too closely for him not to have left striking records of them, but he was also so strongly attached to the fundamental essentials of life and living that he appeals to everyone in all places at all times. His presentation of the features and feelings of the life of his day, his figures with their distinctive racial traits such as *Great Fortune* or the *Knight* armed for the battle of the mind, the moral attitude of his times, have nevertheless an eternal quality, for they also suggest the clamminess of life, the shiver in the flesh, direct contact with immutable nature. It appears that every race, at that moment when it first becomes aware of its individuality, is entrusted with the task of expressing in its own language the general truths that are the common heritage of mankind. During the struggle in which it is able to affirm its own personality only by opposing all that is contrary to it, it produces one or more men who present themselves on its behalf before the council of the mind. Dürer was such a man. He made his appearance at the time when a primitive but tender

Germany, wakened from a long dream, was gathering her forces in order to establish her moral liberty. Humanism and the Reformation are deeply echoed in his work, but he did not act the theologian like Cranach, nor, unlike so many others, did he cast off his German nature in the light of the revelations of Italy. The Reformation gave him a solemn, personal religion. By controlling his faith he enlarged it, by suffering for it he felt it live, and in his eyes Christ's Passion takes on an eternal reality. This is the reason for the strong deep religious element in his work and that apocalyptic thread that leads up to the *Four Apostles*. Humanism enlarged his mind, revealed to him the traditions of art and initiated him in the natural synthesis of mythology. But nevertheless, these were merely currents that bore him along, forces which helped him to gain his independence. The living principle of his art is to be found in the feelings of the people which, in all simplicity, break through the learning of the Meistersinger and burst forth in the German *lied*. Through these feelings, Dürer reaches the heart of his kith and kin. The privacy of the family, the fond attention of wife and mother, the child's love and the pleasures of close friendship, all this soft sweet chamber music runs imperishably through his work. This, indeed, Schongauer had already outlined, but the delicate feelings of the Master of Colmar could command only slender, angular forms. The deep emotions of the soul could only be expressed through indefinite gestures, an uncertain balance and figures that appeared only half real. The intention was exquisite, the sensation timid. Dürer tore down the veil which concealed from man the shape and majesty of nature. Forms became solid, the balance became firm, the rhythm proud. Bodies took on volume, forms filled out the outlines, gestures achieved their purpose and combined with further gestures, the sense of contact became physical and natural curves called to one another and were reunited. The beautiful body of *Amymone* clasps the spine and the sinuous rump of the marine monster that bears her off. The child's tiny hand grips the fruit that it is holding, just as the mother's hands are moulded to the feel of the child's chubby flesh.

The discovery of nature was the proper task and the heroic achievement of Dürer. Thereby he threw off the yoke of the past and repudiated formalism. This strong and enthusiastic love of nature acted as his guide and put him on his guard against the seductive attractions that came to him from abroad or from his own imagination, against vague idealism and against sheer wilfulness. From the time of his first travels abroad he had become intoxicated with the beauty of things. In Italy, Mantegna tempted him with the offer of his imperious epitomes inherited from Antiquity. He understood and admired: he retained the principle but rejected the results. All alone, he walked the path that was to lead him to simple grandeur. His analytical mind enabled him to achieve compositions whose excellence lies in the fact that they succeed in amassing and uniting innumerable details which are felt both in their own right and in relation to the whole. He refuses to sacrifice anything which expresses life, but seizes it entire. Barbari and his sickly charm fail to divert him from his path. At his suggestion, however, Dürer measures, calculates, studies the laws of form and assimilates the logic of living things.

As regards form, what appealed to him most was not that which renders it most pleasing, but what explains it best. What he shows is its reason for existence, the inner principle that supports it, the desire that animates it and makes it grow. He thus gives the impression of perpetual development, of the strivings and aspirations of all things in the life of the universe. The human figure is distinguished from the rest of the world only through a hierarchical selection: the curves of the landscape lead up to it and present it like an unexpected crowning. The same breath of life passes through all the limbs of a vast body. This is what, after ten years of effort, he achieved in the *Nemesis*, *Great Horse* and *Adam and Eve* of 1504. Thereafter, he is master of his thoughts and of his style, which he proceeds to enrich with ever deeper meanings and more complex relations. With ever more strength, wealth and freedom, he evokes the powers of the earth and the energy of growth, and enables the thousand voices of nature's choir to sing to mankind.

Dürer's style is the visible sign and exact transcription of the emotion that things conjured up in him. It is an instinctive emotion which places him in unique, direct contact with nature and which, little by little, prompts him to multiply and to generalize its relations. It is nature which warns him that nothing is alone in the world, that each part is related to its neighbour, and that all are involved in the powerful animation that fills the universe. As long as man sets himself apart in a private world of book-learning and abstract philosophy he remains uncreative, powerless, joyless. By recognizing himself in every living thing, by feeling his own life pulsate in the life that surrounds him, he is magnified and exalted. Nature is no more a logical mechanism but a living concert of passionate and determined will-powers which struggle to achieve balance and harmony. He thereby penetrates into the marvellous region where a thousand tender solemn voices respond to his appeal. Throughout the authority of his genius, he reconquers the Eden of myth and of epic poetry which, through the grace of their innocence, the soul of the common people and of children has never lost. He enters into the poetic realm of analogy.

I do not believe that any artist has ever given us a stronger feeling of this sense of unity and harmony than Dürer has done. His drawings, ingenuous and sensual, scholarly and passionate, embrace and link together all the forms of man, and express the feeling for life through the feeling for shape.

The unity, the truth and the humanity of his drawing are completely admirable. Landscapes, clouds, vegetation, fauna and flora all derive from man and return to man. The gentle flow of the land or the sudden swellings of the soil are underscored by the sturdy growth of vegetation. The trees' groping grasp for the sky and the steady thrust of the sap are expressed in the twisted trunks, the capricious forms of the branches and the swellings and seams in the bark. The human form recalls at once the appearance of the earth in its broad simple lines, its soft furrows and fine ridges, and the vegetation in the tapering roundness of the limbs and the nodules of the muscles. As everything is interconnected in nature, Dürer makes no attempt to separate things out. As every form without its analogy is a form without truth, he moves along the unbroken chain of beings and passes from one to another without any sense of transition. Thus he insists vigorously on the animality of human forms, for he is less in search of formal beauty than organic truth and inner logic. All in all, he goes straight to the substance of things. This powerful synthetic concept provides the gestures with their most relaxed attitudes and the poses their most supple stances. It subjugates the mass of detail to the imperious demands of vital force. This in turn leads to the realization that Dürer possesses a sense of rhythm which he sustains and controls mathematically. In a rough sketch of a nude in Berlin, the pelvis is firmly supported by the legs with impeccable accuracy, just as the abdomen and torso turn on the hips. In *Great Fortune* the lines run into one another, the curve of the abdomen rejoins the bent arc of the thigh and the convex back is linked by the hollow of the loins to the fleshy buttock. Everywhere there is a feeling of strict logic and a deep sense of life.

Dürer was a draftsman and engraver more than a painter, and he knew little of the musical value of tones, the song of colour. Drawing was his real language. But the evocative power of drawing, so complete and so mysterious, is fully apparent throughout his work. This form of expression, which was in perfect keeping with the artist's character, freed him, on account of its simplicity, from any secondary preoccupation and thus brought him to the extreme confine of his passion. The severity of the technique restricted him to the essential truths. By exhausting the resources of a particular art form, he forced it to express everything. A well-placed blow aimed at a particular point sets up a vibration throughout a metal disk: the soul touched by a single firm line resonates likewise. Man perceives the parts as a whole, and cannot separate them out. Furthermore, no sooner is one part of this whole made manifest to our senses than all the others come to life and respond to the one that strikes us, and we reform the total truth which cannot be divided within us. Thus, through the strength of his crayon and burin, Dürer evokes the wholeness of nature.

Maurice Hamel
Albert Dürer, Paris

Grünewald

There, in the ancient convent of Unterlinden, it rises grimly up as soon as one enters and immediately stuns one with the terrifying nightmare of Calvary. It is a whirlwind of art unleashed, which comes and carries you off, and it takes several minutes before one can recover and overcome the impression of pitiful horror which this Christ on the Cross creates, set in the nave of this museum installed in an old deconsecrated church belonging to the cloister.

The scene is arranged in the following manner:

In the centre of the picture a gigantic Christ, disproportionately huge when one compares him with the stature of the people who surround him, is nailed to a roughly stripped tree revealing in places the fresh whiteness of the wood, and the branch forming the cross-piece, drawn down by the hands, bends and, as in the Karlsruhe *Crucifixion*, outlines the taut curve of a bow. The body is similar in the two works. It is livid and shiny, stained with spots of blood, and bristling like a chestnut husk with the thorns of the rods which have remained in the seat of the wounds. At the end of the inordinately long arms, the hands twitch convulsively and claw the air. The legs are forced together so that the knees touch, and the feet, one on top of the other with a nail driven through them, are merely a confused mass of muscles over which the flesh is turning colour while the toe-nails, which have become blue, are putrefying. As to the head, encircled in a gigantic crown of thorns, it sinks upon the baggy, bulging chest, which reveals the pattern of the ribs. This Christ Crucified would be a faithful copy of the Karlsruhe one if it were not for the expression on the face. In fact here Jesus no longer bears the appalling grimace of lockjaw.

It is less horrifying but more humanly debased, dead. The terror of tetanus and of shrieking laughter saved the Karlsruhe panel from the brutishness of the features which is emphasized here by the imbecilic laxness of the mouth. The Man-God of Colmar is merely a poor thief who has been strung up.

But this is not the end of the differences between the two works. The arrangement of the group of onlookers is not, in fact, the same. At Karlsruhe, as elsewhere, the Virgin stands on one side of the Cross and St John on the other. At Colmar, the traditional setting has been disregarded, and Grünewald, the astonishing visionary, reveals his wild and intuitive, his theological yet barbarian nature which sets him apart from other religious painters.

To the right of the cross are three figures: the Virgin, St John the Evangelist and Mary Magdalen. St John, an old German student with a pitiable, beardless face and straw-coloured hair that falls in long dry threads onto his red habit, supports an extraordinary Virgin in a white dress and head-gear who is on the point of fainting, her face as white as a sheet, her eyes closed, her mouth half-open revealing her teeth. Her features are fine and frail and completely modern. If it were not for the dark-green dress which can be glimpsed near the hands, with their brittle clenched fingers, one would take her for a dead nun. She is pitiful and full of charm, young, quite beautiful. In front of her, a really tiny woman bends back on her knees, her arms raised on the air and her hands clasped towards Christ. This little old woman in a pink dress lined with myrtle green, her face veiled to below the eyes and across the base of the nose, is Mary Magdalen. She is ugly and awkward, but her despair is so real that it wrings one's heart.

On the other side, to the left, stands a strange tall figure with a shock of red hair cut straight across the forehead, an unkempt beard, pale eyes, his legs, feet and arms bare, who holds an open book in one hand and points towards Christ with the other.

This man with the face of a Franconian cavalryman, who reveals a mass of hair above his belt tied in a bulging knot and his cloak draped round him in large folds, represents St John the Baptist. He has been brought back from the dead and in explanation of the urgent and commanding gesture of his long index finger, which is slightly curled as it motions towards the Redeemer, an inscription in red letters runs beside his arm: *Illum oportet crescere, me autem minui* (He must increase but I have become less).

John, who became less by making way for the Messiah, who died for having spread the Word, is here restored to life, while he who was living when John himself had died, is here dead. One could say that in his reincarnation he foreshadows the triumph of the Resurrection, and that having once announced the Birth of Jesus before Jesus was born, he now announces his rebirth in heaven, his rising from the dead. He has come back in order to bear witness to the fulfilment of the words of the prophets, to reveal the truth of the Scriptures. He has come back in order in a way to confirm the reality of his words which are later to be consigned to writing by the other John whose place he has taken on the left of the Calvary scene, St John the Apostle, who neither hears nor even sees him, so engrossed is he beside Mary the Mother, as if numbed and paralysed by the bitter fruit of the holy rood.

And alone among the tears, the frightful spasms of the sacrifice, this witness of the before and after, his body bent at the waist, neither weeps nor suffers. Impassibly, he witnesses; with assurance he makes his declaration. And the Lamb of the World whom he baptised lies at his feet, bearing a cross, darting from his breast a jet of blood which falls into a chalice.

This is how the figures are arranged. They are outlined against the falling night. Behind the cross, which stands on a river bank, flows the sad river itself, whose rapid streams are nevertheless the colour of stagnant water, and the rather theatrical aspect of the drama is justified since it is in harmony with this distressful scene, with the dusk that has come to an end and the night that has not yet begun. And the viewer's eye is repelled by the particularly sombre tones of the background and deflected from the vitreous flesh of Christ, whose enormous size is no longer noticed, to settle on the startling whiteness of the Virgin's cloak, which, heightened by the vermilion of the apostle's habit, attracts one's attention at the expense of the other areas and almost makes Mary the principal figure of the work.

It would be a defect in the picture, however, if the balance, which is on the point of being lost and collapsing on the left-hand group, were not nevertheless maintained by the unexpected gesture of John the Baptist, who in turn appeals to one's eye by pointing in the direction of the Son.

One might say that in looking at the scene on Calvary one's eye travels from right to left in order to arrive at the centre.

This effect is certainly intended, as is that which results from the disproportion of the figures, for Grünewald knows how to maintain balance extremely well, and in his other pictures he keeps his proportions.

His exaggeration of the height of Christ is intended to strike the imagination by suggesting the idea of extreme grief and of strength. He has also made it more astounding in order all the same to keep Christ in the foreground and not let him be completely outshone by the great white area of the Virgin in the half-light.

As to her, one feels that he has placed her in the limelight. His choice is understandable, for never had anyone painted so divinely beautiful, so supremely suffering a Mother. And the truth is that she is quite stupefying in this artist's grim work.

She also forms the most outstanding contrast between the various types of individuals that the painter has chosen to represent God and the saints.

Jesus is a thief, St John the Evangelist has come down in the world, while John the Baptist is a mercenary. In fact, they are no more than German peasants. But She is of completely different origin, she is a queen who has entered a convent, she is a wonderful orchid growing among the flowers of a nameless land.

J. K. Huysmans
Trois Eglises
et Trois Primitifs,
Paris, 1908

Hans Baldung Brien

I wish to speak of the fantastic side of Hans Baldung Grien. Born in 1485, a pupil of Dürer's from 1505 to 1509, he executed the main altar of the Cathedral of Freiburg im Breisgau (1512-7), at about the same time as Grünewald was working on the altar-piece for the Antonians at Isenheim) but after 1509 he made Strasbourg his centre, and there he died in 1545. Throughout his career he showed that he was greatly attracted by two subjects—witches and death—and he treated them both with powerful animation and a strange imagination. What were his intentions, what interpretation did he give to his compositions, these are the questions I wish to deal with here.

Let us begin with the subject of witches. A painting in grisaille of 1513, marvellous from the technical point of view, shows the witches' sabbath. Some are riding on a goat, others are busy concocting diabolical potions, all have tormented expressions on their faces. The frantic activity of the scenes, which is almost baroque in style, contrasts strongly with German art of the time. The evocation is tragic, but the artist is ill-informed and the cabbalistic signs that he depicts he has got all wrong. Then there is a drawing of 1514 showing three witches: a shrivelled, dishevelled old fury; a girl who is holding a fire-ball and at the same time, with her legs wide open, triumphantly bestriding the back of a third witch; and the latter, a well-built woman, is bending down in order to reveal her backside from which she lets loose wind and excrement. This disgustingly vulgar and indecent sketch bears the inscription '*Ein gut yar*' (Happy New Year). It was probably earlier, in 1512, that Baldung produced another New Year gift, a religious picture of the risen Christ radiant with nobility and sweetness, but the 1514 greeting is not intended seriously. The fantastic element in witchcraft is merely the excuse for an amusing joke and an outlet for a sensual imagination. And the same applies to a drawing of 1515, in which the pen traces another sabbath scene in white lines on a green background. A buxom woman clasping some ropes is letting a dragon lick her with his pointed tongue, but the dragon's body dissolves into a purely decorative arabesque, and the subject gives rise to meditations on the immorality of sensuality, which is diabolical, but it is clear that Baldung's main intention was to depict an indecent scene and to make a study of a beautiful female nude.

Later, in 1523, Baldung painted the two witches who are now in the museum in Frankfurt. Attracted by the ideals of Antiquity he gives them a novel appearance, an elegant gracefulness and an almost classical majestuousness, while the candelabrum and the transparent vase are in the Renaissance style. But the dark hair, the black, over-large eyes, the staring gaze, the hard, intelligent faces, the extraordinary lighting, the thick black cloud, all serve to give a feeling of uneasiness. The subject has taken on a much deeper significance, except that the humanist attitude of the artist has pushed the scene far into the past, into the pagan world before Christianity which has no point of contact with the reality of his own day. A line drawing, a copy of a contemporary work now lost, shows an old witch holding a fork and brandishing a fire-ball who rises up menacingly behind a young woman stretched out in the foreground. The latter is having her clothes hastily removed by a child while she defencelessly offers up her beautiful body which, though idealized, is nevertheless voluptuous. This vision has nothing in common with the village witches who frequented the forests of the Vosges. Baldung always regards witchcraft with a certain amount of scepticism, and this enables him to indulge his imagination and add a touch of sensuality.

The second subject is death, or rather the Dance of Death. Emile Mâle, and since him various scholars such as Huizinga and particularly A. Tenenti in his delightful work on 'Life and death seen through the art of the fifteenth century' (*Cahiers des Annales*, No. 8, 1952), have enlarged our understanding of the development of this theme, so that obsession with death seems to have been the centre of all moral thought throughout the whole of Europe. Italy prefers the theme of the three dead men and the three living, and feels more deeply the relentless law of death. North of the Alps the preference is for the

Dance of Death, or the dance of the living and the dead, or of Death surprising and seizing the living, but there are many local variants. In Germany, death becomes identified with vanity, or rather, vanity and sensuality are also death. France stresses the fact that death strikes all ages and all social ranks, and this equality in the face of death leads to social satire, it leads also to a search for the meaning of death for the human being, to religious meditations which may assist the Christian to think of the other world and to ease his crossing of the threshold of death. In the region of the Upper Rhine, the theme is very popular, and artists depict as often the Dance of Death as scenes of death and vanity. Baldung treated the subject with such personal imagination, such violence and fantasy, that he influenced artists such as Urs Graf and Nicolas Manuel, but he transformed the theme over the years.

Baldung is surely the author of the little panel in Vienna dated 1510. Still youthful, in the stream of tradition, a little primitive, he amasses detail. A thick forest. A child playing with his little horse and at the same time, screened behind a transparent gauze, bearing witness to the terrible scene. A young girl, naked, doing her hair and about to get dressed while admiring herself in a mirror. Death hangs on to her scarf and holds up aloft the hour-glass, for it is time to die and all is vanity, and this figure with his withered flesh, his skin which is coming away from the bone in thin strips, with his shaggy hair, is typical of German art. Finally, a somewhat indistinct figure, comparatively young, with an abundance of hair, a body not yet mortified, and with a grave expression, holds the mirror up to the young girl without her realizing it. And this figure is not Death but Fatality as conceived in Germany at that time.

There are other works in the same style and in the same spirit. Dating from 1515 or thereabouts is a pen-and-ink drawing touched up in white on brown paper which depicts a young girl doing her hair in front of a mirror while Death enfolds her in his arms and is about to bear her away. Here there is more concision and simplicity, but also a more terrible contrast between the unawareness and nonchalance of this young woman condemned without hope of reprieve, and Death himself who suddenly appears, agile and indefatigable. Even more dramatic is the engraving of 1517 in which Death clasps the young girl to his breast while she wrings her hands, weeps, implores, but all in vain. He seizes her and drags her by the hair, stretches out his arm and imperiously points to an open grave in the foreground, saying ‘ *Hie must du gyn* ’, that is ‘ Here you must go ’. Ghoulishness, sadism and eroticism are combined in a tense frenzy, and all these works reveal a horrible and fantastic imagination.

François-Georges Pariset
Hans Baldung Grien de Strasbourg
et le Fantastique
Journées internationales d'études et d'art
Bordeaux, 1957

Chronology

Date	Political events	Arts	Intellectual life	Religion
1460	First international stock exchange	Grünewald b. *ca* 1460.	Basle university founded.	
1461	Charles VII d. Accession of Louis XI.		First illustrated books printed in Germany.	
1466	Charles the Bold sacks Dinant. Austria revolts against Frederick III.	Quentin Metsys b.		
1471	Louis XI occupies Picardy. Beauvais besieged by Charles the Bold, defended by Jeanne Hachette.	Albrecht Dürer b.	First observatory built at Nuremberg.	
1472	Truce between Louis XI and Charles the Bold: victory of royalty over feudalism.	Lucas Cranach b.		
1478	Unification of France.		Reuchlin first teaches Greek in Germany.	Louis XI suppresses the Inquisition in the Dauphiné.
1480	King René of Anjou d. Louis XI occupies Bar and Anjou.	Altdorfer b.	First tunnel through the Alps, 220 ft long, made at Monte Viso.	
1485		Urs Graf b. Hans Baldung Grien b. Manuel Deutsch b. *ca* 1485.	110 printing presses in Europe.	
1486	Submission of Guyenne.	Jean Clouet b.	Bartholomew Diaz rounds the Cape of Good Hope.	
1488	Battle of Saint-Aubin-du-Cormier: Maximilian transfers trading guilds from Bruges to Antwerp.	Bernard Van Orley b.		Crusade against the Waldenses in Piedmont.
1490	Maximilian I marries Anne of Brittany.	Jean Cousin the Elder b. Dürer's *Portrait of his Father*.	*Introduction to Aristotle's Metaphysics* by Lefèvre d'Etaples.	
1491	Brittany occupied by the French. Maximilian's marriage with Anne annulled. Anne marries Charles VIII. Peasant revolt in Holland.	Schongauer d.		First French seminary founded by Jean Standonck.
1492	Henry VII besieges Boulogne. Treaty of Etaples.		Christopher Columbus discovers America.	
1493	Henry VII transfers the wool market from Antwerp to Calais.	Van Reymerswaele b.		Commission of Tours.
1494	Charles VIII invades Italy.	Lucas Van Leyden b. Rosso Fiorentino b.	Lefèvre d'Etaples' *Ars moralis*.	

Date	Political events	Arts	Intellectual life	Religion
1495	Charles VIII takes Naples.	Jan Van Scorel b.		
1496	Charles VIII loses Naples.	Dürer's *Portrait of Frederick the Wise.*		
1497		Hans Holbein the Younger b.	Giovanni Cabot discovers Nova Scotia.	
1498	Henry VII transfers the wool market back to Antwerp. Charles VIII d. Accession of Louis XII.	Heemskerk b. Lancelot Blondel b.		
1499	Louis XII marries Anne of Brittany. Louis XII invades Italy. Maximilian I acknowledges Swiss independence.	Dürer's *Portrait of Oswald Krell.* Dürer's *Portrait of Hans Tucher.*	Amerigo Vespucci and Hojeda explore the coast of South America.	
1500	Diet of Augsburg.	Dürer's *Descent from the Cross.*	Erasmus's *Adagia.*	
502		Pieter Coeck b. *ca* 1502.	University of Wittenberg founded.	
503	Catharine of Aragon betrothed to Henry, Prince of Wales.	Dürer's *Paumgärtner Triptych.*		Pope authorizes the sale of indulgences by Teutonic Knights.
1504	French lose Naples. Treaty of Blois.	Van Hemmesen b. Cranach's *Repose during the Flight from Egypt.* Dürer's *Adoration of the Magi* and Self-portrait (*ca* 1504).	Erasmus's *Enchiridion Militis Christiani.*	
505	Tours States-General. Claude of France marries François d'Angoulême.	Primaticcio b. Léonard Limosin b. Mabuse's *Adoration of the Magi.*		Luther enters the Augustinian monastery at Erfurt.
506	Philip I of Spain d.	Lambert Lombard b. Cranach's *Martyrdom of St Catharine.*	Reuchlin's *Rudimenta linguae hebraicae.*	
507	Genoa revolts against French domination.	Baldung's *Adoration of the Magi* and *St Sebastian.*		Luther ordained priest.
508	Treaty of Cambrai.	Pieter Aertsen b. Dürer's *Martyrdom of the Ten Thousand Christians.*		

Date	Political events	Arts	Intellectual life	Religion
		Grünewald's *Isenheim Altar-piece* (1508-1514). Van Orley's *Triptych of the Manneton Family* (1508-1512).		
1509	Marriage of Henry VIII and Catharine of Aragon.	Niccolo dell'Abbate b. Cranach's *Holy Family*.	Erasmus's *The Praise of Folly*.	Calvin and Michael Servetus b.
1510		Hieronymus Cock b. Philibert Delorme b. *ca* 1510. Cranach's *Adam and Eve ca* 1510-1512.	Ferro solves cubic equations.	Louis XII and Maximilian decide to hold the conciliabulum of Pisa. Luther goes to Rome.
1511	Julius II forms the Holy League against Louis XII.	Dürer's *Adoration of the Trinity*. Lucas Van Leyden's *Susanna before the Judge*, *Potiphar's Wife* and *The Card-Players*.	Reuchlin's *Augenspiegel*.	Council of Pisa opened and transferred to Milan.
1512	Maximilian I deserts Louis XII.	Dürer's *Portrait* of *Maximilian I*.	Lefèvre d'Etaples' Latin commentary on St Paul's *Epistles*.	Council of Milan disperses Lateran Council 1512-1516.
1514	Peasants' revolt in Wurttemberg.	Lucas Van Leyden's *Lot and his Daughters*.	Guillaume Budé revives the study of jurisprudence in France.	
1515	Louis XII d. Accession of Francis I. Invasion of Italy. Battle of Marignano. Peace declared between Leo X and Francis I.	Mabuse's *St Luke Painting the Virgin*.	Erasmus's edition of *St Jerome*.	
1516	Ferdinand V of Aragon d. Succeeded by Charles V.	Frans Floris b. Hieronymus Bosch d. Baldung's *Coronation of the Virgin*.	Sir Thomas More's *Utopia*. Erasmus's edition of the *New Testament*.	Concordat of Bologna.
1517	Parliament of the University of Paris protests against the Concordat of Bologna. Treaty of Cambrai.	Antonio Moro b. Baldung's *Death and the Woman*. Mabuse's *Hercules and Deianira*.	Ambroise Paré b.	Luther's 95 theses against indulgences.

Date	Political events	Arts	Intellectual life	Religion
1518	Francis I forces the French Parliament to endorse the Concordat of Bologna.	Altdorfer's *Resurrection of Christ.*	Melanchthon's *Greek Grammar.*	Zwingli preaches in Zürich. Luther summoned to Rome to answer for his theses. Melanchthon appointed professor of Greek at Wittenberg.
1519	Charles V elected emperor in favour of Francis I.	Michael Wolgemut d. Holbein's *Portrait of Bonifacius Amerbach.*	Magellan sets out on his first voyage round the world.	
1520	Spain revolts against Charles V's Flemish ministers. The Field of the Cloth of Gold.	François Clouet b. Dürer's *Portrait of Jacob Fugger.*	Luther's *Address to the Christian Nobles of Germany* and *On the Freedom of a Christian.* Straits of Magellan discovered.	Luther is excommunicated and burns the bull of excommunication.
1521	Diet of Worms. Treaty of Lucerne. D'Albrets try to reconquer Navarre. Charles V takes Tournai.	Antoine Caron b. Van Reymerswaele's *St Jerome in his Cell.* Van Orley's *Patience of Job.* Jean Clouet's *Portrait of Charlotte of France.* Dürer's *Portrait of Hans Imhof.*	Discovery of the Philippines and Marianas. Lefèvre d'Etaples' *Psalms.* Machiavelli's *Seven Books on the Art of War.*	Edict of Worms condemns Luther's teachings.
522	Peasants' Wars in Germany. French defeated at Bicocca, Italy, by Colonna and the Imperialists.	Jean Cousin the Younger b.	Censorship of printed books in Germany. Luther's translation of the *Bible* into German. Lefèvre d'Etaples' French version of the *Gospels.* Zwingli's *Architeles.* Erasmus' *Colloquia.* Lefèvre d'Etaples' *Commentarii initiatorii.*	Hadrian VI elected pope. Münzer's disputes with Luther. Inquisition set up in the Netherlands.
523	Constable of Bourbon supports English cause.	Mabuse's *Hercules and Antaeus.*	Ludovicus Vives' *De ratione studii.*	Münzer organizes services in German at Alstedt.

Date	Political events	Arts	Intellectual life	Religion
		Lancelot Blondeel's *Story of Sts Cosmas and Damian.* Guichardin b. Holbein's *Portrait of Erasmus.*	Schöner's *De nuper repertis insulis.* Luther's *Against Henry the English King.* Zwingli's *Kurze Einleitung.*	Hadrian VI d. Clement VII elected pope. Anabaptists appear in Germany.
1524	Battle of the Sesia: Bayard killed. Constable of Bourbon invades Provence. La Trémoille retakes Milan.	Jean Clouet's *Portrait of Francis I ca* 1524. Hans Holbein the Elder d.		Luther attacks Carlstadt. Münzer driven from Alstedt.
1525	Battle of Pavia: Francis I taken prisoner. Peasants' Revolt put down. Catholic League of Dessau formed.	Van Scorel's *Members of the Brotherhood of Jerusalem* 1525-1526. Lucas Van Leyden's *Dance round the Golden Calf.* Grünewald's *Conversation between Sts Erasmus and Maurice* 1525-1526.		Luther condemns the Peasants' Revolt. Matteo di Bassi reforms the Franciscan Order.
1526	Diet of Speyer. Lutherans' Defensive Alliance of Gotha. Treaty of Madrid between Charles V and Francis I.	Philippe Thomassin b. Dürer's *Portrait of Jacob Muffel; Portrait of Hieronymus Holzschuher; The Four Apostles* or *Four Temperaments.* Holbein's *Madonna of Burgomaster Meyer.* Holbein's *Portrait of Sir Henry Wyatt.*	Budé's *Annotationes posteriores.* The Portuguese navigator Meneses discovers New Guinea.	Luther's *Against the Heavenly Prophets; Peaceful Exhortation; Against the Orders.* Order of Capuchins founded. Zwingli disputes with the Catholics at Baden. St Ignatius Loyola's *Spiritual Exercises.*
1527	Margaret Queen of Navarre. Henry VIII seeks an annulment of his marriage to Catharine of Aragon. Rome captured by the Constable of Bourbon. England and France allied against Germany. French defeat in Italy.	Mabuse's *Danae.* Urs Graf the Elder d. Lucas Van Leyden's *Moses Striking Water from the Rocks.*	Protestant university of Marburg founded.	Diet of Oldensee. Diet of Västeras.

Date	Political events	Arts	Intellectual life	Religion
1528	Utrecht annexed to the Netherlands.	Bruegel the Elder b. Holbein's *Portrait of the Artist's Wife and Eldest Two Children.* Grünewald d. Dürer d.	Copernicus proves the sun to be the centre of the universe.	Ignatius Loyola goes to Paris. Balthasar Hübmaier burnt at the stake as an anabaptist. The anabaptists demand the return to primitive Christianity.
1529	Clement VII refuses Henry VIII's divorce petition. Sir Thomas More appointed Lord Chancellor. Charles V rejects the decisions of the Diet of Speyer; the reformers 'protest'. Coalition of Waldshut. Treaty of Kappel.	Cranach's *Portrait of Catharine Bora* and *Portrait of Luther.*	Budé's *Commentaries on the Greek Language.*	Lutheranism spreads to Basle, Saint-Gall, Schaffhausen and Mulhouse. Colloquy of Marburg between Luther and Zwingli. Anabaptism spreads to the Netherlands. Juan de Valdés' *Doctrina Cristiana.* Thomas More's *Dialogue on Heresies.* Luther's *Small* and *Great Catechisms.*
530	Diet of Augsburg. Break between Catholics and Lutherans. Charles V crowned emperor.	Rosso begins to decorate the Francis I Gallery. Quentin Metsys d. Nicolas Manuel's *Self-Portrait ca* 1530. Jean Cousin the Elder's *Scenes from the Life of St Eutropius* Cranach's *Lucretia* and *Judith.* Nicolas Manuel Deutsch d.	Francis I founds the Collège de France.	Confession of Augsburg and Tetrapolitan Confession. Reformation spreads to Neuchâtel.
31	Schmalkaldic League formed.	Lucas Van Leyden's *The Healing of the Blind Man.* Cranach's *Portrait of John-Frederick, Elector of Saxony* and *Venus.*		Zwingli d. Henry VIII declares himself supreme head of the Church of England.

Date	Political events	Arts	Intellectual life	Religion
1532	Brittany united to French monarchy. Peace of Nuremberg. Sir Thomas More resigns.	Martin de Vos b. Heemskerk's *St Luke Painting the Virgin.*	Ariosto's *Orlando furioso.* Clément Marot's *Poèmes.* Rabelais' *Pantagruel.*	
1533	Henry VIII marries Anne Boleyn.	Cranach's *Portrait of Charles V.* Mabuse d. Lucas Van Leyden d.	Erasmus's *De amabili concordia.* Cornelius Agrippa's *De Occulta Philosophia.*	Francis I exiles the doctors of the Sorbonne. Calvin joins the Reformation. Olivetan's French version of the *Bible.*
1534	Treaty of Cadan.		Jacques Cartier discovers Canada and Labrador. Rabelais' *Gargantua.*	Anabaptist communities in Munster put down by united Catholics and Lutherans. Church of England established. Ignatius Loyola makes vow of poverty and chastity. Melanchthon's *Consilium de morandis.*
1535	Military agreement between France and Barbarossa. Renewal of hostilities between Francis I and Charles V.	Germain Pilon b. Jean Clouet's *Person Holding a Volume of Petrarch.*		Reformation accepted in Geneva.
1536	Francis I occupies Bresse and Savoy, takes Turin, and claims Flanders, Artois and Charolais.	Holbein's *Portrait of Richard Southwell.*	Johannes Secondus b. Turquet establishes the silk industry in Lyons. Paracelsus' *Treatise on Medicaments.*	Calvin's *Institutes.*
1537		Cranach's *Jesus in the House of the Pharisee.*	Bonaventura des Périers' *Cymbalum mundi.*	Calvin's *Confessio de Trinitate.* Citizens of Geneva resist Calvin's proposals.
1538	Holy Alliance in Germany against the Protestants.	Altdorfer d.	Strasbourg High School founded.	Reformers persecuted in France.

Date	Political events	Arts	Intellectual life	Religion
		Heemskerk's *Crucifixion* 1538-1543.	Bonaventura des Périers condemned by the Sorbonne.	
539	Ghent revolts against Charles V.	Van Reymerswaele's *Money-Changer and his Wife*. Hans Baldung's *Noli me tangere*. Holbein's *Portrait of Anne of Cleves*.	Mercator's map of the world.	Brandenburg Reform Society of Jesus formally approved.
540	Henry VIII marries and divorces Anne of Cleves.	Hieronymus Francken b.	Sebastian Münzer's *Ptolemy the Geographer*.	Calvin invited back to Geneva.
541	Conference of Ratisbon. Francis I reopens hostilities against Charles V.	Jean Clouet d. Rosso d.	Marot translates the *Psalms*.	Calvin translates his *Institutes* from Latin into French.
542		François Francken the Elder b. Bernard Van Orley d.	Copernicus' *De Revolutionibus* published. Andreas Vesalius' *De corporis humani fabrica*.	Inquisition re-established in Rome. Sebastian Franck advocates complete freedom of thought.
43	Charles V takes Guelderland from the Duke of Cleves.	Holbein the Younger d. François Quesnel b. Ambroise Dubois b. Aertsen's *The Farmer's Wife*. J. Goujon and Lescot: the rood-screen of Saint-Germain l'Auxerrois.		
44	Francis I emancipates the serfs in the royal domain. Diet of Speyer. Battle of Cérisoles. Charles V besieges Saint-Dizier. English besiege Boulogne. Treaty of Crespy.	Ambroise Francken b. Moro's *Two Canons of the Brotherhood of Jerusalem*.	Maurice Scève's *Délie*. Sebastian Münster's *Cosmographia Universalis*.	Calvin's *Brief Instruction* and *Excuse to the Nicodemites*. First Jesuit college in Germany founded in Cologne.

Date	Political events	Arts	Intellectual life	Religion
1545	Massacre of the Waldenses at Avignon.	Hans Baldung Grien d. Lancelot Blondeel's *St Luke Painting the Virgin; The Virgin with Sts Luke and Eligius; Scenes from the Life of the Virgin.* Jan Van Hoey b. François Pourbus b.	Serdio's *General Rules of Architecture.* Ambroise Paré's *Treatise on Surgery.*	Council of Trent opens. Luther's last work, his bitter attack on the Papacy. Calvin's *Against the Libertines.*
1546	Alliance of Maurice of Saxony and Charles V at war with the Schmalkaldic League. Treaty of Ardres.	Aertsen's *Calvary.*	Rabelais' third book published under his own name.	Execution of Etienne Dolet. Luther d. Inquisition established at Naples.
1547	Charles V breaks with Pope Paul III. Francis I d. Accession of Henry II. Revolt against the salt tax in Guyenne. Diet of Augsburg opens.			Council of Trent defines Catholic theology with regard to the Reformation (Counter-Reformation).
1548	Charles V formulates the Interim of Augsburg.	Karel Van Mander b. Delorme builds the Château d'Anet.	Rabelais' fourth book published. Lescot and Goujon's *Fontaine des Innocents.*	Paul III suspends the Council of Trent. Charles V repudiates Paul III. Inquisition executes Burlomacchi.
1549	Margaret of Navarre d.	Moro's *Portrait of Cardinal Granvelle.*	Du Bellay's *Défense et Illustration de la Langue française; Olive.* Vasari's *Lives.*	Paul III d. First large emigration of the French Huguenots to Geneva.
1550	English treaty with France: Boulogne surrendered to the French.	Pieter Coeck d.	Ronsard's *Odes.* Delorme and Bontemps' *Tomb of Francis I.* Pierre Romies' Animadversiones aristotelicanae.	Julian III elected Pope. Jesuit College in Rome founded. Calvin's *Treatise on Scandals.*

Date	Political events	Arts	Intellectual life	Religion
			Goujon's *Caryatids* in the Louvre. Rabelais becomes parish priest of Meduon. Adam Riese's *Treatise of Elementary Calculus.*	
552	Bishoprics of Metz, Toul and Verdun seized by Henry II. Maurice of Saxony occupies Augsburg and the Tyrol. Henry II supports Maurice of Saxony.	Niccolo dell'Abbate begins decorating the Château de Fontainebleau with Primaticcio.	Jodelle's *Cléopâtre captive.* Ronsard's *Amours.*	Council of Trent suspended.
553	Metz successfully defended by the Duke of Guise. Corsica conquered by the French.	Lucas Cranach d.	Postel's *Liber de Causis.* Du Bellay's *Antiquités à Rome.*	Michael Servetus burned at the stake in Geneva. Calvin's *Defence of the Orthodox Faith.* Casinus becomes court preacher in Vienna.
554	French lose Tuscany.	Frans Floris' *Fall of the Rebel Angels.*	Ronsard's *Bocage.*	Sebastian Castellio's *De Haereticis.* Théodore de Bèze's *De Haereticis.*
555	Charles V abdicates in favour of his brother Frederick. Siena rebels against Charles V and calls in the French.	Jean Cousin the Younger's *Descent from the Cross.*		Peace of Augsburg gives equal recognition to Protestants and Catholics in Germany.
556		Aertsen's *Peasants' Repast.*		Ignatius Loyola d.
	Philip of Spain leaves England.	Frans Floris' *Last Judgement.*	Louise Labé's *Sonnets.* Pomponazzi's *De Naturalibus in causis.*	
58	Accession of Queen Elizabeth I. Charles V d.	Otto Van Veen b. Bruegel's *Proverbs* (Antwerp).	Margaret of Navarre's *Heptameron.* Della Porta perfects the *camera obscura* using a converging lens. Du Bellay's *Jeux Rustiques.*	Geneva Academy founded under Théodore de Bèze. Coligny converted to Calvinism.

Date	Political events	Arts	Intellectual life	Religion
1559	Henry II d. Accession of Francis II. Guise family all-powerful in France. Treaty of Cateau-Cambrésis.	Pierre Lescot works on the Louvre. Bruegel's *Proverbs* (Berlin). François Clouet's *Portrait of Henry II.*	Amyot's French translation of Plutarch's *Lives.*	Paul IV d. First Calvinist synod held in Paris.
1560	Francis II d. Accession of Charles IX. Huguenot conspiracy suppressed at Amboise.	Jean Cousin the Elder d. Bruegel's *Children's Games.* Thomas Leu b.	Théodore de Bèze's *Treatise on the Authority of the Magistrate.*	
1561	States-General of Orleans.	Toussaint Dubreuil b.		Synod of the reformers meets at Poitiers.
1562	Edict of Saint-Germain.	Van Scorel d.	Ronsard's *Discours sur la Misère de ce Temps.*	Council of Trent reassembled.
1563	François de Guise assassinated. Plague breaks out in London.	Bruegel's *Tower of Babel* and *Fall of Icarus ca* 1563.	Barnabe Googe's *Eclogs, Epitaphs and Sonnets.*	
1564	Edict of Roussillon. Ferdinand I d. Treaty of Troyes.	'Hell' Bruegel b. Bruegel's *Bearing of the Cross.* Martin Fréminet b.	Rabelais' fifth book published. William Shakespeare b.	Calvin d. St Teresa of Avila's *Way of Perfection.*
1565		Bruegel's *Hunters in the Snow; Gloomy Day; Hay Making; The Harvesters;* and *The Return of the Herd.*	Goudimel composes his *Psalms* in a Calvinist spirit. Henri Estienne's *Treatise on Conformity.*	Pius IV d.
1566	Gowrie Conspiracy.	Lambert Lombard d. Bruegel's *Numbering at Bethlehem; Massacre of the Innocents; Sermon of St John; Conversion of St Paul; Seascape.* Bruegel's *Peasants' Dance; Village Fair; Noah's Rest* 1566-1568.	Nicholas Udall's *Ralph Roister Doister.*	Pius V elected Pope. Catechism of the Council of Trent. St Teresa's *Thoughts on Divine Love.*
1567	Revolt of the Netherlands. French Protestants take up arms.	Jean Goujon d. Van Reymerswaele d. Bruegel's *Land of Cockaigne.*	Birth of the *Commedia dell'arte.*	

Date	Political events	Arts	Intellectual life	Religion
1568	Peace of Longjumeau and new revolt of the French Protestants. Michel de L'Hospital disgraced. Duke of Alba sets up the 'tribunal of the troubles' in Antwerp. Maximilian II protests to Philip II of the Duke of Alba's excesses.	'Velvet' Bruegel b. Bruegel's *Misanthrope; Beggars; The Parable of the Blind.*	Mendaña discovers the Solomon Is. Jean Bodin's *Reply to Paradoxes.*	
569	Louis Condé defeated at Jarnac, taken prisoner and shot.	Bruegel the Elder d.	Mercator's map of the world published.	
570	Peace of Saint-Germain.	Hieronymus Cock d. Frans Floris d. Philibert Delorme d. Primaticcio d.	Ortelius' *Theatrum orbis terrarum.* Giodano Bruno teaches that the world is actuated by internal forces and not from without.	
571	Act for incorporation of Oxford and Cambridge.	Niccolo dell'Abbate d. François Bourbus' *Wedding of the Painter Hoefnagel.*	Printers in Paris and Lyons go on strike.	Akbar, Mogul emperor of India, convokes an assembly of representatives of all the religions.
572	Massacre of St Bartholomew. William of Orange becomes Governor of the Netherlands. Henry married Margaret of Valois and becomes a Catholic.	François Clouet d. François Pourbus' *Christ among the Doctors.*	Henri Etienne's *Thesaurus linguae grecae.* Ronsard's *La Franciade.* John Donne b.	Pius V d. Coligny, the Huguenot leader, assassinated by the Guises.
74	Charles IX d. Accession of Henry III. Renewal of Wars of Religion in France.	Martin Heemskerk d. Corneille de Lyon d.	Ronsard's *Sonnets pour Hélène.* Jean Bodin's *Discussions on Economics.*	St Teresa's commentary on the *Song of Songs.*
75	Battle of Dormans	Léonard Limosin d. Pieter Aertsen d.	Jacob Boehme b.	
76	Duke of Guise forms the Holy League to assert the supremacy of Catholicism in France. Confederation of Delft. Don Juan becomes Governor of the Netherlands. Pacification of Ghent. Maximilian II d.	Antonio Moro d.	Jean Bodin's *The Republic.* Sir Humphrey Gilbert's *Discourse of a New Passage to Cataia.* Tycho Brahe builds the Uraniborg observatory on the island of Hveen.	

Date	Political events	Arts	Intellectual life	Religion
1581	States of The Hague declare their independence.	François Pourbus d. Lancelot Blondeel d.	Vincenzo Galilei's *Dialogue of Ancient and Modern Music.* Tasso's *Gerusalemme Liberata.*	
1585	Cardinal Richelieu b. Leicester's expedition to the Netherlands. Sixtus V rejects the Protestant Henry of Navarre's claims to the French throne.		Cervantes' *Galatea.* Simon Stevinus outlines decimal system for currency, weights and measures.	Gregory XIII d. Sixtus V elected Pope.
1590	Battle of Ivry. Henry IV besieges Paris. Alessandro Farnese raises the siege.	Germain Pilon d.	Spenser's *Faerie Queene* bks i-iii.	Sixtus V d. Urban VII, then Gregory XIV, elected pope.
1593	States-General of the Louvre. Conference of Suresnes.	Ambroise Dubois decorates the Queen's Chamber from 1593. Delft enamelware produced.	Shakespeare's *Venus and Adonis.* Christopher Marlowe d.	Luis de Molina's *Of Justice and the Law.*
1594	Henry IV professes Catholicism. Jean Chastel assassinated.	Jean Cousin the Younger d.	Shakespeare's *Lucrece.* Hooker's *Laws of Ecclesiastical Polity.*	Paris Parliament bans the Jesuits.
1596	Archduke Albert becomes Governor of the Netherlands.		Descartes b. Raleigh's *Discovery of Guiana.* Kepler's *Mysterium cosmographicum.* Spenser's *Faerie Queene* bks iv-vi.	
1598	Edict of Nantes. Philip II d. Lord Burghley d. Treaty of Vervins between France and Spain.	Ambroise Francken's *Multiplication of Pains.*	Lope de Vega's *Arcadia.* Shakespeare's *Henry IV* pt i and *Love's Labour's Lost.* Hakluyt's *Principall Navigations, Voyages and Discoveries.*	Clement VIII forbids communion under both kinds in the Austrian states.
1599		Antoine Caron d.	Shakespeare's *Julius Caesar.*	

Date	Political events	Arts	Intellectual life	Religion
1600	Henry IV marries Marie de Medici.		Shakespeare's *Henry IV* pt ii, *Henry V*, *Merchant of Venice*, *Midsummer-Night's Dream*, *Much Ado about Nothing* and *As You Like It*. Calderón b.	Giordano Bruno burnt at the stake in Rome.
1602	Alliance between France and the Swiss Cantons renewed.	Toussaint Dubreuil d. Gobelins factory founded.	Bodleian Library opened. Shakespeare's *Merry Wives of Windsor*.	St Francis of Sales consecrated Bishop of Geneva. Henry IV permits the return of the Jesuits.
603	Queen Elizabeth I d. Accession of James I. Henry IV arranges an alliance between the Grisons and Venice.	Martin de Vos d.	Shakespeare's *Hamlet* and *Troilus and Cressida*. Dutch East India Company founded.	
606	Henry IV arbitrates in the conflict between Venice and the Pope.	Joachim von Sandrart b. Karel Van Mander d.	Pierre Corneille b. John Lyly d.	
607	Navarre united with Béarn.		Honoré d'Urfé's *Astrée*.	
608	German Evangelical Union formed against Lutherans and Calvinists.	Fréminet begins decorating the chapel of the Trinity at Fontainebleau.	Shakespeare's *King Lear* and *Coriolanus*. John Milton b.	St Francis of Sales' *Introduction to the Devout Life*.
610	Henry IV assassinated. Accession of Louis XIII. Marie de Medici becomes regent of France. Alliance between the Holy League and Spain.	Hieronymus Francken the Elder d.	Galileo invents the telescope. Galileo's *Nuntius Siderius*. Shakespeare's *Tempest*, *Cymbeline* and *Winter's Tale* acted 1610-1612.	
612	Marie de Medici makes peace with Spain. Louis XII betrothed to Anne of Austria.	Thomas de Leu d. Salomon de Brosse builds the Palais du Luxembourg in Paris.	Jacob Boehme's *Aurora*. Webster's *The White Devil*. Francisco Suarez' *Tractatus de Legibus*.	

Date	Political events	Arts	Intellectual life	Religion
1614	Condé's revolt. French States-General complain of mismanagement of finances.	Ambroise Dubois d.	Isaac Casaubon d. Jonson's *Bartholomew Fair* acted.	Leonard Brusher's *Peace of Religion.*
1615		Jan Van Hoey d.	Chapman completes his translation of the *Odyssey*.	
1616	Treaty of Loudon. Richelieu becomes Secretary of War. Condé arrested.	Franck Francken d. Jacques Callot's *Battles of the Medicis.*	William Shakespeare d. William Harvey expounds the theory of the circulation of the blood to the College of Surgeons.	St Francis of Sales' *Treatise on the Love of God.* Inquisition forbids Galileo to expound his doctrines.
1618	Thirty Years' War 1618-1648.	Francken the Elder d.	Salon of the Marquise de Rambouillet held in Paris. Sir Walter Raleigh executed.	
1619	Christine of France married Victor-Amedeus of Savoy.	Martin Fréminet d. François Quesnel d.	Bank of Hamburg founded. Kepler's *Harmonice Mundi Purchas his Pilgrim* published.	
1620	Navarre annexed to France. Treaty of Ulm.		Francis Bacon's *Novum Organum.* Pilgrim Fathers emigrate to America.	
1625	Accession of Charles I. Frederick of Nassau d.	'Velvet' Bruegel d.	Grotius' *De jure belli et pacis.*	
1629	Richelieu's campaign in Piedmont. Treaty of Lübeck between the Emperor and Denmark.	Otto Van Veen d.	Pierre Corneille's *Mélite.* Giovanni Branca's project for a steam engine.	Richelieu deprives the Protestants of political rights but grants them religious freedom.
1630	'Day of Dupes': Richelieu overcomes the opposition of Marie de Medici and the House of Guise. Diet of Ratisbon. Richelieu seizes Pinerolo and takes Savoy.		Tirso de Molina's *El Burlador de Sevilla*, the first play dealing with Don Juan.	

Date	Political events	Arts	Intellectual life	Religion
1638	Treaty between France and Sweden.	Poussin paints *The Shepherds of Arcadia* in Rome. 'Hell'Bruegel d.	Pierre Corneille's *La Veuve* and *La Suivante*. Shakespeare and Fletcher's *Two Noble Kinsmen* published.	St Vincent de Paul founds the Sisters of Charity.
1683	Colbert d. Mouis XIV married Mme de Maintenon. Turks lay siege to Vienna.	Joachim von Sandrart d.	Newton demonstrates his theory of gravitation. Dryden's translation of Plutarch.	

Museography

Name	Place	Museum	Title	Year	Material	Dimensions
Abbate, Niccolo dell' (*ca* 1509-1571)	Fontainebleau	Château	Decorations in collaboration with Primaticcio	From 1552	Frescoes	
	Fontainebleau	Château	*Landscape with Men Threshing Wheat*		Canvas	39″ × 56″
	Château de Fontenay-en-Cotentin	Private Collection	*Ulysses and the Sirens*		Canvas	59″ × 81″
	Paris	Private Collection	*Harvesting Corn*		Canvas	39″ × 56″
Aertsen, Pieter (1508-1575)	Antwerp	Museum	*Calvary*	1546		
	Antwerp	Museum	*Peasants' Repast*	1556	Wood	55″ × 78″
	Antwerp	Museum	*Dance of the Eggs*	1557	Wood	33″ × 68″
	Antwerp	Museum	*The Pancake-Maker*		Wood	37″ × 65″
	Berlin	Museum	*Christ Bearing the Cross*			
	Brussels	Museum	*Christ with Martha and Mary*			
	Brussels	Museum	*The Cook*	1559	Wood	50″ × 32″
	Brussels	Museum	*The Cook*			
	Lille	Museum	*The Farmer's Wife*	1543		
	Uppsala		*The Butcher's Stall*			
Altdorfer, Albrecht (*ca* 1480-1538)	Berlin	Museum	*Holy Family at the Fountain*			
	Florence	Uffizi	*St Florian Altar-piece*		Wood	30″ × 26″
	Munich	Pinakothek	*St George and the Dragon*		Wood	26″ × 30″
	Munich	Pinakothek	*Birth of the Virgin*			
	Munich	Pinakothek	*Susanna at the Bath*			
	Munich	Pinakothek	*Battle of Alexander*			
	Munich	Pinakothek	*Danube Landscape near Regensburg*		Wood	18″ × 24″
	Vienna	Museum	*Resurrection of Christ*	1518	Wood	28″ × 15″
Anonymous artists of the School of Fontainebleau	Aix-en-Provence	Museum	*Allegory of Peace*			
	Dijon	Museum	*The Courtesan*		Canvas	38″ × 29″
	Geneva	Museum	*Sabina Poppaea*		Wood	32″ × 24″
	Hartford	Wadsworth Athenaeum	*The Tepidarium*		Wood	37″ × 50″

Name	Place	Museum	Title	Year	Material	Dimensions
	New York	Wildenstein Collection	*Night*		Wood	20″ × 26″
	New York	Wildenstein Collection	*Ceres and Vulcan*		Wood	24″ × 17″
	Paris	Louvre	*Gabrielle d'Estrées and the Duchess of Villars*		Wood	38″ × 50″
	Paris	Louvre	*Artemis*		Wood	18″ × 12″
	Rome	Museum	*The Middle-Aged Woman*			
Baldung Grien, Hans (*ca* 1485-1545)	Basle	Museum	*Woman and Death*	1517		
	Basle	Museum	*Death Kissing a Woman before an Open Tomb*			
	Berlin	Museum	*Adoration of the Magi*	1507		
	Berlin	Museum	*St Sebastian*	1507		
	Darmstadt	Museum	*Noli me tangere*	1539		
	Frankfurt	Museum	*The Witches' Sabbath*			
	Freiburg	Cathedral of Notre-Dame	*Coronation of the Virgin Altar-piece*	1516		
	Vienna	Museum	*Young Girl and Death*			
Blondeel, Lancelot (1498-1581)	Amsterdam	Rijksmuseum	*Saint's Martyrdom*	1558		
	Bruges	Museum	*Story of Sts Cosmas and Damian*	1523		
	Bruges	Museum	*St Luke Painting the Virgin*	1545		
	Bruges	Museum	*The Virgin with Sts Luke and Eligius*	1545		
	Bruges	Museum	*Scenes from the Life of the Virgin*	1545		
Bosch, Hieronymus (*ca* 1450-1516)	Berlin	Dahlem Museum	*St John in Patmos*		Wood	21″ × 16″
	Ghent	Museum	*Bearing of the Cross*		Wood	30″ × 32″
	Ghent	Museum	*St Jerome at Prayer*		Wood	30″ × 23″
	Lisbon	Museum	*Temptation of St Antony*		Wood	52″ × 46″
	London	National Gallery	*The Crowning with Thorns*		Wood	29″ × 23″
	Madrid	Prado	*The Hay-Wain* central panel volets		Wood	54″ × 40″ 54″ × 19″

Name	Place	Museum	Title	Year	Material	Dimensions
	Madrid	Prado	*The Cure of Folly*		Wood	19″ × 14″
	Madrid	Prado	*Seven Deadly Sins*		Wood	47″ × 60″
	Madrid	Prado	*Garden of Earthly Delights*		Wood	87″ × 77″
	Madrid	José Lazaro Collection	*St John the Baptist in the Wilderness*		Wood	20″ × 16″
	Paris	Louvre	*Ship of Fools*		Wood	22″ × 13″
	Philadelphia	Museum of Art	*Epiphany*		Wood	30″ × 21″
	Rotterdam	Boymans Museum	*St Christopher*		Wood	44″ × 29″
	Rotterdam	Boymans Museum	*Prodigal Son*		Wood	Diam. 71″
	Saint-Germain-en-Laye	Museum	*The Conjuror*		Wood	20″ × 26″
	Vienna	Museum	*Last Judgement* central panel volets		Wood Wood	65″ × 50″ 66″ × 24″
Bruegel the Elder (*ca* 1525-1569)	Antwerp	Museum	*Netherlandish Proverbs*	1558	Wood	30″ × 38″
	Antwerp	Museum	*Dulle Griet*	1564	Wood	54″ × 63″
	Berlin	Museum	*Netherlandish Proverbs*	1559	Wood	46″ × 64″
	Brussels	Museum	*Landscape with Icarus*	*ca* 1563	Canvas	29″ × 44″
	Brussels	Museum	*The Fall of the Rebel Angels*	1562	Wood	46″ × 64″
	Brussels	Museum	*Numbering at Bethlehem*	1570	Wood	46″ × 65″
	Budapest	Museum	*Sermon of St John the Baptist*	1565–1567	Wood	37″ × 63″
	Madrid	Prado	*Triumph of Death*	1565–1567	Wood	46″ × 64″
	Munich	Museum	*Land of Cockaigne*	1567	Wood	20″ × 31″
	Naples	Museum	*Parable of the Blind*	1567	Canvas	34″ × 61″
	Naples	Museum	*The Misanthrope*	1568	Canvas	Diam. 35″
	New York	Metropolitan Museum	*The Harvesters*	1565	Wood	46″ × 64″
	Paris	Louvre	*Cripples*	1568	Wood	7″ × 8″
	Prague	Museum	*Hay Making*	1565	Wood	45″ × 62″

Name	Place	Museum	Title	Year	Material	Dimensions
	Vienna	Museum	*The Return of the Herd*	1565	Wood	46″ × 64″
	Vienna	Museum	*Massacre of the Innocents*	1566	Wood	44″ × 63″
	Vienna	Museum	*Conversion of St Paul*	1565–1567	Wood	43″ × 61″
	Vienna	Museum	*Storm at Sea*	1565–1567	Wood	28″ × 38″
	Vienna	Museum	*Children's Games*	1560	Wood	46″ × 63″
	Vienna	Museum	*Fight between Carnival and Lent*	1559	Wood	46″ × 65″
	Vienna	Museum	*Tower of Babel*	1563	Wood	45″ × 65″
	Vienna	Museum	*Procession to Calvary*	1564	Wood	49″ × 67″
	Vienna	Museum	*Hunters in the Snow*	1565	Wood	46″ × 64″
	Vienna	Museum	*Wedding Banquet*	*ca* 1568	Wood	45″ × 65″
	Vienna	Museum	*Peasant Dance*	*ca* 1568	Wood	45″ × 65″
	Vienna	Museum	*The Gloomy Day*	1565	Wood	46″ × 64″
3runswick Monogrammist	Brunswick	Museum	*The Meal of the Poor*		Wood	23″ × 20″
	Paris	Louvre	*Abraham's Sacrifice*		Wood	16″ × 12″
;aron, Antoine 1521-1599)	Paris	Private Collection	*Triumph of Summer*		Canvas	31″ × 70″
	Paris	Private Collection	*Triumph of Winter*		Canvas	31″ × 70″
	Paris	Private Collection	*Meeting of Abraham and Melchizedek*		Wood	31″ × 37″
	Paris	Private Collection	*Astronomers Observing an Eclipse*			
	Paris	Private Collection	*Apotheosis of Semele*			
	Paris	Private Collection	*Elephant Tournament*			
	Paris	Louvre	*Augustus and the Sibyl of Tibur*			
	Paris	Louvre	*Massacres under the Triumvirate*			
louet, François efore 1520-1572)	Chantilly	Museum	*Margaret of France as a Child*		Wood	12″ × 9″
	Chantilly	Museum	*Jacques of Savoy, Duke of Nemours*		Wood	13″ × 9″
	Florence	Uffizi	*Henry II*	1559	Wood	12″ × 7″

Name	Place	Museum	Title	Year	Material	Dimensions
	Paris	Louvre	*Henry II*		Wood	13″ × 9″
	Paris	Louvre	*Pierre Quthe*		Wood	12″ × 9″
	Paris	Louvre	*Elizabeth of Austria*		Wood	12″ × 8″
	Paris	Louvre	*Charles IX*		Wood	13″ × 7″
	Rouen	Museum	*Diane in her Bath*			
	Tours	Museum	*Diane in her Bath*			
	Vienna	Museum	*Charles IX*		Canvas	87″ × 45″
Clouet, Jean (*ca* 1486-1540)	Antwerp	Museum	*The Dauphin François*		Wood	6″ × 5″
	Florence	Uffizi	*Francis I on Horseback*		Wood	11″ × 9″
	Hampton Court	Palace	*Person Holding a Volume of Petrarch*	*ca* 1535		
	Lyons	Museum	*Guillaume de Montmorency*			
	Paris	Louvre	*Francis I*	*ca* 1524	Wood	38″ × 29″
	Paris	Louvre	*Guillaume de Montmorency*			
	Paris	Thomson Collection	*Charlotte of France*	1521		
Corneille de Lyon (*ca* 1500-after 1574)	Chantilly	Museum	*Madame de Lausac*		Wood	7″ × 6″
	Chantilly	Museum	*Catharine de Medici, Dauphine of France*		Wood	6″ × 5″
	Chantilly	Museum	*Francis II, Dauphin of France*			
	Chantilly	Museum	*Margaret of Savoy*			
	Paris	Louvre	*Duke of Montpensier*			
Cousin the Elder, Jean (*ca* 1490-*ca* 1561)	Paris	Louvre	*Eva Prima Pandora*			
	Sens	Cathedral	*Scenes from the Life of St Eutropius*	1530	Stained glass	
	Sens	Cathedral	*The Sibyl of Tibur Consulted by the Emperor Augustus*			
Cousin the Younger, Jean (1522-1594)	Paris	Rupilly Collection	*Descent from the Cross*	*ca* 1555-1560	Wood	25″ × 18″
	Paris	Louvre	*Last Judgement*			
Cranach, Lucas (1472-1553)	Berlin	Museum	*Portrait of the Wife of Stephan Reuss*	1503	Wood	20″ × 15″
	Berlin	Museum	*Rest during the Flight into Egypt*	1504	Wood	27″ × 20″

Name	Place	Museum	Title	Year	Material	Dimensions
	Bonn	Museum	*Jesus in the House of the Pharisee*	after 1537	Wood	31″ × 43″
	Dresden	Museum	*Martyrdom of St Catharine*	1506	Wood	50″ × 55″
	Florence	Uffizi	*Martin Luther*	1529	Wood	15″ × 9″
	Florence	Uffizi	*Catharine Bora*	1529	Wood	15″ × 9″
	Frankfurt	Museum	*Holy Family*	1509	Wood	47″ × 39″
	Leningrad	Hermitage	*Venus*		Wood	67″ × 29″
	Lugano	Von Thyssen Collection	*Charles V*	1533	Wood	20″ × 14″
	Munich	Pinakothek	*Crucifixion*	1503	Wood	54″ × 39″
	Munich	Pinakothek	*Adam and Eve*	*ca* 1510-1512	Wood	19″ × 14″
	Munich	Pinakothek	*Lucretia*	*ca* 1530	Wood	76″ × 30″
	Naples	Capodimonte	*Jesus and the Woman Taken in Adultery*		Wood	22″ × 30″
	Nuremberg	Museum	*Johann Stephan Reuss*	1503	Wood	21″ × 15″
	Paris	Louvre	*John-Frederick, Elector of Saxony*	1531	Wood	20″ × 14″
	Rome	Galleria Borghese	*Venus*	1531	Wood	67″ × 29″
	Stuttgart	Museum	*Judith*	*ca* 1530	Wood	34″ × 23″
	Winterthur	Reinhart Collection	*Portrait of Johannes Cuspinian*	1503	Wood	23″ × 18″
	Winterthur	Reinhart Collection	*Portrait of Anna Putsch, Cuspinian's First Wife*	1503	Wood	18″ × 23″
	Winterthur	Museum	*'Let the Little Children come unto Me'*		Wood	34″ × 48″
Dubois, Ambroise (1543-1614)	Fontainebleau	Château	Decoration of the Queen's Chamber	after 1593	Frescoes	
Dubreuil, Toussaint (1561-1602)	Saint-Germain-en-Laye	Château	*Ancient Sacrifice; Woman Greeted by a Warrior*		Frescoes	
Dürer, Albrecht (1471-1528)	Berlin	Museum	*Frederick the Wise*	*ca* 1496	Canvas	30″ × 22″
	Berlin	Museum	*Jacob Muffel*	1526	Wood transferred to canvas	19″ × 14″
	Berlin	Museum	*Hieronymus Holzschuher*	1526	Wood	19″ × 14″

Name	Place	Museum	Title	Year	Material	Dimensions
	Florence	Uffizi	*Adoration of the Magi*	1504	Wood	39″ × 44″
	Florence	Uffizi	*Portrait of Dürer's Father*	1490	Wood	48″ × 35″
	Madrid	Prado	*Hans Imhof*	1521	Wood	19″ × 15″
	Madrid	Prado	*Adam and Eve*	1507		
	Munich	Pinakothek	*Four Apostles*	1526	Wood	80″ × 29″
	Munich	Pinakothek	*Self-portrait*	*ca* 1504	Wood	26″ × 19″
	Munich	Pinakothek	*Jacob Fugger*	*ca* 1520	Canvas	27″ × 20″
	Munich	Pinakothek	*Oswolt Krell*	1499	Wood	19″ × 15″
	Munich	Pinakothek	*Paumgärtner Triptych* central panel: *Nativity* left volet: *St George* right volet: *St Hubert*	*ca* 1503	 Wood Wood Wood	 60″ × 48″ 60″ × 34″ 60″ × 34″
	Munich	Pinakothek	*Descent from the Cross*	1500	Wood	60″ × 47″
	Paris	Louvre	*Self-portrait*	1493	Vellum mounted on canvas	
	Vienna	Museum	*Martyrdom of the Ten Thousand*	1508	Canvas	39″ × 34″
	Vienna	Museum	*The Trinity and All Saints*	1511	Wood	57″ × 52″
	Vienna	Museum	*Portrait of Maximilian I*	1512	Wood	29″ × 24″
	Weimar	Museum	*Hans Tucher*	1499		
Floris, Frans (*ca* 1516-1570)	Antwerp	Museum	*The Fall of the Rebel Angels*	1554		
	Berlin	Museum	*Venus and Mars Entangled in Vulcan's Net*			
	Brunswick	Museum	*The Falconer*			
	Brussels	Museum	*The Last Judgement*	1556		
	Caen	Museum	*Portrait of an Elderly Woman*			
	Stockholm	Museum	*Venus and Adonis*			
	Stockholm	Museum	*Banquet of the Sea-Gods*			
Francken, Ambroise (1544-1618)	Antwerp	Museum	*The Multiplication of Pains*	1598		
	Antwerp	Museum	*Martyrdom of Sts Crispin and Crispinian*			
Fréminet, Martin (1564-1619)	Fontainebleau	Chapel of the Trinity	Decoration	from 1608	Oil on plaster	

Name	Place	Museum	Title	Year	Material	Dimensions
Grünewald, Matthias (1445/1460-*ca* 1528)	Basle	Museum	*Crucifixion*			
	Colmar	Unterlinden Museum	*Isenheim Altar-piece*	1508-1514	Wood	
	Frankfurt	Museum	*St Cyriacus the Recluse; St Lawrence*			
	Karlsruhe	Museum	*Crucifixion*			
	Munich	Pinakothek	*Mocking of Christ*			
	Munich	Pinakothek	*Sts Maurice and Erasmus*	*ca* 1525-1526		
Heemskerk, Martin (1498-1574)	Amsterdam	Museum	*Pieter Bicker and his Wife Anna Codde*	1529	Wood	33″ × 26″
	Berlin	Museum	*Story of Momus*			
	Brunswick	Museum	*Baptism of Christ*			
	Ghent	Museum	*Crucifixion*			
	Haarlem	Museum	*Annunciation* and *Adoration of the Magi and Shepherds*			
	Haarlem	Museum	*St Luke Painting the Virgin*	1532		
	Kassel	Museum	*Family Portrait*			
	Linköping (Sweden)	Cathedral	*Crucifixion*	1538-1543		
Holbein, Hans (*ca* 1497-1543)	Basle	Museum	*The Artist's Family*	*ca* 1528	Paper mounted on wood	30″ × 25″
	Basle	Museum	*Dead Christ*		Wood	79″ × 16″
	Basle	Museum	*Bonifacius Amerbach*	1519	Wood	11″ × 11″
	Basle	Museum	*Jakob Meyer, Burgomaster of Basle*		Wood	15″ × 12″
	Basle	Museum	*Dorothea Kannengiesser, Wife of Jakob Meyer*		Wood	15″ × 12″
	Berlin	Museum	*Georg Gisze*		Wood	17″ × 12″
	Darmstadt	Museum	*Madonna of Burgomaster Meyer*	*ca* 1526	Wood	13″ × 11″
	Florence	Uffizi	*Richard Southwell*	1536	Canvas	19″ × 15″
	London	National Gallery	*The Ambassadors*			
	Paris	Louvre	*Nicholas Kratzer*		Wood	15″ × 12″

Name	Place	Museum	Title	Year	Material	Dimensions
	Paris	Louvre	*Erasmus*	1523	Wood	17″ × 23″
	Paris	Louvre	*Anne of Cleves*	1539	Vellum on canvas	26″ × 19″
	Paris	Louvre	*Sir Henry Wyatt*	1526-1528	Wood	21″ × 17″
	Rome	Palazzo Barberini	*Henry VIII*		Canvas	34″ × 29″
	São Paulo	Museum	*Henry Howard, Earl of Surrey*		Wood	21″ × 17″
Lucas Van Leyden (1494-1533)	Amsterdam	Museum	*Sermon in Church*	*ca* 1530	Canvas	52″ × 38″
	Berlin	Museum	*The Game of Chess*			
	Berlin	Museum	*Susanna before the Judges*	*ca* 1511		
	Berlin	Museum	*Potiphar's Wife*	*ca* 1511		
	Berlin	Museum	*The Card Players*	*ca* 1511	Wood	13″ × 19″
	Brunswick	Museum	*Self-portrait*			
	Leningrad	Hermitage	*The Healing of the Blind Man*	1531		
	Leyden	Museum	*Last Judgement*	1526	Wood	104″ × 30″
	Leyden	Museum	*Dance round the Golden Calf*	*ca* 1525		
	Nuremberg	Museum	*Moses Striking Water from the Rock*	*ca* 1527		
	Paris	Louvre	*Lot and his Daughters*	*ca* 1514	Wood	23″ × 13″
Lombard, Lambert (1506-1566)	Liège	Church of Saint-Denis	*Life of Christ; Legend of Denis*			
Mabuse (Jan Gossaert) (*ca* 1478-1533)	Berlin	Museum	*Malvagna Triptych*		Wood	13″ × 9″
	Berlin	Museum	*Christ on the Mount of Olives*	after 1509		23″ × 25″
	Berlin	Museum	*Neptune and Aphrodite*	1516	Wood	74″ × 49″
	Berlin	Museum	*Hercules and Dejanira*	1517	Wood	10″ × 4″
	Berlin	Museum	*Hercules and Antaeus*	1523	Wood	18″ × 14″
	Brussels	Museum	*Adam and Eve*		Wood	67″ × 45″
	Copenhagen	Museum	*The Children of Christian II of Denmark*		Wood	14″ × 20″
	London	National Gallery	*Adoration of the Magi*	*ca* 1505		70″ × 63″
	Munich	Pinakothek	*Madonna*	1527	Oval wood	12″ × 9″

Name	Place	Museum	Title	Year	Material	Dimensions
	Munich	Pinakothek	*Danae*	1527		45″ × 37″
	Paris	Louvre	*The Chancellor Jean Carondelet*	1517	Oval wood	17″ × 11″
	Prague	Museum	*St Luke Painting the Virgin*	1515	Wood	91″ × 81″
Manuel, Nicolas (*ca* 1485-1530)	Basle	Museum	*Death Embracing a Prostitute*			
	Basle	Museum	*Judgement of Paris*		Canvas	88″ × 63″
	Basle	Museum	*Pyramus and Thisbe*		Canvas	60″ × 63″
	Basle	Museum	*Bathsheba's Bath*			
	Berne	Museum	*St Luke Painting the Virgin*		Wood	46″ × 32″
	Berne	Museum	*Battle of the Giants*			
	Berne	Museum	*Beheading of St John the Baptist*			
	Berne	Museum	*Birth of the Virgin Mary*		Wood	46″ × 32″
	Berne	Museum	*Self-portrait*	*ca* 1530	Wood	14″ × 10″
Master of Flora	New York	Metropolitan Museum	*Birth of Cupid*			
	Zürich	Feilchenfeldt Collection	*Triumph of Flora*			
Metsys, Quentin 1465-1530)	Paris	Jacquemart-André Museum	*Old Man*		Wood	15″ × 12″
	Paris	Louvre	*Madonna*		Wood	27″ × 20″
	Poznan	Museum	*Virgin and Child*		Wood	26″ × 19″
	Rome	Palazzo Barberini	*Judith*		Wood	37″ × 47″
	Rome	Palazzo Barberini	*Erasmus*		Canvas	22″ × 18″
Moro, Antonio *ca* 1517-1576)	Berlin	Museum	*Two Canons of the Brotherhood of Jerusalem*	1544	Wood	36″ × 40″
	Brunswick	Museum	*Jan Van Scorel*		Wood	36″ × 33″
	Brussels	Museum	*Hubert Goltzius*		Wood	35″ × 31″
	Brussels	Museum	*The Duke of Alba*		Wood	35″ × 30″
	Kassel	Museum	*William of Orange*		Wood	36″ × 31″
	Madrid	Prado	*Maximilian II*		Wood	41″ × 33″
	Madrid	Prado	*Mary Tudor*	1554	Wood	43″ × 33″
	Madrid	Prado	*Pereson, the King of Spain's Jester*		Wood	41″ × 33″

Name	Place	Museum	Title	Year	Material	Dimensions
	Paris	Louvre	*Cardinal de Granvelle's Dwarf*			43″ × 33″
	Vienna	Museum	*Portrait of Cardinal de Granvelle*	1549		43″ × 35″
Pourbus, François (1545-1581)	Antwerp	Museum	*The Wedding of the Painter Hoefnagel*	1571		
	Düsseldorf	Museum	*Viglius Ayta*			
	Ghent	St Bavo's	*Christ among the Doctors*	1572		
Primaticcio (1505-1570)	Fontainebleau	Château	Decoration of the Queen's Chamber, Golden Gate, Duchesse d'Etampes' Bedchamber, and Ballroom	from 1532	Frescoes	
	London	Private Collection	*Ulysses and Penelope*		Canvas	45″ × 48″
	Paris	Private Collection	*Jean de Dinteville as St George*		Canvas	66″ × 47″
Rosso (1494-1541)	Fontainebleau	Château	Decoration of the Francis I Gallery	from 1530	Frescoes	
	Paris	Louvre	*Pietà*			
Van Hemessen, Jan (*ca* 1540-before 1567)	Antwerp	Church of Saint-Jacques	*Last Judgement*			
	Brussels	Museum	*The Prodigal Son*	1536		
	Brussels	Museum	*The Calling of St Matthew*	1536		
	Karlsruhe	Museum	*Dissolute Company*			
	Munich	Museum	*Ecce Homo*			
	Paris	Louvre	*Tobias Healing his Father*	1555		
Van Orley, Berard (*ca* 1488-1542)	Antwerp	Museum	*Last Judgement* and *Seven Works of Charity*			
	Bonn	Museum	*Triptych of the Manneton Family*	*ca* 1508-1512		
	Brussels	Museum	*Dr George Zelle*	1519	Wood	15″ × 13″
	Brussels	Museum	*The Trials and Patience of Job*	1521		
	Brussels	Museum	*The Incredulity and Death of St Thomas*			
	Brussels	Museum	*Election and Beheading of St Matthew*			
	Brussels	St Gudula's	*Charles V and Elizabeth of Portugal, Louis of Hungary and his Wife*		Stained glass	

Name	Place	Museum	Title	Year	Material	Dimensions
	Paris	Louvre	*Holy Family*			
	Vienna	Museum	Central panel of the *Sts Thomas and Matthew Altar-piece*			
Van Reymerswaele (*ca* 1495-after 1567)	Berlin	Museum	*St Jerome in his Study*	1521	Wood	31″ × 42″
	Louvain	Museum	*Two Tax-Gatherers*		Wood	33″ × 37″
	Lugano	Von Thyssen Collection	*The Calling of St Matthew*		Wood	28″ × 35″
	Madrid	Prado	*The Money-Changer and his Wife*	1539	Wood	33″ × 38″
Van Scorel, Jan (1495-1562)	Amsterdam	Museum	*Bathsheba*		Wood	41″ × 80″
	Amsterdam	Museum	*The Queen of Sheba's Visit to King Solomon*			
	Amsterdam	Museum	*Mary Magdalen*		Wood	26″ × 30″
	Rome	Palazzo Doria-Pamphili	*Agatha Van Schoonhoven*			
	Utrecht	Museum	*Van Lochorst Triptych*			
	Utrecht	Museum	*Members of the Brotherhood of Jerusalem*	1525-1526	Wood	30″ × 65″
Van Veen, Otto (1558-1629)	Antwerp	Museum	*The Calling of St Matthew*			
	Antwerp	Museum	*Zachariah in the Fig-Tree*			
	Bordeaux	Museum	*The Marriage of St Catharine*			
	Schleissheim	Museum	*Triumph of the Catholic Church* (six paintings)			
Vos, Martin de (1532-1603)	Amsterdam	Museum	*Giles Hoffman and his Wife Margaretha Van Nispen*		Wood	46″ × 55″
	Antwerp	Museum	*The Incredulity of St Thomas*			
	Antwerp	Museum	*Triumph of Christ*			
	Antwerp	Museum	*Caesar's Tribute*			

Dictionary

Abbate, Niccolo dell' (*ca* 1509-71)

Born in Modena, died in France. Niccolo dell'Abbate was first apprenticed to his father, and then went to study under the sculptor Antonio Begarelli. He may also have been a pupil of Correggio. According to one tradition, he became a soldier, but did not follow the military life for long. In 1537 he took up his brushes again and assisted Alberto Fontana on the frescoes for the butcher's shops in Modena, and then went on to decorate some of the public buildings on his own. From this period are supposed to date various frescoes painted in castles, among others that of Sarudiano. Beneath a portico he painted subjects taken from the poems of Ariosto, and in a closet twelve pictures corresponding to the twelve books of the *Aeneid.* In 1547, Niccolo dell'Abbate was summoned to Bologna to decorate the Palazzo Torfanini and the Palazzo Poggi. In this he was extremely successful, and he was later praised in a famous sonnet by Agostino Caracci. On the advice of Primaticcio, Henry II invited him to France, where he arrived at the beginning of 1552. In May of that year, he was granted a pension on the strength of his portraits of the king and queen, and sent for his wife and three children in Italy. During the eighteen years that he spent in France, Niccolo dell'Abbate acted as Primaticcio's right-hand man. From this association there resulted a number of works on a grand scale, some of them executed at Fontainebleau. These included eight large pictures for the St Louis Chamber, the decoration of the Ballroom and the Henry II Room. Besides all this, he also painted frescoes, either alone or in association with Primaticcio, for the former Meudon Pavilion, which was destroyed during the reign of Louis XIV, for the chapel of the Hôtel de Guise (later to become the Hôtel de Soubise and then the National Archives), the Hôtel de Toulouse, the Hôtel de Montmorency, the house of Councillor Le Tellier at Chantilly, and the Château de Beauregard near Blois. He was also a landscape-painter who had a considerable influence on French painting. The City of Paris requested him to work on paintings, and to construct triumphal arches at the Porte Saint-Denis, the Ponceau Fountain, etc., on the occasion of the solemn entry in 1571 of Charles IX and of his queen Elizabeth of Austria. He died in the same year.

Niccolo dell'Abbate
Amorous Conversation
Musée des Beaux-Arts, Algiers

Aertsen, Pieter (1508-75)

Born and died in Amsterdam. Pieter Aertsen was the son of a stocking manufacturer. At first he worked for a painter called Alart Claeszoon, and then at the age of eighteen he moved to Antwerp where he lodged with a painter and compatriot, Jan Mandyn. In 1535, he was admitted master to the Painters' Guild of Antwerp under the name ' Lange Pier ' (Long Peter), given him on account of his height.

His biographer states that ' he paid little attention to himself and seemed a complete peasant '. Vasari mentions him and calls him ' Pietro lungo ', but it is not known whether he ever travelled to Italy. In 1542 he married the aunt of his faithful follower Joachim Beuckelaer, and in the same year became a citizen of Antwerp, being described as ' Peeter Aerts, Peetersone Van Amsterdam, schilder ' (Peter Aerts, son of Peter of Amsterdam, painter). In 1557 he returned to his birthplace and remained there for the rest of his life. He had three sons, all of whom were painters.

Aertsen is above all a genre-painter: he painted interiors and in particular kitchens, which had a great success, as did his still-lifes. He also produced a number of religious works for Notre-Dame in Amsterdam, depicting the *Death of the Virgin*, the *Adoration of the Magi* and the *Nativity*, and he decorated many religious buildings. But many of these works were destroyed by the iconoclasts in 1566. He also painted country scenes, such as the *Peasants' Repast* (1556), the *Pancake-Makers* and the *Dance of the Eggs*. His pictures are among the earliest examples of paintings of familiar scenes to be found in Holland. As a painter of the common people, sometimes in aggressive attitudes, he is the forerunner of Jan Steen.

Altdorfer, Albrecht (*ca* 1480-1538)

Born at Amberg, a small village in Bavaria, died at Ratisbon. It is generally supposed that he was the son of the painter Ulrich Altdorfer. In 1505, Albrecht Altdorfer, at the age of twenty-five, became a citizen of Ratisbon, where his abilities were quickly appreciated. In 1508, he received official employment, and the following year the Town Council is recorded as settling an account for a picture he had painted for the choir of St Peter's. In 1526, he became a town councillor, being already the corporation architect. He was responsible for the ramparts surrounding Ratisbon, which were built to withstand the attacks of the Turks. He also drew up the plans for the slaughterhouse, which still exists to-day. Altdorfer took an active part in public affairs, and it was he who signed the decree for the expulsion of the Jews. Towards the end of his life he became an ardent follower of Luther. In about 1510, he painted his *Holy Family* and a *St George*. Then he executed the *St Florian Altar-piece* and his *Susanna at the Bath*. In 1529 he produced his masterpiece, *The Battle of Alexander*. By now he had given up his official functions in order to devote himself entirely to painting. Towards the end of his life he painted his *View of the Region of the Danube*, which is considered the first example of pure landscape-painting.

Anamorphosis

An apparently shapeless figure consisting of a number of distorted lines and con-

Hans Baldung Grien
Portrait of a Young Man
Museum, Strasbourg

fused colours which in fact are combined according to the laws of optics in such a way that, when viewed from a particular angle, they reveal to the eye a regular image.

Antonello da Messina (*ca* 1430-*ca* 1479)

Born and died in Messina. The son of a sculptor, Antonello moved to Rome in order to complete his training, returned to Palermo, and then moved on to Naples, where he came to know Antonio Solario, called the Zingaro. He afterwards went back to Messina for a few months, and later settled in Venice (1474), where he had a sensational success. All the great men of the day wished to have their portraits painted by him, and he achieved a considerable reputation.
Antonello opened his workshop to all those who wished to learn the secrets of Flemish art, which he himself had learnt in Naples.
After a fairly long period spent in Sicily (1465-70), where he had a number of pupils including Sobo Antonio, Giovanni Borghese and Pino da Messina, he returned to Venice in 1471. The Republic commissioned him to paint a number of frescoes and pictures. During the last twenty years of his life he succeeded in achieving a happy combination of the styles of Flemish and Venetian painting.

Augustus and the Sybil of Tibur by Antoine Caron

This depicts a scene from the *Mystery of the Incarnation and Nativity of our Lord and Saviour Jesus Christ* in which the Emperor Augustus, having questioned the sybil about his reign, is shown in the heavens the Virgin holding her Son, who will be the new emperor of the world. In the background one sees the crowd of spectators massed behind a balustrade, and in the centre of them Catharine de Medici, who presides over the scene. Further in the distance on the right, a tourney is being held in the presence of Henry II.

Baldung Grien, Hans (1485-1545)

Born at Gmünd in Swabia, died in Strasbourg. Hans Baldung was the son of an official attached to the Bishopric of Strasbourg. He first studied painting in Alsace, and then settled at Nuremberg, where from 1502-6 he was employed in Dürer's work-

shop. He continued to remain in touch with his teacher, who, during his travels in the Netherlands, took away with him a large number of Baldung's engravings to sell at the Frankfurt fair. In 1509 he became a citizen of Strasbourg, and thereafter remained in that city except when he went to Freiburg to paint the altar-piece of the *Coronation of the Virgin* (1511-2). During this period he made the acquaintance of Grünewald, who was painting the *Isenheim Altar-piece.* He stayed in Freiburg for four years, and returned to Strasbourg in 1517 where he remained for the rest of his life. The Bishop of Strasbourg employed him as official painter. Among his works are *Death and the Young Woman* (1517), *Death Dragging a Woman to the Tomb*, the *Seven Ages of Life* and *Noli Me Tangere* (1539). He also worked for Christopher, Margrave of Basle, whose portrait he engraved on wood (1511). Baldung also produced a series of very impressive wood-engravings depicting the apostles, a witch, etc. A large number of remarkable drawings by him have survived.

Ballroom at Fontainebleau

The subjects depicted are a *Bacchanal*, *Parnassus*, *The Three Graces Dancing in the Presence of the Gods*, *Discord at the Marriage of Thetis and Peleus*, *Philemon and Baucis*, *Phaeton*, *Vulcan Forging the Features of Love* and *Ceres and the Harvest*. The décor also includes smaller subjects which show numerous Olympian divinities, nymphs, heroes and allegorical figures. The entire room was painted by Niccolo dell'Abbate. 'Primaticcio drew the figures from life, and one or two of these served for each subject; Niccolo dell'Abbate added the details and even transformed the designs themselves, as in the case of the god Pan, for example, to whom he added goat's feet' (Louis Dimier). Unfortunately these paintings have been spoilt by later restoration.

Barbari, Jacopo de' (*ca* 1440/50-*ca* 1515)

Also known as Jacob Walch or the Master with the Caduceus, he was born in Venice. It is now established that Barbari and Walch, who were formerly considered two separate artists, were in fact one and the same person, who was called 'Walch' (that is to say, 'foreigner') in Germany because of his Italian origin. In one of his letters from Venice written in 1506, Dürer mentions that Jacopo is no longer in the city. In fact, that year he accompanied Philip of Burgundy to the Netherlands, and stopped at Nuremberg, where he had already lived from 1494 to 1500. After these travels in the Netherlands, there is no further mention of him until 1510, when he appears in the account-books of Margaret of Austria, then regent of the Netherlands. Here he is referred to as 'groom and court painter'. In 1511, he was granted a pension on account of his 'debility and old age'. Jacopo de' Barbari's work is the meeting-point between the Italian and German Schools, but his style is above all that of a Germanized Italian. His subjects are mainly taken from classical mythology, and he treats them with completely classi-

Hieronymous Bosch
The Conjuror (detail)
Musée Municipal, Saint-Germain-en-Laye

cal gracefulness and feeling. His figures are slender and elegant. He exerted a considerable influence on Mabuse as well as on Dürer. The latter came to know him in Venice and from 1506 onwards regarded him as a person worth imitating. His paintings include the *Virgin at the Fountain* in the Louvre, the *Mathematical Demonstration* in Naples, and the *Madonna and Child* in Berlin.

Blondeel, Lancelot (*ca* 1498-1581)

Born at Poperinghe. Blondeel began life as a mason, and this explains why he included a trowel in his monogram. In 1519 he was admitted as master painter into the Bruges Guild. Thereafter his career was brilliant. In 1520 he married Catherine Seriees. She bore him a daughter who later married Pieter Pourbus, one of his pupils. Like the Italian masters, Blondeel was not only a painter but also a sculptor, architect, engraver and engineer. He drew up the plans for a new port at Bruges which, though not used in his own day, were taken up again in the nineteenth century. His works include *The Story of Sts Cosmas and Damian*, executed for the Surgeons' Guild in Bruges, *St Luke Painting the Virgin* and the *Virgin between St Luke and St Eligius* (1545), painted for the Saddlers' Guild in Bruges, *Scenes from the Life of the Virgin* and a *Saint's Martyrdom* (1558).

Bosch, Hieronymus (1460/4-1516)

Born and died in 's Hertogenbosch. Hieronymus Bosch's real name was Van Aken, but he took his surname from his birthplace. Apart from innumerable copies and variations on the same theme, all that has come down to us of his work consists of some forty panels and some drawings. Since the sixteenth century the most famous of these have been in Spanish collections, while there are some in Venice. A first group of works all of which show a similar technique, are

probably youthful experiments. Bosch treats in turn a variety of traditional religious subjects, such as *The Epiphany* (Philadelphia), *The Wedding at Cana* (Rotterdam), *The Crucifixion* (Brussels) and *Ecce Homo* (Frankfurt), and genre scenes which contain a new style of realism, such as *The Seven Deadly Sins*, *The Cure of Folly* (Prado), and *The Conjuror* (Saint-Germain-en-Laye). He observes the world with a sharp, cunning eye. Like Erasmus during the same period, he is haunted by the theme of human folly. He studies its manifesta-

Velvet Bruegel's Workshop
Basket of Flowers (detail)
Musée de l'Hôtel Sonddi, Saint-Omer

tions in *The Ship of Fools* (Louvre) and *The Hay Wain* (Prado). The treatment of these two panels is already masterly. Among the works of maturity are *The Last Judgement* (Vienna), *The Temptation of St Antony* (Lisbon), and *The Garden of Earthly Delights* (Escorial). Here Bosch discloses a fantastic universe teeming with monsters in nightmarish settings. No subject could suit him better than *The Temptation of St Antony*, of which he painted several versions. Towards the end of the fifteenth century this subject, which had long been abandoned by painters, found favour again among the congregation of Antonians. Alongside the temptation scenes are certain pictures of ascetics, such as *St John on Patmos* (Berlin), *St Jerome* (Ghent), and *St Christopher* (Rotterdam), which form a mystical counterbalance to the diabolical outbursts of *The Temptation of St Antony* and *The Garden of Earthly Delights*. The theme of the Passion inspired a series of expressionist panels which are quite distinct from the rest of Bosch's work. For instance, *The Crowning with Thorns* (National Gallery and Escorial) and *Bearing of the Cross* (Ghent) present a stupefying and hallucinating impression. The final easing of his mind is shown in two calm and restrained works, one religious, the *St Antony* in the Prado, and the other profane, *The Prodigal Son* in Rotterdam.

Bruegel, Jan (known as Velvet Bruegel) (1568-1625)

Born in Brussels, died in Antwerp. The son of Bruegel the Elder, Jan Bruegel followed in his father's footsteps, and indeed during his own lifetime his reputation was as great as that of his father. He was first a pupil of his grandmother, Maria Vane Bessemer, the widow of Pieter Coeck, who looked after him when his father died. He then worked for Pieter Van Goetkint. He soon began to specialize in painting still-lifes. He visited Italy, passing through Cologne on his way, and as a result his manner changed considerably. He started to paint landscapes. On his return to Flanders, his style had become completely transformed and he had a great success. He settled in Antwerp and married Isabella Van Jode. This marriage resulted in the birth of a son, Jan II, in 1601, who also became a painter, and a daughter, Paschasia, who later became the wife of Van Kessel. In 1609, Jan Bruegel, whose first wife had by now died, married Catharina Van Marienburg. He had two children by his second wife, Ambrosius, who was also a painter, and Anne, who became the first wife of David Teniers. Jan Bruegel became dean of the Antwerp Painters' Guild in 1602, and he was also a member of a society called ' The Violet '. He was a friend of Rubens, who often asked his help in painting the landscapes and flowers in his own pictures. The most important example of this collaboration is to be found in a canvas in The Hague depicting *Adam* and *Eve in the Garden of Eden*. His son Jan II learnt to imitate his style so well that it is sometimes difficult to distinguish the work of the son from that of the father. Velvet Bruegel's major works include the *Bowl of Flowers* in Antwerp, *The Garden of Eden*, *The Creation of Eve* and *Noah's Ark* in Budapest, *The Four Elements* in Florence, and *The Bridge of Talavera* in the Louvre.

Bruegel, Pieter, the Elder (called Peasant Bruegel) (*ca* 1528-69)

Peter Bruegel
Drawing
Frits Lugt Collection, The Hague

Possibly born at a place called Brueghel, died in Brussels. The date and place of birth of Pieter Bruegel are uncertain. It is known only that he was the son of a peasant. In about 1545, he was apprenticed to his first master, Pieter Coeck, a Romanist and pupil of Van Orley, who had travelled widely in Italy and the Near East. Coeck instructed him in the style of Italian art. He was then employed in the workshop of Hieronymus Cock, who was an engraver, printseller and picture dealer. At this time Cock was taking into his workshop the finest artists of the day. Pieter Bruegel engraved some of his own productions for Cock, as well as reproducing the pictures of Hieronymus Bosch, who had a profound influence on him and remained one of his faithful followers. In 1551 Bruegel was admitted to the Painters' Guild in Antwerp, and shortly afterwards left for Italy. In 1553, he was still in Rome, as is proved by some of his drawings. He remained abroad for a matter of years, and during this period he produced his famous *Naval Battle in the Straits of Messina*. When he returned to Flanders in 1554, he brought back with him quantities of drawings depicting the countryside through which he had travelled. These sketches of landscapes led Van Mander to remark that, in crossing the Alps, Bruegel had ' devoured the rocks and mountains in order, on his return, to disgorge them onto his panels and canvases '. He went back to work with Cock, but now as his collaborator and no longer as his pupil. Bruegel mixed in humanist circles. He was on close terms with Abraham Ortelius, one of the greatest geographers of his day, the printer Christophe Plantin, and the painter and numismatist Hubert Goltzius. In 1563, he married Mayken Coeck, the daughter of his first master, who bore him a son and a daughter, both of whom became painters. Pieter Bruegel himself turned to painting late in life. The first painting that can be ascribed to him with

Bruegel the Younger
Summer (detail)
Private Collection, Paris

certainty, the *Netherlandish Proverbs*, was executed *ca* 1558. Between 1562 and 1565, he produced a number of pictures on a variety of subjects, including *The Tower of Babel* (1563), *Landscape with the Fall of Icarus* (1563), *The Procession to Calvary* (1564), and various ' diabolical ' pictures, such as *The Fall of the Rebel Angels*, *The Triumph of Death* and ' *Dulle Griet* ', in which the influence of Hieronymus Bosch predominates.
In 1565, a banker called Jonghelinck commissioned a series of paintings from him to make up a calendar, of which five have survived. Then, from 1565 to 1567, Bruegel produced his *Sermon of St John the Baptist* and *Conversion of St Paul.* In 1566 he painted the *Hunters in the Snow*, which as its title suggests consists of a study of a snow-scene, *The Numbering at Bethlehem* and *The Massacre of the Innocents*, and in 1567, *The Land of Cockaigne*, a work of social protest, and various other pieces reflecting the manners of the day. In *The Misanthrope* (1568), Bruegel is once again solemn and pessimistic. *The Cripples* and *The Parable of the Blind* are his last major works.

Bruegel, Pieter II (called Hell Bruegel)
(*ca* 1564-1637/8)

Born in Brussels, died in Amsterdam. Son of Pieter Bruegel the Elder, he first studied his art under his grandmother, the miniaturist Maria Verhulst. He then worked for Gilles Van Conincxloo in Antwerp until 1585, when he was admitted to the Painters' Guild. In the same year he married. He had a number of pupils, including his son Pieter III, Gonzales Cocques, Tripon and André Daniels in 1599, and Jan Garet in 1608. One of his friends was Joos Van Momper. Pieter II frequently copied his father's works. Among his own paintings the most notable are *The Burning of Troy* in Besançon, *The Massacre of the Innocents* in Dresden, *Virgil and Dante in Hell* in the Uffizi, and *Christ Sleeping in the Temple* in Milan.

Caron, Antoine (1521-99)

Nothing is known about Antoine Caron's early years, except that he worked in his native town of Beauvais making designs for stained-glass windows for churches and painting religious pictures. He then entered the service of Francis I between

Antoine Caron
Duc d'Aumont
Louvre, Paris

1540 and 1550. During this period he worked under Primaticcio and was influenced by Niccolo dell'Abbate. In 1560 Catharine de Medici appointed him court painter. He was entrusted with organizing royal entertainments and recording them in his drawings. As a result, he found himself in the company of the greatest artists and poets of the day. In 1561, he was employed on the decoration of the Porte Saint-Denis in Paris for the solemn entry into the city of Charles IX, which had in fact to be postponed. In 1573, he was one of those responsible for the arrangements for the reception in honour of the Duke of Anjou, who had just been crowned king of Poland. In 1581, he was one of the team of artists who organized the entertainments for the marriage of the Duc de Joyeuse and Margaret of Lorraine. Nevertheless, despite his fame, his works soon became lost among the vast number of unsigned pictures of the period which were attributed to Flemish or Italian artists. However, some of his engravings, signed, are to be found in a French translation by Blaise de Vigenère of the works of Philostratus, which appeared in 1617. Also ascribed to him are a *Portrait of Henry IV* and several drawings. In 1936, a scholar called Gustave Lebel succeeded in authenticating the picture entitled *Augustus and the Sybil of Tibur*, which he came across in a Paris auction-room. Since then a few more works by this curious artist have been revealed, including a series of Triumphs (*Summer*, *Winter*), *Astronomers Studying an Eclipse*, the *Meeting between Abraham and Melchizedek*, the *Apotheosis of Semele*, the *Tournament of the Elephants* and the *Massacres under the Triumvirate*.

Chamber of the Duchesse d'Etampes at Fontainebleau

Here stucco-work overflows onto the frescoes. The stucco is used to depict twenty female figures with slender lines, though the softness of the moulding gives the impression that they have been modelled from life. Sets of three infants hold up garlands over the medallions which enclose the paintings. The latter have been almost completely ruined by restoration. The subject of the series was the story of Alexander, and included the following scenes: *Alexander Offering a Crown to Campaspe*, *Alexander Taming Bucephalus*, *Alexander Clasping the Works of Homer*, *Apelles Painting Campaspe* and *Alexander Surrendering Campaspe to Apelles*. Alexander and Campaspe naturally stand for Francis I and his mistress whom Primaticcio intended to honour. In the preparatory designs for the frescoes—which alone can give us some idea of what the original paintings were like—one notices the influence of Parmigianino in the extremely slender forms of the figures. In fact, it

François Clouet
Marguerite de Valois, Queen of Navarre
Musée Condé, Chantilly

was just about this time that Fantuzzi, who had stolen a number of Parmigianino's drawings, brought them to France where he sought refuge, and he found employment as one of Primaticcio's numerous assistants. This explains how Primaticcio came to be influenced by Parmigianino's style.

Chapel of the Trinity at Fontainebleau

The decoration of the vaulted ceiling consists of five panels with four ovals between them, showing the *Four Elements.* In the panels the artist has depicted *Noah Entering the Ark*, *The Fall of the Rebel Angels*, *God the Father in His Glory*, *The Angel Gabriel Appearing to Mary* and *The Ancient Fathers of the Church Rejoicing at the Coming of Jesus Christ.* Fréminet also painted under an arch behind the altar an *Annunciation* and on the areas between the windows the kings of Jerusalem alternating with the patriarchs and prophets treated in camaieu. The emblems of Religion, Faith, Hope and Charity decorate the angles of the vaulted ceiling.

Clouet, François (before 1520-72)

Born at Tours, died in Paris. Clouet's date of birth is still uncertain, but it is known that on his father's death he was given the titles of court painter and groom. Another document states that his annual salary was 240 francs. He had therefore achieved considerable fame while still very young. On the death of Francis I in 1547, he was entrusted with the funeral arrangements and with painting a portrait of the king. Henry II confirmed Clouet in his appointments, and shortly afterwards awarded him the lucrative post of commissioner at Châtelct. François Clouet was also employed on the arrangements for the funeral of Henry II. His successor, Francis II, likewise treated Clouet with great respect. He became very wealthy and his output was extremely large. François Clouet was first employed in his father's workshop, and it is therefore sometimes difficult to decide whether a drawing is by father or son. However, he soon developed a style of his own, as can be seen in the portrait in oils, dated 1562, of the apothecary *Pierre Quthe*, now in the Louvre, and the curious picture of the same year showing a lady in her bath. Collections of his drawings are to be found in the Bibliothèque Nationale, the Musée de Chantilly and the British Museum. These include portraits of Henry II and Charles IX, as well as their wives and children and members of the court. These drawings belong to the years 1538-72. They formed the basis for full-length portraits on wood or canvas of *Henry II* and *Charles IX* (1566), a half-length portrait of *Charles IX* (1561) and two half-lengths of *Henry II*; as well as portraits of *Madame de Roannais*; *Elizabeth of Austria*; *Jeanne d'Albret, Queen of Navarre* (1570); *Margaret of France at the Age of Eight*; *Madame de Savoie*; and *Madame de Bouillon*.

Clouet, Jean (*ca* 1486-1540)

Possibly born in Brussels, died in Paris. The exact date of Jean Clouet's birth is unknown, but it is, however, agreed that he was of Flemish extraction. Some scholars believe that his father was a certain Jehan Cloët, a painter from Brussels who carried out work for the Duke of Burgundy. It is not known when he settled in France. Nevertheless, at the death of Louis XII in 1515, he already had the title of court painter, along with Bourdichon and Perréal, and they had two assistants, Nicolas Belin of Modena and Barthélémy Guety. He first went to Tours, where in 1521 he married Jeanne Boucout, daughter of a goldsmith. She bore him a son, François. From 1529 up to his death in 1540 he and his son shared a house in the Rue Sainte-Avoye in Paris. As court painter he also held the position of groom of the bedchamber, for which he first received an annual sum of 180 francs, which was increased to 240 francs in 1523. On two occasions in 1528, he received further payments ' for several portraits and sketches from life '. Large numbers of his drawings have survived, and the Musée de Chantilly alone possesses a remarkable collection of some 300, which had once belonged to Catharine de Medici. These drawings in crayon were considered not simply as preparatory sketches for portraits, but in fact as works in their own right. The few paintings by Jean Clouet that have come down to us show that he continued the tradition of the great primitive painters. For example, there are the miniatures depicting the *Champions of Marignano* which illustrate a manuscript in the Bibliothèque Nationale entitled *The Gallic War*, and the portraits of *Charlotte of France* (1521) and *The Dauphin François*. In 1524, Clouet painted a portrait of *Francis I*, and two portraits of *Guillaume de Montmorency* are attributed to him. It is thought that the strange *Person Holding a Volume of Petrarch* was painted *ca* 1535. His portrait of *Guillaume Budé* was discovered in England in 1923. Among his later works to have survived is the *Equestrian Portrait of Francis I*.

Cock, Hieronymus (*ca* 1510-70)

Hieronymus Cock travelled in Italy, studying the painters of the Renaissance. He was influenced particularly by Raphael. He returned to Antwerp and was admitted to the Painters' Guild *ca* 1546. He then made a second trip to Italy. Hieronymus Cock was one of the masters of Pieter Bruegel the Elder. He was not only a painter but above all an engraver, printseller and picture dealer. In Antwerp he kept a shop at the sign of ' The Four Winds ', which was the meeting-place of artists and patrons. His engravings were distributed throughout

Corneille de Lyon
Portrait of a Dark-haired Man

Europe. Bruegel executed many engravings for him, including copies of the paintings of Hieronymus Bosch.

Coeck, Pieter (1502/7-1550)

Born at Aelst, died in Brussels. Pieter Coeck was a pupil of Bernard Van Orley in Brussels from 1517 to 1521, and travelled in Italy *ca* 1521. He was admitted as master painter to the Antwerp Guild in 1527. He was invited by the Sultans of Constantinople to go and design cartoons for tapestries, and he returned from this visit with a number of studies of oriental costumes. In 1534, he is found to be court painter to Charles V. In 1535, he sailed with the emperor's fleet and was present at the capture of Tunis. In 1537 he became dean of the Antwerp Guild, and made sketches for the stained-glass windows of the church of Saint-Nicolas de Notre-Dame. In 1548 he decorated the Moelnere Palace in Antwerp, and in the following year he worked on the decorations for the entry of Charles V and his son Philip. Pieter Coeck was the father-in-law of Pieter Bruegel the Elder.

Corneille de Lyon (beginning of XVIth century-1574)

Born in The Hague. We know that Corneille had already settled in Lyons by 1534, since the Latin poet Johannes Secundus, author of *Basia*, states that he visited him there in that year. In 1540, he was appointed by letters patent painter to the dauphin, who was later to reign as Henry II. In 1547, he received his letters of naturalization. In 1551, the Venetian ambassador, Giovanni Vapelli, saw in his house in Lyons, ' besides many beautiful paintings ', the whole ' Court of France, both lords and ladies, portrayed in many small pictures as naturally as one could imagine '. In 1546, Catharine de Medici visited the painter's workshop in Lyons. When Henry II died, Charles IX confirmed Corneille in his privileges. The last mention of him is in a decree issued in 1574, in which the Consulate of Lyons states that he is to continue ' in the enjoyment of the privileges, exemptions and liberties such as are enjoyed by the other grooms of the bedchamber and members of His Majesty's household'. In his famous gallery he displayed to his clients portraits of the celebrities of the day. He employed a large number of assistants and it is therefore difficult to discover which of the pictures attributed to him are in fact in his own hand. His works include portraits of *Margaret of France*; *Claude Gouffier*; *Suzanne d'Escars, Dame de Pompadour*; *Beatrice Bacheco, Comtesse d'Entremont*, lady-in-waiting to Queen Eléonore; *Charles de Cossé, Comte de Brissac*; of a *Young Man in Black*; the *Marquise d'Elbeuf*; *Jean d'Albon*; and *Jacques Bertrant*.

Court, Jean de

There is very little information about this painter. It is known that he was active as a portrait-painter at the French court *ca* 1572, when he succeeded François Clouet as official court painter. In 1574 he painted a portrait of Henry III, then still Duke of Anjou. Certain authorities consider that he is the same person as the enameller, Jehan de Cour, who was active in 1555. On the other hand, the latter has sometimes been identified with Jehan Courteys.

Cousin, Jean, the Elder (*ca* 1490-1560)

Born in the village of Soucy, just outside Sens. Jean Cousin's parents were modest vine-growers. Between 1512 and 1515, he had two masters, Jacques Hympe and Tassin Gassot, who had come to Sens to work on the stained-glass windows of the cathedral. In 1526 Jean Cousin became a qualified painter-surveyor. In about 1530, the monastery of Vauluisant commissioned him to paint an altar-piece, which has not survived. He continued, however, to practise the art of stained-glass painting. Indeed, according to tradition he was responsible for two of the beautiful stained-glass windows in Sens Cathedral, one in the chapel of Saint-Eutrope showing *Scenes from the Life of the Saint and his Martyrdom* (1530), and the other in the chapel of Our Lady of Loretto, depicting *Augustus Consulting the Sybil of Tibur* (1542).
With his reputation firmly established, Jean Cousin decided *ca* 1540 to settle in Paris. He acquired a large piece of land on the corner of the Rue de Seine and the Rue des Marais. Here he built a magnificent house and workshop. Thereafter he prepared the designs and plans for all sorts of work which was then carried out by professional craftsmen. These included the cartoons for the tapestries in the cathedral of Langres. He also executed a large number of wood-engravings. The only painting of his that has come down to us is the *Eva Prima Pandora* in the Louvre.
When Charles V visited Paris in 1540, Jean Cousin helped to decorate two imposing triumphal arches which were set up in the Rue Saint-Antoine. Nine years later, when Henry II entered his capital, Jean Cousin was commissioned to work on the city's decorations.
Jean Cousin wrote two learned works on art theory. In his *Treatise on Perspective* (1560) he reveals a fine knowledge of mathematics. In his *Book of Portraiture*, which appeared in 1571, after his death, he explains how to draw the human body in perfect proportion. Jean Cousin the Elder died in Paris in 1560.

Cousin, Jean, the Younger (1522-94)

Born in Soucy, near Sens, died in Paris. Jean Cousin the Younger first studied at the University of Paris and then worked for his father. When the latter died, he took his place. He illustrated a *Livre de Fortune*, made embroidery patterns for a *Livre de Lingerie* (1584), designed stained-glass windows, etc. Jean Cousin's masterpiece is the celebrated *Last Judgement* which for a long time hung in the sacristy of the Minorites of Vincennes, but is now in the Louvre, and which shows a marked influence of Michelangelo. Also attributed to Jean Cousin the Younger is a *Descent from the Cross* which bears a number of analogies with the illustrations in the *Livre de Fortune*.

Cranach, Lucas, the Elder (1472-1553)

Born in Kronach, died at Weimar. Lucas took his surname from his birthplace of Kronach, bear Bamberg. It is thought that he received his training from his father, who was also a painter. The earliest of his works to have come down to us is a *St Jerome with a Crucifixion*, painted in Vienna and dated 1503. In Vienna he moved in intellectual circles. He painted portraits of *Dr Reuss*, rector of the university, and of the humanist *Johannes Cuspinian and his Wife*. His *Repose in Egypt* is one of his last pictures painted in Vienna. By 1504, he must have made his reputation, for in that year he was invited by Prince Frederick the Wise to become court painter in Wittenberg. In 1506 he executed the *St Catharine Altarpiece*. In the following year he finished the great Venus now in the Hermitage. He painted a number of pictures portraying *Venus*, *Nymphs*, *Diana*, *Bathsheba* and *Judith*, since they gave him the opportunity of producing his own style of nude study. In 1508, Cranach visited the Netherlands, probably on a diplomatic mission. There he painted the portrait of the future *Charles V*, then aged eight. This contact with the art of the Netherlands is reflected in his *Holy Family Altar-piece*, painted in 1509. After 1510, paintings definitely from the hand of Cranach become more and more rare. The many commissions that flowed in to him he often passed on to his sons, Hans and Lucas the Younger, who were helped by numerous assistants. ' Reaching almost the level of an industry,' wrote Adeline Hultftegger, ' Cranach's output appears to have been organized along the lines of mediaeval craftsmanship, the master producing the design which his assistants then carry into effect, following the instructions that he has given them.' In 1519 he was elected to the Wittenberg town council, and on two occasions, in 1537 and 1540, he served as Burgomaster. In 1520, he acquired an apothecary's shop, for which the Elector granted him special privileges. He also controlled a printing-press which issued engravings and a large number of Lutheran tracts. Cranach was in fact a close friend of Luther, and was a witness to his mar-

Lucas Cranach
Love Scene
Museum, Barcelona

riage. Luther in turn stood godfather to one of his children. In his old age, Cranach became the recognized painter of the Reformation. His workshops turned out many evangelical pictures, such as *Jesus Driving the Merchants from the Temple*, *Jesus and the Woman Taken in Adultery*, '*Let the Little Children Come unto Me*' and *Jesus in the Pharisee's House*. He also painted *Luther and Catharine Bora*. Cranach painted a number of excellent portraits, such as the *Portrait of a Young Man*, *Sybil of Cleves* (1526), *Charles V* (1533) and a *Self-Portrait* in the Uffizi (1550). In 1547, Cranach's protector, John-Frederick, was taken prisoner by Charles V at the Battle of Muhlberg and borne off to Augsburg. Cranach shared his master's captivity and interceded for him with the emperor. When John-Frederick was released, Cranach followed him to his new residence at Weimar, where he remained till his death.

' **Cripples, The** ' by Bruegel the Elder

'This,' says Charles de Tolnay, 'is a parody of society: one can recognize the priest by his paper tiara, the prince by his cardboard crown, the soldier by his cap, the townsman by his béret and the peasant by his bonnet.' With their crutches and pattens and wooden legs, which seem to be part of their bodies, they appear to belong to a sub-human race. These social outcasts move about in the light of spring, and this contrast heightens the impression of despair mixed with irony which emerges from this work.

D

' **Dance of Death** ' by Nicolas Manuel Deutsch

Unfortunately we know this work only from a seventeenth-century copy on a reduced scale. This strange painting seems to be derived from old examples of the Dance of Death which Manuel saw in the cemetery at Basle. But he succeeds in giving the subject a new twist. It is not simply a sad and painful representation of the end of man, whether rich or poor. Manuel had a sharp satirical sense and he was an active supporter of the Reformation. He therefore used the theme as a means of defending Luther and attacking Rome. The pope, cardinals, monks and novices, all the clergy in fact, were treated with distaste. Satirical verses accompanied the various scenes, which were painted along a series of arches.
Each scene showed Death, a fleshless corpse capering about with macabre gestures and inviting someone to dance with him. The backgrounds consisted of excellent Swiss landscapes.

Delorme, Philibert (*ca* 1510-70)

Born in Lyons, died in Paris. Philibert Delorme was the son of an architect who taught him his profession. He travelled in Italy where he studied the art of the ancients. Here he stayed a long time, and succeeded in acquiring sufficient knowledge and experience to be employed by Pope Paul III. Cardinal du Bellay invited him to Lyons, where he remained for several years, working on private com-

Philibert Delorme
Figure Symbolizing Architecture

missions. His patron then summoned him to Paris and entrusted him with the construction of the Château de Saint-Maur. The cardinal's patronage brought him to the attention of the king. On 3rd February 1545, Francis I appointed Philibert Delorme 'master architect and general overseer of the buildings and edifices, works and fortifications' in Brittany. Shortly afterwards he was appointed king's councillor, was given a number of abbeys and received the title of almoner. In 1548, Henry III made him inspector of the royal buildings at Fontainebleau, Saint-Germain, etc. When Henry died, however, Delorme fell into disgrace, for Diane de Poitiers, who had been his protector, was estranged from the court. In fact, Catharine de Medici never forgave him for having built the Château d'Anet for the king's favourite. By letters patent, dated 22nd June 1559, he was deprived of his official post, which was given to his mortal enemy Primaticcio, leader of the Italian faction at Fontainebleau. Delorme died in his house in the cloister of Notre-Dame in Paris on 8th January 1570. He left two illegitimate children.

Philibert Delorme's achievement as an architect is considerable. His finest work was the Château d'Anet, built for Diane de Poitiers. All that remains of it today is the chapel and the left wing: numerous alterations at various periods have completely altered its original appearance. He also drew up for Catharine de Medici magnificent designs for the Tuileries, but was able to build only a part of the façade facing the gardens, and this was completely altered in the reign of Louis XIV. The Château de Saint-Maur-les-Fossés, which Cardinal du Bellay commissioned him to build, was destroyed well before the French Revolution. The tomb of Francis I at Saint-Denis is the only work by Delorme that has come down to us in its almost original state. He also did work at Saint-Germain-en-Laye and at Fontainebleau. At Chenonceaux he designed the bridge and gallery, and at Vincennes he was responsible for the vaults and the coping of the chapel. In Paris he built the town-house of the banker Patouillet in the Rue de la Savaterie; another house in the Rue de la Cerisaie; and the Tournelles stables. He also provided the plans for the Château de Valençay, the main façade of the Château d'Uzès, and the Château de Meudon, and rebuilt Saint-Eloi de Noyon.

Philibert Delorme wrote two books on architecture. The first, which appeared in 1561, is dedicated to Charles IX and bears the title *New Inventions for Building Well and at Little Expense*. The second came out in 1567, under the title *The First Volume of the Architecture of Philibert de l'Orme*. It is dedicated to Catharine de Medici.

Dubois, Ambroise (1543-1614)

Born in Antwerp, died at Fontainebleau. It is not known whom Ambroise Dubois studied under in his native city, but his style shows that he was associated with the group around Frans Floris. At the age of twenty-five he went and settled in France, but it was not till *ca* 1593 that the king summoned him to Fontainebleau. In 1595 he was appointed king's painter, and subsequently he became in turn painter in ordinary and then ' painter to His Majesty at his Château of Fontainebleau '. In 1601, he became a French citizen. Five years later, Marie de Medici became his patron and protector. Most of his work was executed at Fontainebleau, where he was aided by two other Flemish painters, Jan Dhoey and Josse Van Voltigeant. Of the numerous works that Dubois produced there, there remain only a few paintings in the chapel of Saint-Saturnin and some of the pictures depicting *The Story of Tancred and Clorinda* which he had done for the queen's apartments. The *Gallery of Diana*, which was considered his masterpiece, has unfortunately been completely destroyed. It contained twenty-three large pictures representing the victories of Henry IV and his love for Gabrielle d'Estrées.

Ambroise Dubois died at Fontainebleau at the age of seventy-one, leaving two sons, both of whom were painters. The first was entrusted with maintaining his father's pictures, while the second was put in charge of the paintings of Fréminet.

Dubreuil, Toussaint (1561-1602)

Born and died in Paris. Toussaint Dubreuil was a pupil of Fréminet the Elder, and became painter in ordinary to Henry III. His work has been almost entirely destroyed. In the Canopy Pavilion at Fontainebleau he painted *Mars and Venus* over a fireplace and fourteen frescoes representing the *Story of Hercules*. He was engaged to restore the paintings in the Ulysses Gallery. At Saint-Germain-en-Laye he executed seventy-eight pictures of which two survive—an *Ancient Sacrifice* and a *Woman Greeted by a Warrior*. He also worked on the decoration of the Kings' Gallery in the Louvre, which was burnt down in 1661. A magnificent collection of his drawings has come down to us, together with a picture in the Louvre, *Angelica and Medoro*, and this is all that we have from which to gain an idea of his style.

Dumoustier, Geoffroy

The date of birth of this artist is unknown. We know that he was working on the paintings of the Château de Fontainebleau between 1537 and 1540, under the supervision of Rosso Fiorentino. He was also a miniaturist, engraver and painter on glass. Besides a number of portraits, several engravings in the Bibliothèque Nationale are ascribed to him. Mention should be made of an etching, the *Standing Madonna Holding the Infant Jesus* (1543), and of a *Figure of a Woman Standing* seen full face and bearing in one hand the orb of the sun and in the other the orb of the moon (1547).

Dürer, Albrecht (1471-1528)

Born and died in Nuremberg. Albrecht Dürer was the third of eighteen children of one of the craftsmen for whom Nuremberg was famous. At the age of fifteen he was apprenticed to Michael Wolgemuth, the most celebrated painter in Nuremberg at the time. Three years later he had gained sufficient knowledge and experience for his father to authorize him to set out on his travels, which were to last for four years. He stayed in Colmar, Basle and Strasbourg, and travelled through Venetia. Among the works painted during his wanderings, the most important is his *Self-Portrait* on vellum, dated 1493. In 1494, he returned to Nuremberg, where he married Agnes Frey, who brought him a dowry of two hundred florins. He then opened a workshop in his parents' house, where he painted altar-pieces and votive pictures in the local tradition. At this stage his work is clearly influenced by Mantegna. Examples include a triptych now in Dresden, *The Paumgärtner Triptych* in Munich, and *The Adoration of the Magi* in the Uffizi. During this period he also produced a number of portraits including those of *Frederick the Wise*, *Hans Tucher* and *Jacob Fugger*, as well as a *Self-Portrait*. He also made a series of wood-engravings representing *The Revelation of St John* and *The Life of the Virgin*, and copper engravings showing the *Holy Family*, *The Prodigal Son*, etc. These engravings were such a success that they were quickly copied by the Italians. Dürer therefore travelled once again to Italy, where he was able to compare his work with Italian painting. For the Venetians who were building the ' Fondaco dei Tedeschi ', he painted the *Festival of the Rose Garlands*. Dürer returned to Nuremberg in 1507, and proceeded to paint two large canvases, *Adam and Eve* (1508) and *The Massacre of the Ten Thousand Christians*. From 1508 to 1511 he worked on the magnificent *Adoration of the Trinity*. Other paintings produced during this period include *The Virgin with a Pear*, *The Virgin of the Lily* and the portraits of *Charlemagne* and of *Sigismund*. But by about 1510 he was so discouraged by how little his pictures were earning him considering the time that he spent on them, that he decided to give up painting. In 1513 and 1514, he made copper-engravings of three of his major works, *The Knight, Death and the Devil*, *Melencolia* and *St Jerome in his Study*. At this time (1512) Dürer was employed by the Emperor Maximilian, and he continued to work for him until 1519. For the *Triumphal Arch* he produced ninety-two blocks. In 1520-1, the plague broke out in Nuremberg, and Dürer decided to travel to the Netherlands, where he was triumphantly received. He spent a year in Antwerp and made short trips to Brussels, Aix-la-Chapelle, Cologne, Zeeland, Ghent, Bruges and Malines. Despite the tempting offers of the town council of Antwerp, he preferred to return to his native city. Here he was commissioned to make cartoons for the decoration of the great chamber in the Town Hall. The actual decorating was carried out by one of his pupils. During his last years, Dürer devoted himself to the study of the human face. Examples are his portrait of *Hans Imhoff* in the Prado, and those of the councillors *Jacob Muffel* and *Hieronymus Holzschuher* (1526), and that of *Johann Kleberger*. His last major work. *The Four Apostles*, is also his spiritual testament. He had many famous friends, including Luther, Melanchthon and Raphael—the two painters exchanged their portraits. He wrote a *Treatise on Human Proportions* and *Instructions in Measurement*. He died in Nuremberg in 1528.

'Elizabeth of Austria' by François Clouet

Brantôme wrote of the young wife of Charles IX that she 'was a very beautiful princess with a complexion as beautiful and delicate as that of any lady of her court and most pleasing. She was very sensible, very virtuous and very good.' Clouet shows us a child (she was seventeen) more charming than beautiful, devoid of affectation or coquetry. The complexion of her frail face is fresh, her eyes are clear, intelligent and good, her brow is pensive, the expression of her mouth sweet and child-like. A slight veil of melancholy is spread over her countenance, as if the young princess already had foreknowledge of the sadness to come. She soon lost her husband, Charles IX, and she died at the age of thirty-eight after living in retreat in the Convent of St Clare which she had founded in Vienna.

Elzevier

A celebrated family of booksellers and printers in the sixteenth and seventeenth centuries, who had businesses at Leyden, The Hague, Utrecht and Amsterdam. The founder of this line was Louis Elzevier, who was born in Louvain *ca* 1540 and died in Leyden in 1617. He became a bookbinder, and followed his father to Antwerp, where the latter was employed from 1565 to 1588 as a typographer in the printing-works of the famous Christophe Plantin. Louis was a zealous Protestant, and consequently in 1568 he had to flee abroad to escape the persecutions of the Duke of Alba. He found refuge in Wesel, in the duchy of Cleves. Profiting from an amnesty, he settled in Douai, but was obliged to leave again in 1580, when he established himself permanently in Leyden. To the profession of bookbinder he added that of bookseller, and in this capacity, he rendered considerable service to the university, which rewarded him by appointing him beadle in 1586. The following year he received permission to set up a stall on university land, and this humble shop was the foundation of the Elzeviers' fortunes. In 1594 he became a citizen of Leyden. Thereafter, he became an active publisher and particularly a dealer in books, full of ideas but not over-scrupulous in his manner of putting them into effect. Nevertheless, he enjoyed a considerable reputation and was on close terms with a number of famous scholars. He produced some hundred volumes in Latin, French, Flemish and even German. He was the publisher of his most famous fellow-countrymen, such as Meursius, Heinsius and Puteanus. Louis Elzevier had nine children, including seven sons, who, for the most part, followed in his footsteps.

Erasmus, Desiderius (1467-1536)

One of the greatest humanists of the Renaissance, born in Rotterdam, died in Basle. An illegitimate child, he was left, at his father's death, to the care of guardians who squandered his fortune and forced him to enter a monastery. After three years he left to become a private secretary. Eventually he reached Paris where he studied at the Collège Montaigu. Here he was extremely unhappy, for the teaching of scholastic theology he found dull. He had an English pupil, Lord Mountjoy, who brought him to England and gave him an allowance of a hundred crowns a year.
Here Erasmus got to know the leading humanists, such as Sir Thomas More, John Colet and William Grocyn. Early in 1499 he returned to France and then lived variously in Paris, Orleans, Louvain and Rotterdam, making a study of the Greek and Latin classics. Like most scholars of the time, he lived from day to day by his pen. In 1506 he set out for Italy, and in the same year was awarded the degree of Doctor of Letters by Bologna university. After Pope Julius II had released him from his monastic vows, he visited Aldus Minutius, the Venetian printer who published some of his writings. In 1509, when Henry VIII, who was fond of him, came to the throne, Erasmus was invited to England. During the journey he wrote his immortal satire *The Praise of Folly.* At Cambridge Erasmus taught Greek and lectured on the Church Fathers and the New Testament. But he disliked the climate and returned to the continent, where he travelled widely before going back to his own country. Here Charles V gave him the title of councillor and a pension of 400 florins, without insisting on his residing in the Netherlands. Erasmus was now relieved of having to earn a living, and could travel where he liked and work at his ease. In 1521, he settled permanently in Basle where Froben proceeded to print all his writings. He found the atmosphere in Basle congenial to him, for it was a city in which both Catholics and Protestants were able to live in comparative peace. Erasmus watched the Reformation taking place without himself becoming involved, except that he did quarrel with Luther whom he accused of excessive violence, while the latter complained of his half-heartedness. In the winter of 1535 he suffered an attack of gout, and died on 11th or 12th July in the following year. He spent his last days philosophically, and

Jean Cousin
Eva Prima Pandora (detail)
Louvre, Paris

never lost his calm serenity. His friends asked him what they could do for him, so he gave orders for his coffin. In his will he left all his possessions ' to the poor, the aged and infirm, to young orphans and to young men of promise '. He was buried in Basle Cathedral.

Erasmus had a greater influence than any other humanist. The corpus of his writings is enormous and of an amazing variety. His chief works are the *Adagia*, a collection of sayings culled from classical authors; the *Colloquies*, editions of which sold in vast quantities throughout the sixteenth and seventeenth centuries, and which reveal that acute observation and caustic wit which have earned him the title of ' the Renaissance Voltaire '; and *The Praise of Folly*, which was made popular by the illustrations of Hans Holbein. Here he enthusiastically derides every form of human stupidity and gleefully attacks theologians, monks, the high dignitaries of the Church including the popes, as well as princes and other great men. Equally important is his *Correspondence* with the leading figures of his time. Erasmus was also one of the most notable editors of classical texts. He published excellent editions, carefully collated with the manuscripts, of Suetonius, Cicero, Pliny the Elder, Seneca, Livy, Terence, Demosthenes, Aristotle and Ptolemy.

' **Eva Prima Pandora** ' by Jean Cousin the Elder

This allegorical painting shows a naked woman seated in a grotto. One hand bears a branch from the fatal Tree of Knowledge, and lies beside a skull. The other rests on an urn which represents Pandora's box, while a serpent encircles both arm and urn. In the background is a dark forest and beyond that a rough sea. On a block of stone in the centre of the picture is a vase. From this rises a coil of smoke in which one could formerly see a cloud of evil geniuses spreading forth over the world, representing the ills that have come from the box or have sprung from the eating of the apple. ' The remains of the symbolism which one can pick out here and there in this work,' wrote Louis Gillet, ' are the first manifestation in France of the independence of art. The study of form, knowledge of the human body conceived as the essential element in the language of plastic art, the problems of composition, modelling and expression which this study implies, all that the Florentine painters had been striving to achieve for a century – that is the real subject of this piece . . . The slenderness of this Eve outdoes even that of Primaticcio's nymphs, and in this rather paradoxical excess itself one feels something personal or individual, that almost visionary gracefulness of some of Ingres' *Odalisques*, and above all that manner of using the pure form and the architecture of the human machine, as of a delicate musical instrument.'

Frans Floris
The Holy Family (detail)

First School of Fontainebleau

'It is true,' writes Louis Dimier (and what he says also applies to Niccolo dell'Abbate), 'that neither Rosso nor Primaticcio belongs to the first rank of the Italian Renaissance. Our imagination, roving through the great glories of the school, is inclined to pause at other names. But the reason for this is that we are inclined to forget our chronology. Those artists whom we tend to prefer were for the most part already dead. During this period of the Italian Schools, with the exception of the Venetian, the painters of the first rank had nearly all ceased to exist. One must be satisfied with their followers. One must also admit that the tasks made demands that did not suit every painter, however eminent. Artists were required who had studied in Rome or Florence.' The art of Fontainebleau represents perfectly the epicurism of the age. It has a strange charm about it which is slightly worrying on account of its mixture of sensuality and erudition. French restraint here tempers Italian exuberance. This art is particularly concerned with elegance and variations of the human form. The figures are elongated and tend towards the gracefulness of Parmigianino. One result of the influence of the First School of Fontainebleau on French painting was that mythological scenes came to replace Biblical subjects. The female nudes who appear in the very frank pagan scenes reflect the famous beauties of the day, such as Mme d'Etampes, Diane de Poitiers and Gabrielle d'Estrées. Fontainebleau had an immense influence throughout Europe, and many foreign painters, particularly Flemish, went to study in what was considered then as a second Rome.

Floris, Frans (Frans de Vriendt) (1516-70)

Born and died at Antwerp. Frans Floris came of an artistic family. His father and his grandfather were sculptors, while his brother Corneille was a celebrated architect. Floris began his career by studying sculpture, but his talent for painting soon became evident. He went to Liège to work under Lambert Lombard. When he returned to his native city in 1540, he was admitted into the Guild as a master painter, but he left shortly afterwards for Italy. There he studied the works of Michelangelo and the Antique. He may have been present at the unveiling of the *Last Judgement* in the Sistine Chapel, but in any case he did a lot of work in red chalk in the manner of the Sistine frescoes. On his return to Antwerp he rapidly acquired a considerable reputation throughout the Netherlands and even in Spain. His patrons and protectors included the

Prince of Orange and the Counts of Hoorn and Egmont. His workshop became so renowned that, according to Van Mander, he had a hundred and twenty pupils. His pictures were mass-produced by his assistants, he himself painting merely the more subtle areas. He became extremely wealthy and lived in grand style. The city of Delft commissioned him to paint a *Crucifixion* for one of the main churches. When Charles V re-entered Antwerp in 1549, Floris was engaged with Jan Van Vries to paint the triumphal arches along the emperor's route, and he carried out similar work for Philip II's visit. In 1554 he produced his most famous work, *The Fall of the Rebel Angels*. In 1559 he did work for the church of Notre-Dame in Antwerp, producing an *Assumption*, which has disappeared, and a *Nativity*.
His *Last Judgement* (1566) shows the influence of Michelangelo. For Nicolas Jonghelingh, a wealthy citizen of Antwerp, he produced in 1568 some remarkable decorations consisting of *The Labours of Hercules* and ten other large pictures. He then returned to religious subjects. On his death he left unfinished a *Christ on the Cross and Resurrection* which he had begun in 1570 for the Grand Prior of Spain.

Francis I Gallery at Fontainebleau

This gallery was built for court assemblies. Its décor seems to have been suggested by the king himself. The lower part consists of carved walnut panelling, a masterpiece of woodcarving by Scibec de Carpi. This rises to arm level, and above runs a frieze of frescoes alternating with stucco bas-reliefs, the whole work being by Rosso Fiorentino. The subjects depicted are shown within projecting panels richly ornamented with vases, garlands, shells, masks, ram's skulls, fruits and fantastic animals. Included here and there among these decorations are smaller panels containing miniature frescoes. Sometimes in the gaps between the ornaments the wall surface is painted with various designs enhanced with gold. Rosso's frescoes have been restored so often that nothing remains of the original designs or colours. In order to gain some idea of what these were really like one has to study Rosso's drawings, contemporary engravings, and also some tapestries in the Kunsthistorisches Museum, Vienna, which were copied from the original frescoes.

Francken the Elder, Ambroise (1544-1618)

Born at Herenthals, died at Antwerp. Ambroise Francken the Elder belongs to the second generation of a family that produced five successive generations of painters. He was the third of the four sons of Nicolas (1520-96), who was the first of the line. Ambroise had an active life and enjoyed great success. All three brothers were pupils of Frans Floris, who was the same age as their father. Van Mander states that Ambroise was invited to go to Tournai by the bishop of the diocese. It appears that he also visited Italy. We find him in Flanders in 1569, and the following year he went to Fontainebleau, as is shown by the records

Francken the Elder
Noah Entering the Ark
Tési Museum, Le Mans

of the town of Avon where the artist attended a baptism and acted as godfather. He therefore had first-hand knowledge of the frescoes of Rosso and Primaticcio. On his return to Antwerp he became a master painter of the Guild in 1573, at the age of twenty-nine. In 1577 he became a citizen, and in 1581 he was made dean of the Guild. Thereafter he remained in Flanders, where he died on 16th October 1618, at the age of sixty-four.
Ambroise Francken was twice married but left no children. His nephew Hieronymus II (1578-1623), son of his brother Frans, was one of his pupils. Ambroise Francken's works include *The Martyrdom of Sts Crispin and Crispinian*, *The Woman Taken in Adultery* and the *Resurrection of Jairus' Daughter*. In 1608 he painted a *Holy Trinity* and a *Christ on the Cross*. His engravings include *Man Sustained by Grace and Enlightened by Virtue* (1578) and eight designs depicting *The Struggle between the Vices and the Virtues* (1579).

Francken the Elder, Frans (1542-1616)

Born at Herenthals, died at Antwerp. Frans Francken the Elder was the second son of Nicolas Francken (1520-96). From Frans sprang three further generations of painters. He himself was first taught by his father and then by Frans Floris, whose manner he kept to more closely than did his brother Ambroise. He became a citizen of Antwerp in 1567. He was admitted to the Guild as a master painter, and later became dean in 1588, as his younger brother had been before him. He married in 1573, and his wife bore him four sons—Thomas, Jerom, Frans II and Ambroise II, all of whom became painters. Besides his own sons, Frans Francken the Elder had several other outstanding pupils, including Goltzius, Jan Van Wall and Herman Van der Maest. He never left Antwerp and died there in his seventy-fourth year. His works include the vast triptych in Antwerp Cathedral, of which the centre panel represents *Jesus among the Doctors*, while the volets depict *The Miracle of Elias at Sarepta* and *St Ambrose Baptising St Augustine* (1587). Mention should also be made of the two volets showing the *Entombment* and the *Apparition of Jesus to Mary Magdalen* in the church of Saint-Jacques in Antwerp.

Francken the Elder, Jerom (1540-1610)

Born at Herenthals, died at Antwerp. Jerom was the eldest son of the painter Nicolas Francken. He studied under Frans Floris, and then travelled to Italy where he stayed some time. Then he moved to Paris where he had a great success at the French court. Henry III com-

Martin Fréminet
Mercury Ordering Aeneas to Abandon Dido
(detail)
Louvre, Paris

missioned him to paint his portrait. Christophe de Thou, president of the Parliament of Paris, became his protector and commissioned from him a painting of *The Adoration of the Shepherds* (1585), which has since disappeared. Jerom returned to Antwerp *ca* 1590. He was recalled to Paris by his protectors in 1595, and remained there for the rest of his life, dying there *ca* 1610. He was married to a Frenchwoman, who bore him two sons and three daughters. Most of Jerom Francken's works have disappeared. His most famous painting is the *Abdication of Charles V* in Amsterdam.

Fréminet, Martin (1564-1619)

Born in Paris, died at Fontainebleau. Martin studied under his father, Médéric Fréminet, who specialized in crewel-work. While still very young he went to Paris where he executed a *St Sebastian* for the church of Saint-Josse, but this work is now known only from a contemporary engraving. Then, at the age of twenty-eight, he travelled to Rome, where he struck up a friendship with Giuseppe Cesari, better known as Cavaliere d'Arpino. Martin Fréminet studied the work of Michelangelo in particular, and was much influenced by him. However, he was also interested in the paintings of Parmigianino, and his friends included Mathurin Régnier and Philippe Thomassin. After working in Rome for six years, he visited Venice, where he greatly admired Tintoretto and Veronese. He also spent a long time in Lombardy and, before returning to France, painted several pictures in Turin, including a *St Martin* for Duke Charles-Emmanuel of Savoy. In 1603 he returned to Paris. His great reputation quickly led to his being appointed painter in ordinary and groom of the bedchamber to Henry IV. In 1606 he painted a portrait of the dauphin, the future Louis XIII, whose drawing-master he became. In 1608 Fréminet began to decorate the Chapel of the Trinity at Fontainebleau with paintings depicting *Noah Entering into the Ark*, *The Fall of the Rebel Angels*, *God the Father in His Glory*, *The Annunciation*, *The Ancient Fathers of the Church Rejoicing at the Coming of Christ*, *The Archangel Gabriel Appearing to Mary*, *The Kings of Jerusalem*, *The Patriarchs*, *Prophets*, and various *Emblems*. The artist worked on this series until 1618. When he had finished it, Marie de Medici appointed him Knight of the Order of St Michael. Fréminet then worked for private patrons. He decorated the square room in the Château de Richelieu with eight paintings depicting the *Evangelists* and *The Fathers of the Church*. He died in 1619 and was buried in the abbey of Barbeaux, near Fontainebleau. He had indeed executed a number of paintings for this abbey, but they were all destroyed in 1793.

Funeral of Francis I

François Clouet was urgently summoned to Rambouillet where the king had died. He made a drawing of the king's face, and also a death mask in wax. On his return to Paris, he and his workmen made a model of the head, based on the mask, out of paper pulp and wax and affixed to it a false beard and hair. The face was then painted in oils, using the original drawing as a guide. Clouet also modelled two pairs of hands, ' one closed and the other joined '. Finally, a wicker-work frame was made and this was clothed. When the whole thing was put together the likeness was perfect. This effigy was borne on a ceremonial palanquin during the funeral.

Gallery of Diana, Fontainebleau

The twenty-three large pictures by Ambroise Dubois represented the victories of Henry IV and various mythological scenes which were conceived in such a way that they recalled—through the clever use of allegory—the king's love-affair with Gabrielle d'Estrées. These panels were separated by figures of gods and demi-gods on Olympus, painted in camaieu. The vaulted ceiling was richly adorned with arabesques and grotesque figures, copied from those in the Ulysses Gallery, which served as frames for twenty large pictures depicting mythological scenes or celebrating the virtues of Henry IV. Ambroise Dubois here revealed an extraordinarily fertile imagination and a genius for decoration. One can get some idea of this work from the water-colour copies which Percier, the celebrated architect under the Empire, made, and which retain something of the complex and masterly arrangement of the décor.

Golden Gate of Fontainebleau

In 1535 Primaticcio painted two pictures on the subject of *The Story of Hercules* for the Golden Gate, which formed the entrance to the château. In one the hero allows himself to be dressed in women's clothes by Omphale, and in the other he repulses the god Pan who was chasing Omphale in his sleep (an episode drawn from Ovid's *Fasti*). These paintings were entirely redone in the nineteenth century, but Primaticcio's preparatory sketches are now in the Louvre. At a much later date, in 1554, Primaticcio also decorated the vestibule that follows on from the porch. Here he depicted *Aurora in her Chariot*, *Jupiter Hurling Thunderbolts at the Titans*, *Hercules and the Argonauts* and various other subjects. Unfortunately these compositions were also repainted in the last century and altered in the most arbitrary way by a mediocre academic painter.

Goujon, Jean (d. *ca* 1567)

Architect and sculptor, born in Rouen, died in Paris. His first work was carried out in Rouen for the church of Saint-Maclou and for the cathedral, in 1541 and 1542. In 1543, Goujon went to Paris, where he carved the rood-screen for Saint-Germain-l'Auxerrois in 1544. Also for the Town Hall he painted representations of the twelve months of the year on large wooden panels, which were destroyed in 1871. At about this time he was working on the decoration of the Château d'Ecouen for the Constable of Montmorency. For the Hôtel Carnavalet he carved *Fame*, *Children Supporting Scrolls*, *Force* and *Vigilance*. But it is the work that he carried out in the Louvre that gives us the best idea of his genius. In 1550 he was commissioned to carve four caryatids for the Salle des Suisses. Between 1555 and 1562, the royal accounts show that 4,880 francs were paid to him, which implies that he produced another series of works. All the sculptures on the front façade of the courtyard of the Louvre can be ascribed to him. His other works include a *Bust of Henry I*, *Diana Leaning on a Stag*, *The Deposition of Christ*, *The Four Evangelists*, *Tritons and Nereids* and the *Naiads* which decorate the Fountain of the Innocents.

Matthias Grünewald
Portrait of a Donor

Grünewald, Matthias (1455/1460-*ca* 1528)

Born in Würzburg, died in Halle. There is considerable uncertainty about Grünewald's life, but a great deal of research has been carried out recently, and has resulted in a number of new theories. The latest and most widely accepted is based on the research of Zülch, H. N. Naumann and Haug. According to them, documents in the Frankfurt archives regarding the painter's estate suggest that his real name was Matthis Nithardt, called Gothart, and that he was the son of an engineer in Würzburg. Grünewald was the protégé of a canon called Heinrich Reitzmann of Aschaffenburg. In 1490, he was working with a sculptor in Worms. In 1501 he became a master painter. In 1508 he was official court painter and artistic adviser to the archbishop of Mainz, Uriel von Gemmingen. It is known that he twice stayed in Alsace: in 1479-80 he was in Strasbourg and between 1513 and 1515 he lived at Isenheim, where he painted the famous altar-piece now in the Unterlinden Museum in Colmar. When Albert of Brandenburg succeeded Urie von Gemmingen as archbishop in 1514, Grünewald was confirmed in his post. A few years later he attended the corona-

tion of Charles V at Aix-la-Chapelle, which was the occasion of his meeting Dürer. In 1525, as a result of the Peasant Wars, Grünewald lost his appointment in Mainz and was forced to flee to Frankfurt. He then went on to Halle, which was a Protestant city, where he worked as a hydraulic engineer. He probably died there in 1528.
Grünewald's earliest works are *The Mocking of Christ* and a small *Crucifixion* in Basle. The representations of *St Cyriacus* and *St Lawrence* in Frankfurt formed part of an altar-piece which was commissioned by the art-patron Jacob Heller for the Dominican convent chapel in Frankfurt. In 1508 he began work on his masterpiece, the *Isenheim Altar-piece*, which took him five to six years to complete. His later works include a *Madonna* (1519) and a volet representing the *Foundation of St Mary Major* (Fribourg Museum), a *Crucifixion* (Karlsruhe), and *Sts Maurice and Erasmus* (1525-6), Grünewald's last work.

Guichardin, Louis (1523-89)

Born in Florence. Louis Guichardin, who was the nephew of the famous historian François Guichardin, was variously employed by Cosimo the Great. Later he travelled widely, staying for a long time in Antwerp, where he was favoured by the Duke of Alba. However, he published a work in which he condemned the Duke's form of government, and for this he was condemned to prison for several months, and was only freed through the personal intervention of the Grand-Duke of Tuscany. He had a number of powerful enemies who were jealous of his talents, and they succeeded not only in getting him dismissed from the Florentine court but also in stopping him from returning. His principal work is his *Description of all the Netherlands, otherwise called Lower Germany*, which appeared in Antwerp in 1567. This curious publication includes some interesting details concerning the arts in the Netherlands during the Renaissance.

Heemskerck, Martin (1498-1574)

Born in Heemskerck near Haarlem, died in Haarlem. Martin Heemskerck was the son of a farmer who first apprenticed him to Cornelis Willems of Haarlem, but then summoned him back to work in the fields. Shortly afterwards Heemskerck

Martin Heemskerck
Ceres
Musée de l'Ecole des Beaux-Arts

fled to Delft, where he worked under a second-rate artist called Jan Lucas. He soon left the latter to study under Van Scorel. One of his most important works of this period is his *St Luke Painting the Virgin* (1532). At the age of thirty-four he travelled to Italy, where he stayed for three years. On his return he settled in Haarlem, where he was highly regarded among the painters of his time. His paintings were mainly commissioned for public buildings, for example his *Crucifixion* in the church of St Lawrence at Alkmaar (1538-41). He became a churchwarden in his local parish. The civil war forced him to flee, together with his friend and pupil Jacob Rauwerts. He spent two years in Amsterdam, but returned to Haarlem at the end of his life. His most important works are an *Annunciation*, *The Adoration of the Magi and Shepherds*, *The Story of Momus* and *The Baptism of Christ*. He also painted portraits including a *Family Portrait* in the Kassel Museum, a portrait of his wife *Anna Codde* and a *Self-Portrait* (1544).

Holbein the Elder, Hans (1460/1465-1524)

Born in Augsburg, died in Isenheim. Hans Holbein the Elder was the son of Michael Holbein, a breeches-maker who had settled in Augsburg in 1448. It is thought that Holbein the Elder was employed for a time in Martin Schongauer's workshop in Colmar, and that he was influenced by Rogier Van der Weyden. He seems to have led a difficult life. It appears that for most of his career he refused to accept the ideas of the Renaissance. In 1449, Hans Holbein was back in his place of birth. His early works include the murals in the abbey of Weingarten and two small *Madonnas*, now in Nuremberg. In 1449 he became a citizen of Ulm. From that year dates his *Death of the Virgin* (Basle) and thirteen scenes from the *Passion*. In 1501 he visited Frankfurt, where he did some important work, including *The Last Supper*, *Christ's Entry into Jerusalem*, *Christ Driving the Money-Changers from the Temple* and *The Tree of Jesse*. In 1502, he decorated the abbey of Kaisheim with some twenty paintings, including a *Descent from the Cross*. In 1503-4 he produced the scenes from the *Life of St Paul* in which he painted his own portrait and those of his two sons. Holbein spent the years from 1506 to 1508 on work for the church of St Maurice in Augsburg. His masterpiece is the *St Sebastian Altar-piece* which he painted for the abbey of St Catharine in Augsburg. Despite his enormous output, Hans Holbein the Elder was unable to remain in Augsburg and he left for Isenheim, while his two sons settled in Basle in 1514.

Holbein the Younger, Hans (1497-1543)

Born in Augsburg, died in London. Hans Holbein the Elder taught his two sons the art of painting. Ambrosius, the elder, died in 1518 at the age of twenty-five, leaving behind a few beautiful drawings. He and his younger brother Hans had decided to settle in Basle in 1514. It is likely that the two young men had chosen this city in the hope of finding work there as draftsmen and wood-engravers among

Hans Holbein the Younger
Portrait of Bonifacius Amerbach
Museum, Basle

the local printers, who included Adam Petri, Cratander, Wolff and Jean Froben. In fact, Hans and Ambrosius did succeed in supplying numerous illustrations and designs for title-pages, particularly for Jean Froben. Hans Holbein made pen drawings for a copy of Erasmus's *The Praise of Folly* and illustrated Sir Thomas More's *Utopia*. His first known work, *The Madonna and Child* (Basle) is dated 1514. It also appears that he profited from a stay in Luzern to visit Como and Milan. Five years later he travelled through France in the company of his friend Bonifacius Amerbach, a scholar and art-collector. This enabled him to gain first-hand knowledge of the French Renaissance. In 1516 he produced the first examples of the brilliant style of portraiture which he was to maintain throughout his life: the portraits of *Jacob Meyer* and his wife, *Dorothea Kannengiesser*, the even better portrait of *Bonifacius Amerbach* (1519), and then one of his finest works, the portrait of *Erasmus* (1523). While he was still in Basle he painted murals for the Town Hall and various houses. He made designs for stained-glass windows, and also for goldsmiths and gunsmiths. Finally, he produced various religious paintings, the best known of which are the *Dead Christ* and the *Madonna of the Burgomaster Meyer*. In 1525, when the iconoclasts began to destroy religious images, Holbein decided to come to England. In 1526, with an introduction from Erasmus, he was made welcome by Sir Thomas More. After this date, Holbein concentrated on portrait-painting and became the most fashionable artist at court. During this period he painted the portraits of *William Warham*, who was Archbishop of Canterbury; the Bishop of Rochester, *John Fisher;* the astronomer *Nicholas Kratzer; Sir Brian Tuke*, treasurer of the household, with the figure of Death cackling behind him; and *Sir Henry Guildford*, comptroller of the household. In 1528 Hans Holbein returned to Basle and bought a house for three hundred florins. Here he stayed for four years, during which time he painted the famous portrait of his wife and two children. He rejected various offers that were made to him, and returned to England in 1523, and remained there for the rest of his life. The merchants of the Steelyard commissioned him to paint '*The Triumphs of Wealth and Poverty*'. In 1536 Holbein became attached to the court. He first painted a portrait of *Henry VIII* and then one of *Lady Jane Seymour*. After the latter's death, the king ordered Holbein to paint portraits of the aspirants to her position, *Christina of Denmark* and *Anne of Cleves*. Later he painted *Catharine Howard*. In 1543 the plague broke out in

London: Holbein made his will in favour of his mistress and her two children, without any mention of his family in Basle. Shortly afterwards he died.

Hooy, Jan Dammesz Van (1545-1615)

Born in Leyden, died at Avon, near Fontainebleau. Jan Dammesz was the son of Dammesz Claesz Van Hooy and grandson of Lucas Van Leyden. He was the pupil of his brother Lucas. He travelled first in Italy and then in France, where he became a French citizen in 1750. He entered the Household of Henry IV, who employed him on decorating the Château de Fontainebleau in collaboration with Ambroise Dubois, and appointed him director of his gallery of paintings. Jan Dammesz also did work for the abbey of Barbeaux. Conrelisz Vorom appears to have been a pupil of his in Paris.

Humanist

The name is applied particularly to the philologists (Latinists and Hellenists) of the period that runs from Petrarch to Casaubon. These scholars completely revived interest in the classics. Throughout the fifteenth century the humanists occupied the chairs of rhetoric, law, medicine, mathematics and philosophy in nearly all the universities in Italy. They were employed to teach Latin and Greek. Humanist ideas rapidly spread throughout Europe. The humanists themselves also became private tutors in royal or noble households. At first, humanism remained completely within the Church. The most famous humanists rejected the schoolmen and went back to ancient sources, but they were concerned in spreading knowledge of both the holy scriptures and classical texts. Marsilio Ficino attempted to combine platonic philosophy with Christianity. Erasmus raised Socrates to the level of the saints. He edited and translated the pre-Christian moral philosophers, the Fathers of the Church and the New Testament.

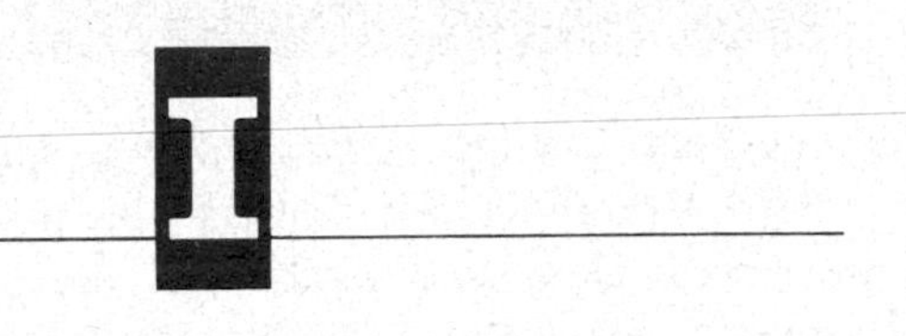

Isenheim Altar-piece by Matthias Grünewald

The *Crucifixion* is terrifyingly realistic. Half-dead, bruised, streaming with blood, contorted, Christ hangs pitifully from the Cross, which itself is distorted by the weight of his body. Around him is the dark night and a feeling of terror,

Matthias Grünewald
Hermits Antony and Paul in Converse
Isenheim Altar-piece
Unterlinden, Colmar

the world overthrown by a supernatural storm. Against this cataclysmic background, a haggard Mary Magdalen clasps her hands in despair, while in front of her St John the Baptist points his finger up at Christ and with the Holy Scriptures in his hand points to the fulfilment of the Old Testament prophecy. Opposite him is the Virgin Mary, her beauty strained by emotion, supported in the arms of St John the Evangelist, who is himself completely exhausted. However, this picture is not completely discouraging. In this lugubrious scene the cross stands out as a symbol of hope, a sign of great love and pity against the cloudy horizon which is so dark and empty that it foretells the coming dawn. This in fact leads to the *Resurrection*. The Saviour, with a halo painted in lively colours, arises transfigured, immaterial, his body dissolving in the fiery light. Shedding his fleshly body, the Son returns to God the Father. *The Virgin Adored by Angels* is delightful in the beauty of its colours and is extremely delicate in execution. Within the garden of the *Song of Solomon*, the Virgin Mary, surrounded by ordinary household objects, leans tenderly over the Child whom she holds in her arms. On the left-hand side in a rather strange sanctuary with Gothic arches, a host of angels play music to her on stringed instruments. The left volet depicts an *Annunciation* which, though violent, remains traditional in type.
In *The Temptation of St Antony*, a hallucinating troop of monsters, demons and unclean animals, including a bird of prey, a tortoise and a shark, harass the wretched saint, scratching him, biting him, and tearing him to pieces. On the other hand, *Hermits Antony and Paul in Converse* gives an impression of calm and freshness, while the figures themselves display that tranquillity of spirit that comes from great faith. They talk together of divine matters, while the crow that brings St Paul his food each day, warned of the arrival of a guest, bears a double portion in its beak. The peaceful landscape, which seems to be still wet with dew, is also full of beatitude. The *Entombment* on the predella reveals the same shocking realism as the *Crucifixion*. Dr Richier has remarked that in the body of Christ 'the attention to detail is pushed to the point of indicating small haloes of flame around the wounds'.

Johannes Secundus (Jan Evraerts) (1511-36)

Born in The Hague, died in Tournai. Jan Evraerts was the son of a jurist and early in life became fascinated by Latin studies. His father sent him to study law at Bourges under Alciati. He took his doctor's degree in 1533. On his return to Malines, where his family lived, he became secretary to the archbishop of Toledo, in order that he might have an opportunity of travelling. He was attached to the entourage of Charles V and joined the expedition against Tunis in

1534. However, the African climate affected his health and he had to return to his native land. He then took the post of secretary to Georges d'Egmont, bishop of Utrecht, who was living in Tournai. He died at the age of twenty-five of a disease that he had contracted in Tunis. Johannes Secundus, to use his Latin name by which he is best known, owes his celebrity to his Latin poems, the *Elegies, Epigrams and Odes*, but above all the *Basia* (*Kisses*), a collection of delightful and sensuous poems, many of which were imitated by Ronsard.

King's Chamber and Queen's Chamber at Fontainebleau

The decoration by Primaticcio consists of twenty pairs of terminals at the angles and on either side of the windows, with trophies between them suspended from a satyr's mask, and in four places children bearing coats of arms. The large pictures depict scenes from the *Siege of Troy*, and the small ones the fable of Proserpine. Shortly afterwards, Primaticcio painted the Queen's Chamber, of which there remains only the chimney-piece with its stucco work and a fresco representing the *Marriage of Venus and Adonis*.

Land of Cockaigne by Bruegel the Elder

This picture illustrates a Flemish folk-tale about Luilekkerland, a utopian land of lazy guzzlers. In the background one can see the hero struggling out of a hill of flour towards the promised land in which cacti have become biscuits. The picture is full of food, such as a roasted pig with a knife in its side ready for cutting it up, a roast chicken falling into a plate, a boiled egg running on a pair of legs, hedges of sausages, and flans covering the roof of a building. A tree supports a table loaded with delicious dishes, and beneath this three lazy guzzlers are snoring in their sleep—a noble armed from head to foot, a peasant lying on his flail, and a schoolboy who has cast aside his books.

Life of Christ and Legend of St Denis by Lambert Lombard

Of this group of panels, *Christ's Arrest*, *Christ before Pontius Pilate* and the *Ecce Homo* in the church of Saint-Denis were carried out by a follower of Lambert Lombard. Only *The Adoration of the Shepherds*, *The Last Communion of St Denis* (both in the church of Saint-Denis), the *Jewish Sacrifice* (Liège Museum) and *The Martyrdom of St Denis* can be considered definitely in the hand of Lombard himself. 'The plastic invention of these paintings,' Léo Van Puyvelde rightly remarks, 'is banal. The colours and the treatment do not rise above the ordinary standards of the German painters of the period, with this

Léonard Limosin
The Great Monsieur de Guise
Louvre, Paris

difference, that Lombard exaggerates the contrast of tones and accentuates the projected shadows. The costumes and the architectural constructions show that the painter was keen to display his archaeological knowledge, but it should be noted that he was not inspired only by the sculptures and monuments that he saw in Rome, but also by his studies of Romano-Gallic art, to which, as we know, he was passionately devoted.'

Limosin, Léonard (*ca* 1505-75)

Léonard Limosin was born in Limoges, the son of an innkeeper, François Limosin. It is agreed that he was a pupil of Nicole Pénicaud. Some art-historians believe that he came to Fontainebleau in 1527, though neither Rosso nor Primaticcio had settled there by that date. Limosin's earliest works as an enamellist show German influences. From 1530 onwards he was painter to the king and carried out a considerable amount of enamel-work for churches, including in 1532 eighteen plaques after Dürer's *Passion*.
In 1537 he enamelled a large number of cups and chess-boards (now in the Louvre), which are masterpieces of their kind. In 1541 he settled in Limoges with his brother, and he gained a considerable reputation. He made portraits of all the famous people of his day, including the queen, her children, and the king's mistress (*Story of Diane of Poitiers*). In 1545, the painter Michel Rochetel produced for him a series of drawings of the twelve apostles which he reproduced for the Château d'Anet. In 1548 he was appointed groom to the king. In 1551 he did an oil painting of *The Unbelief of St Thomas*. In 1558 Henry II commissioned him to execute forty-six plaques for the Sainte-Chapelle. At this time he also produced a *Nude with Fair Hair* and a *Goddess at the Table of the Gods*, and then a series of portraits of *Francis II*, *Marguerite de Valois* and the *Cardinal of Lorraine*. Intoxicated with success, he worked too fast and the quality of his work began to decline. Under Francis II he retained his position as groom of the bedchamber with its pension of eighty francs per annum. He was also a surveyor. In 1571 he was appointed a consul at the same time as the enameller Jean Pénicaud. Limosin's last enamels are dated 1574: they are not of the same quality as his earlier work. Limosin's output was considerable, and today 1,840 enamels are ascribed to him.

Lambert Lombard
Vision (detail)

Lombard, Lambert (1506-66)

Born and died in Liège. Lambert Lombard was the son of a butcher and was apprenticed to Jean Demeuse. Later, attracted by the work of Albrecht Dürer, he travelled in Germany. He completed his training under Mabuse, who was at this time living in Middelburg, and who introduced him to Italian art. On his return to Liège, Lombard entered the service of the prince-bishop, Evrard de la Marck, a humanist and patron of the arts. In 1537 his protector got him attached to the suite of Cardinal Reginald Pole, who had incurred Henry VIII's enmity as papal legate and was returning to Rome. Thus Lombard was able to visit Italy, where he stayed two years. It is assumed that he returned to Liège shortly after his protector's death in 1538. It is not easy to obtain a clear idea of the quality of Lombard's work, for a large amount of it disappeared during the sack of Bonn in 1703 and also during the French Revolution. He painted murals for the churches of St Peter and St Paul, but these soon disintegrated since the size that he used for the white background was not resistant to humidity. His surviving works consist basically of a few panels dispersed in the eighteenth century, which accompanied a large carved altar-piece in the church of Saint-Denis in Liège. Also attributed to him is what is considered as a self-portrait.

' **Lot and his Daughters** ' by Lucas Van Leyden

While one of his daughters is caressed by her father, the other fills a jug with wine. In the distance the sky reflects the flames from Sodom on fire. The Italian influence is to be noted in the strong contrast of the figures, the chiaroscuro suggesting night, and Lot's tent which is reminiscent of that in *Constantine's Dream*. But there is no lack of features recalling an earlier epoch—for example, the fantastic landscape and rocks, the fiery sky and the dull greyish colours are in the tradition of Hieronymus Bosch, while the still-lifes in the foreground foreshadow those of the next generation of Dutch painters.

Lucas Van Leyden (1494-1533)

Born and died in Leyden. Lucas was a pupil of his father, Hugo Jacobsz, a talented painter. Then in 1508 he was employed in the workshop of Cornelis Engebrechtsz, founder of the Leyden School and a transitional artist who was

Lucas Van Leyden
Portrait of Bartolo
Bibliothèque Nationale, Paris

already slightly influenced by the Italians. Lucas was an infant prodigy: Karel Van Mander states that he was already a remarkable engraver at the age of nine and that when he was twelve he astonished all the painters in Leyden by his masterly tempera painting of *The Story of St Hubert*. The lord of Lockhorst for whom he had painted this picture paid him twelve golden florins, one for each year of his life. In 1517, Lucas married Lysbeth Van Boschhuyzen, daughter of one of the noblest families in Leyden, who had borne him a daughter the previous year. His wife brought him a large fortune as dowry. Thereafter he lived a life of luxury and was fêted and praised wherever he went. In 1521 he travelled to Antwerp to meet Dürer, who was staying in the city, and the two painters admired each other's work. It was through Dürer's works that Lucas Van Leyden began to discover Italy. He stayed on in Antwerp until 1522, and then returned to work in Leyden. He left again in 1527, having bought and equipped a barge for travelling along the canals. At Middelburg he visited Mabuse. Lucas Van Leyden died at the age of thirty-nine.

Lucas was not only a great painter but also a great engraver. The majority of his pictures have disappeared. One of the earliest is probably *The Game of Chess. Susannah before the Judge* and *Potiphar's Wife Displaying Joseph's Clothes* date from 1511, as does *The Card Players.* His *Self-Portrait* comes a little later. The small picture of *Lot and his Daughters* is dated *ca* 1514. *The Last Judgement*, painted *ca* 1526, summarizes Lucas Van Leyden's studies. From the same period date *The Dance round the Golden Calf* (1525) and *Moses Striking Water from the Rock* (*ca* 1527). *The Healing of the Blind Man* (1531) is one of his last works.

Luther, Martin (1483-1546)

Born and died at Eisleben, Thüringen. Luther was born into a peasant family, and spent his childhood at Mansfeld. At the age of fourteen he was sent to the Latin school in Magdeburg, and then to that at Eisenach. He continued his studies at the university of Erfurt, and in 1505 received the degree of master of philosophy. In the same year he entered the Augustine monastery, and in 1507 he became a priest. He was disgusted by the morals at the papal court when he visited Rome between 1511 and 1512.
From 1507 to 1517 he lived the life of a mystic, and during this time he was able to build up his revolutionary brand of theology, based on his concept of Fallen Man, deprived of God, forever incapable of escaping from his self-made void, yet saved by the grace of God alone. In an attack on the inquisitor Tetzel in 1571, Luther condemned the sale of indul-

gences. He was hounded out and had to seek refuge at Wittenberg, where he sought and received the protection of Frederick, Elector of Saxony. Drawing the conclusions from his ideas, he proceeded to repudiate in turn the authority of the pope, the Church hierarchy, the celibacy of priests, monastic vows, the cult of the saints, the concept of purgatory, and the mass itself. He was excommunicated in 1521, and promptly burnt the papal bull in public in the main square of Wittenberg on 16th December. Summoned to appear before the Diet of Worms (1521), Luther attended but refused to submit and was put under the ban of the Empire. His protector, Frederick of Saxony, hid him for ten months in the castle of Wartburg, where he proceeded to write a number of pamphlets. Then, from 1522 to 1526, he travelled throughout Germany preaching the Reformation. In 1525 he married Catharine Bora. From 1526 to 1529, he set about organizing his own Church with the help of Melanchthon, the main author of the *Augsburg Confession* (1530).
The Peasants' Revolt endangered his work, but the League of Schmalkalde (1530) served to consolidate it. In 1534, the Anabaptists' revolt broke out, but it was suppressed. Luther spent his last years in developing his doctrines and countering the excesses and wrong interpretations that were placed on them.
Luther's main works are the *Letter to the German Nobles* (1520), *The Babylonian Captivity of the Church* (1520), *Against the Bull of Anti-Christ* (1520) and the *Exhortation to Peace* (1525). Luther's friends gathered together the master's words and jokes, which they published in 1566 as the *Table-Talk*. Luther was not only the founder of the Reformation, but also one of the leading writers of his day who did much to stabilize the German language, mainly through his celebrated translation of the *Bible*.

Mabuse (Jean Gossaert) (*ca* 1478-1533)

Born at Maubeuge, died in Antwerp. Jan Gossaert received the surname of Mabuse when he moved to the Flemish-speaking area, for this was how the name of his birthplace, Maubeuge, was pronounced in Ghent, Bruges and Antwerp. He was the son of a binder of the chapter of Sainte-Aldegonde in Maubeuge. The earliest mention of Mabuse is to be found in the records of the Painters' Guild in Antwerp, which report that a certain Jennyn Van Henegouwe (John of Hainault) became a master painter in 1503. This is none other than Mabuse himself. But it is only after he entered the service of Philip of Burgundy that Mabuse's life is at all clear to us. Philip, the illegitimate son of Philip the Good, was ' high admiral of the Sea of Zetland and Governor of Guldre and Zutphen '. In 1508 he went on an embassy to Julius II, taking with him a brilliant train of men of letters and artists, amongst whom was Mabuse. Philip was well received in Verona and

Florence. In Rome Julius II welcomed him, and offered him canvases and marble statues. Philip of Burgundy accepted only two statues, however, one of Julius Caesar and the other of the Emperor Hadrian. He made Mabuse paint the ancient monuments which he visited in Rome. In 1509 he returned to the Netherlands.

The dating of Mabuse's works has not yet been properly established. *The Adoration of the Magi* is an early work painted for the abbey of Grammont in about 1505. From the same period probably dates the excellent *Christ on the Mount of Olives*. The famous triptych in Palermo was painted during his stay in Rome. *St Luke Painting the Virgin* is a work that definitely shows the triumph of Italian influences. Now the main altarpiece in Prague Cathedral, it was originally commissioned for the chapel of the Painters' Guild in Malines, and was completed in 1515. Subsequently, Mabuse painted a number of very human *Virgins*. He then introduced mythological compositions into the painting of the Netherlands, as for example *Neptune and Amphitrite* (1516), *Hercules and Omphale* (1517), *Hercules and Antaeus* (1523), a series of *Adam and Eve*s, and a *Danae* dated 1527. He also painted portraits, including those of the *Chancellor Jean Carondelet* and of *The Children of Christian II of Denmark*.

Marcantonio, Raimondi (*ca* 1480-1527/1534)

Born at Argius near Bologna, died in Bologna. Marcantonio was a famous line engraver. He studied under Raibolini, who employed him on niello-work. By *Small Passion* and a copy of the beautiful print of *Adam and Eve*. These copies were sold as originals. The fraud gave rise to court proceedings, and Marcantonio was ordered by the Venetian tribunal to add his mark to that of the real author. In 1510, Marcantonio was in Florence where he engraved a plate of 1505 he had already engraved his famous plate of *Pyramus and Thisbe* and had travelled in Northern Italy, visiting in particular Venice. From 1508 to 1510 he lived in Venice, engraving Dürer's works. He made seventeen engravings of *The Life of the Virgin*, thirty-seven of the *Small Passion* and a copy of the beautiful print of *Adam and Eve*. These copies were sold as originals. The fraud gave rise to court proceedings, and Marcantonio was ordered by the Venetian tribunal to add his mark to that of the real author. In 1510, Marcantonio was in Florence where he engraved a plate of Michelangelo's *War of the Pisans*. He then moved on to Rome where, after making further imitations of Dürer's works, he found his real *métier* by working under Raphael. For eight or nine years he reproduced the latter's masterpieces and thereby revealed the full range of his talent. He set up a workshop where his pupils included Marco Dente da Rovina and Agostino di Musi. When Raphael died Marcantonio began to make engravings of Giulio Romano's work. The erotic engravings after Romano that he made to illustrate the sonnets of Aretino roused the wrath of Pope Clement VII, and he was imprisoned. On being released through the intercession of Hippolytus de Medici and of Bandinelli, he had a serious dispute with the latter concerning his engraving of the *Martyrdom of St Lawrence* after Baccio. The siege and sack of Rome in 1527 brought ruin to Marcantonio. He fled to Bologna and nothing further was heard of him. His prints were sold throughout Europe and played an important part in spreading the new aesthetic ideals of Italy.

Malvagna Triptych by Mabuse

The central panel shows a *Virgin and Child* which owes much to the ideas of Gérard David. The Virgin is surrounded by a canopy of sculptured and gilded wood like a stall in flamboyant Gothic style. Through three apertures one perceives a background consisting of a wooded landscape with buildings in a mixed Renaissance and Byzantine style. But the delightful little angels who are playing music round the Madonna's throne are really Italian ' putti ' inspired by the Venetians, perhaps by Bellini. As to *St Dorothea* and *St Catharine* on the volets, their costumes and their attractiveness recall the manner of the Renaissance saints.

Mannerism

This was an international art movement which occurred between classicism and the baroque. Jean Leymarie has defined it as follows: ' The death of Raphael in 1520 coincides with the beginning of a crisis on every level which threw Italy into confusion and shook the whole of Europe. Man attempted once again to define his role and position in a universe torn by the religious schism of the Reformation and by political conflicts, while at the same time the world was suddenly being enlarged by maritime discovery and scientific knowledge. That spontaneous unity of life and style, the confidence between artist and society, were broken. Separated from their content, the classical forms of the great masters were in a way turned back on themselves with refined frenzy, through exasperation and a dissociation of their constituent elements. The result is a composite, technically skilful art which has a strange attraction, as realist in detail as it is unreal in the whole, which reveals at once the unrest of the period and its sceptical detachment, its frantic nervousness, and its intellectual passion.' Imported from Italy, Mannerism spread rapidly across Europe to France and the Netherlands and even as far as Germany and Prague.

Mantegna, Andrea (1431-1506)

Born in Isola di Carturo near Padua, died in Mantua. Mantegna was early employed in the workshop of Squarcione. He came under the influence of the works executed in Venetia by Andrea del Castagno, Paolo Uccello and Donatello. In 1454 he married the daughter of Jacopo Bellini in Venice. Between 1454 and 1459 he was in charge of the painting of frescoes for the Ovetari chapel in the church of the Eremitani in Padua. From 1460 up to his death he lived at the court of Mantua. For Lodovico Gonzaga he

Nicolas Manuel Deutsch
Self-portrait
Museum, Berne

decorated the ' Camera degli Sposi ' in the castle at Mantua. In 1488 he went to Rome to decorate the chapel of the Belvedere for Innocent VIII. On returning to Mantua he painted the *Triumph of Caesar*, a series of nine pictures each nine feet square, originally intended for a theatre but now in Hampton Court Palace. At the end of his life he was commissioned by Isabella d'Este to paint the *Victorious Wisdom of the Vices* and *Parnassus*. Mantegna was also a collector of antiquities and a learned archaeologist, as well as being an engraver and sculptor. His influence on other painters was considerable, and one notices evidence of it in Memlinc, Gérard David, and above all Dürer.

Manuel Deutsch, Nicolas (*ca* 1485-1530)

A pupil of Mit der Neefie and of Hans Fries, the Swiss artist Manuel Deutsch must be included among those known as the ' painters of lansquenets ' on account of the paintings in which he shows German mercenaries of the period. He visited Italy on several occasions and was therefore well aware of the developments of the Renaissance. In fact, he fought with the Swiss troops in the Italian campaign. His most important works are *The Dance of Death, Death Embracing a Prostitute, The Judgement of Paris, Pyramus and Thisbe, The Beheading of John the Baptist* and *The Fight of the Giants.*

Master of Flora

The Master of Flora was a follower of Primaticcio, from whom he obtained his sense of graceful outline, but he has an even more refined feeling than his master for the harmony of the lines of the female body, which for him is a combination of extremely voluptuous arabesques. Among the works attributed to him are *The Triumph of Flora* in a private collection and the *Birth of Cupid* in the Metropolitan Museum, New York.

Melanchthon (Philipp Schwarzerd) (1497-1560)

Born in Bretten in the Palatinate, died at Wittenberg. Melanchthon was the great-nephew of the famous humanist philosopher Reuchlin, and himself became one of the leading spirits of the age. He entered the university of Heidelberg when he was twelve, took his bachelor's degree when he was fourteen and his master's degree at Tübingen in 1514. He then began to study theology. In 1518 he became professor of Greek at Wittenberg, and then a bachelor of theology in 1520, the year in which he

Quentin Metsys
Erasmus of Rotterdam
Palazzo Barberini, Rome

married. He was attracted by the personality and ideas of Luther, and accompanied him to the Leipzig Disputation. In 1521 he published his first Protestant work. In 1526 he was appointed professor of theology. Thereafter he stood by Luther in every way possible. In 1529 he attended the Colloquium of Marburg. He was mainly responsible for the *Augsburg Confession* and the *Apology for the Augsburg Confession.* In 1535 he took part in the Colloquium of Kassel and subsequently in all the great assemblies which led to the formation of the Lutheran church. After Luther's death, he became the leading figure of the Reformation, but, deprived of his master, he took a weak line on every great occasion and made concessions to the Catholics as well as to the Protestants themselves. These struggles embittered him and brought unhappiness to his last years.

Melanchthon was also a great humanist and was the founder of classical education among the Protestants of the sixteenth century. His *Greek Grammar* (1518), his *Rhetoric* (1519) and his *Dialectic* (1535) are major works. He edited and commented on a number of classical authors, including Cicero, Pliny the Younger, Plutarch and Tacitus.

Metsys, Quentin (ca 1466-1530)

Born at Louvain, but lived all his life in Antwerp. According to tradition, Metsys was the son of a smith and he himself was an expert metalworker and made the well in Antwerp. He became a painter because of a love affair—he fell in love with the daughter of the painter Van Tuylt, who would not let her marry anyone except a painter. So the smith left his forge, travelled in Germany and England and, thanks to his determination and his exceptional ability, became a reputable painter. His early works include *St Veronica's Veil*, *The Holy Face* and a *Madonna*. His earliest dated work is the *Legend of St Anne* or *The Genealogy of the Virgin*. Metsys' principal religious work is certainly the *Entombment* in Antwerp Museum (1508), a picture commissioned by the Cabinetmakers' Guild. Some of his work consists of sharp caricatures such as *The Courtesan*, *The Old Man and the Misers* and *The Banker and his Wife*. Metsys brings to an end the great period of Flemish primitive painting in Antwerp. During his last years he adopted the innovations of the Romanists.

' Misanthrope, The ' by Bruegel the Elder

The glass sphere surmounted by a cross, within which is a petty thief with a wicked grin on his face, represents the world. The thief is cutting the strings of the pessimistic old philosopher's purse, while the latter is lost in his meditations. Bruegel painted the following two lines in Gothic letters underneath:

Om dat de werelt is oes ongetru
Daer om gha ic in den ru.
(Because the world is so faithless
I am going into mourning.)

Moro, Antonio (or Mor Antonis, Antonio Van Dashorst) (*ca* 1517-*ca* 1576)

Antonio Moro
Cardinal Granvelle's Dwarf
Louvre, Paris

Born in Utrecht, died in Antwerp. Antonio Moro was the nephew of Van Scorel, to whom he became apprenticed. He then settled in Antwerp, where he became a master painter in 1547. He travelled to Italy and was working in Rome *ca* 1550. On the recommendation of Cardinal Granvelle, minister to Charles V and the painter's protector, the Emperor sent him to Lisbon to paint the royal family. From there he went on to Spain where he painted portraits of the leading figures at court. In 1554 he visited England in order to paint the portrait of *Mary Tudor* on the occasion of her marriage to Philip II of Spain. In 1555 he was once more in the Netherlands where he remained for the rest of his life, apart from one short visit to Spain. He resided in Utrecht but made regular visits to Brussels and Antwerp, where he was the favourite painter of the Duke of Alba. He died in Antwerp towards the end of 1576. Moro's earliest known work is dated 1544 and is a portrait of *The Two Canons of the Brotherhood of Jerusalem.* In 1549 he painted the portrait of *Cardinal Granvelle.* Moro's most successful works are his portraits of *William of Orange*, the *Duke of Alba*, *Maximilian II* and *Mary Tudor.* The Prado contains forty-six of his portraits. Towards the end of his life Moro turned from formal portraits to more personal ones of middle-class people, for example *The Musician Jean Lecoq*, *Jan Van Scorel* and *Hubert Goltzius.*

Neoplatonists

Among the Greek scholars who attended the Council of Florence convoked by Pope Eugenius IV in 1439 with the object

Lucas Cranach
Venus
Louvre, Paris

of reunion with the Greek Church, was Gemistus Plethon, a great admirer of the works of Plato. He was enthusiastically received in Florence by the Medicis. He succeeded in getting them to share his enthusiasm and he inspired Cosimo with the idea of founding an academy to revive the study of Platonic philosophy. While invoking Plato's name above all others, it seems that he was really inspired by the School of Alexandria, and he is in fact much nearer to Plotinus and Proclus than to Plato himself. Following his Alexandrian teachers, he took a deep interest in stoicism, whose moral philosophy he regarded as finer than that of the Christians. In his efforts to combine a number of doctrines in an eclectic type of mysticism, he attempted to form a synthesis of the doctrines of Plato and those of Zoroaster. The Platonic Academy in Florence counted among its members John Argyropoulos, another Greek scholar, and the Hellenists Angelo Poliziano and Cristoforo Landino. Cosimo wanted a trained exponent of Plato's philosophy, and eventually appointed Marsilio Ficino to the task, making him president of the academy. Ficino regarded Platonism and Christianity as mutually harmonious. Furthermore, he considered Plato to be a forerunner of Jesus Christ. From his professorial chair he recommended the faithful to read the works of Plato. He even tried to introduce passages from Plato's works into the services and prayers of the Church. The followers of Platonism were called by him ' brothers in Plato '. The concepts of the Neoplatonists in Florence, which affirm the pre-eminence of the human conscience and of innate ideas over the objective world, had a considerable influence on the art of the Cinquecento. These ideas were held by the majority of humanists throughout Europe, and Erasmus went so far as to suggest that Socrates should be ranked among the saints.

Nudes by Cranach

The rhythmical style, the sinuous outlines of these human bodies have suggested that Cranach was influenced by Botticelli, whose works he could easily have been familiar with through the large number of copies which circulated in his day. On the other hand, perhaps one should agree with Salomon Reinach that the painter borrowed this form of the female figure from wood-engravers, who themselves had taken it from the French ivory-carvers of the fourteenth century; or else take Louis Réau's point of view, that Cranach received his ideas from the miniaturists of the Danube region. We prefer to think that these goddesses and Biblical heroines with their deceptively innocent expression, sprang quite unconsciously from Cranach's own mind.

Bruegel the Elder
The Parable of the Blind
Capodimonte, Naples

'Parable of the Blind, The' by Bruegel the Elder

This picture is inspired by the words in the Gospel of St Matthew, xv, 14: 'If the blind lead the blind, both shall fall into the ditch'. Bruegel shows the poor creatures with their dull faces and vacant eyes turned to heaven, being driven along as it were by an invisible force towards their fatal destiny. The artist has admirably succeeded in rendering the increasing expressions of horror on their faces. As in *The Cripples*, nature, beautiful but indifferent, is contrasted with the tragic buffoonery of the scene. Bruegel certainly wished to depict the blindness of a century which lacked any sense of where it was going, and which was rushing through uncertainty and darkness towards its own destruction. But this painting also expresses more than anything else Bruegel's conception of the human situation.

Patenier, Joachim (*ca* 1485-1524)

Born either in Dinant or in Bouvines, on the other bank of the Meuse. Patenier became a member of the Painters' Guild in Antwerp in 1515.
He was married first to Françoise Buyst, and then in 1521 to Jeanne Noyts. Albrecht Dürer attended his second marriage. He greatly admired Patenier's work, and painted his portrait. Patenier probably died shortly before October 1524, for in that month his widow and children sold the house he had bought five years previously. Patenier was the first Flemish painter to give more importance in his works to the landscapes than to the figures peopling them. His religious pictures also served as a pretext for expressing an original attitude to nature. Although one finds Italian influences in his work, he kept close to the traditional style of the Netherlands from which his ideas sprang. He retained the concepts of composition, attention to detail and the speckled colours of the primitives. Among his principal works are *Landscape with the Flight into Egypt* (Antwerp), *St Jerome* (Louvre), *Repose during the Flight into Egypt* (Berlin), and *St Christopher Carrying the Infant Christ* (National Gallery).

Pilon, Germain (*ca* 1535-90)

Born and died in Paris. Germain Pilon was the son of a sculptor who taught him the sculptor's art. Later he became a person of importance at court. Early on, he worked with his father at the abbey of Solesme. From 1558 to 1559 he worked on the *Tomb of Francis I* in the abbey of Saint-Denis. He was then engaged to do the sculptures for the *Tomb of Henry II*

François Pourbus the Elder
Eleonora of Mantua
Pitti Gallery, Florence

in the same abbey, and worked on them from 1564 to 1583. In 1571 he was appointed official sculptor to Charles IX and, according to a document dated 1573, he became 'clerk and general manager of the art of engraving with regards to the coins of the realm'. Pilon also produced sculptures for the garden of the Palais de Fontainebleau. In 1585 he carved the *Tomb of Ludovico Birago* in the Val des Ecoliers. During this period he worked with Pierre Lescot on the decoration of the courtyard of the Louvre and completed his sculptures for the 'dial' of the Palais de Justice. He also did work for the Château d'Anet. In Mans Cathedral he carved the *Tomb of Guillaume Gaugey de Belley*. His impressive statue of *St Francis in Ecstasy* is in the church of St Francis in Paris.

Portraits by Jan Van Scorel

Among the remarkable portraits by Jan Van Scorel are that of *Agatha Van Schoonhoven*, the painter's mistress, who bore him six children; the *Portrait of a Schoolboy*, astonishing for its sensitive use of colour, a painting which reveals humanist interest (' Who is rich? He who is free of desire. Who is poor? The miser', says a Latin inscription, while through the transparent paper which he holds in his hand one can read in mirror writing, 'God gives all, and yet His riches never diminish'); the *Portrait of a Pilgrim*, which is thought to be a self-portrait; and *George Van Egmont*, before he became bishop of Utrecht, cold, and full of ecclesiastical unction.

Pourbus the Elder, François (1545-81)

Born in Bruges, died in Antwerp. François Pourbus was the son of Pieter Pourbus the Elder (1524-87). He belonged to a remarkable family of painters, though their styles were all very traditional. François Pourbus the Elder was the pupil of Frans Floris. He became a member of the Painters' Guild in Antwerp in 1569. A contemporary writer relates that when Pourbus went to Ghent on the eve of his departure for Italy, he fell in love with his master's daughter, Suzanne Floris, and decided not to go on. He married her in 1569, and she bore him one son. He contracted a second marriage in 1578 with Anna Mahieu. He was standard-bearer of the city guards, and it is said that he found the task so exhausting that it made him ill and he died. One of Pourbus' most important religious works is the altar-piece of the Viglius funerary chapel in St Bavo's, Ghent, showing *Christ among the Doctors* (1572). Like his father before him, Pourbus was mainly a portrait-painter. Examples of his por-

Primaticcio
Sitting Woman with Drapes
Louvre, Paris

traits include his *Viglius Ayta*, *The Marriage of the Painter Hoefnaegel* (1571), *Gilles de Schmidt* and *Jan Van Hembyse.*

Primaticcio, Francesco (1505-70)

Born in Bologna, died in Paris. Francesco Primaticcio came from a noble family, and was very early in life apprenticed to a painter. He first studied under Innocenzo da Immola, and then under Bagnacavallo, who belonged to the Roman School and was a follower of Raphael. At the age of twenty-one, Primaticcio moved to Mantua in order to work under Giulio Romano, whose style greatly influenced him. When the latter was engaged by Federigo Gonzaga to build and decorate the Tea Palace, Primaticcio was employed on painting and stucco-work, following Romano's designs. There are several examples of stucco-work from this series which can be definitely attributed to Primaticcio, and notably the frieze representing *The Triumph of the Emperor Sigismund.* In 1532, Francis I asked Giulio Romano to go to France and work for him, but he sent Primaticcio in his stead. On his arrival at Fontainebleau, Primaticcio found that Rosso had already been there a year. Primaticcio was employed on the decoration of the king's chamber, but all the work he did for it has since disappeared. Shortly afterwards he decorated the queen's chamber. In 1535 he painted two scenes from *The Story of Hercules* for the Golden Gate at the entrance to the château. Primaticcio worked with Rosso on the Pomona Pavilion in the gardens of Fontainebleau, as well as on the paintings

in the Canopy Pavilion. Vasari reports that the two painters hated each other, but this appears to be an exaggeration, though they were certainly rivals. In 1540 the king entrusted Primaticcio with a mission to Italy to collect ancient and modern works of art. He returned with one hundred and twenty-five statues and busts, and mouldings of such famous ancient sculptures as the *Laocoon* of the Tiber, the *Commodus Hercules* and the Cnidos *Venus*, of which bronze casts were made in France.
Rosso died during his absence abroad, and on his return in 1542, Primaticcio was made overseer of all the work being carried out at Fontainebleau. Francis I appointed him abbot of Saint-Martin and also made him general commissioner responsible for buildings and works of art. He first completed the gallery, which Rosso had not been able to finish, by painting a *Danae* and a *Semele*. He then decorated the bedchamber of the Duchesse d'Etampes. This series of paintings was based on the *Story of Alexander*. He then carried out considerable work

Rosso Fiorentino
Magical Scene
Musée de l'Ecole des Beaux-Arts, Paris

for the bathing apartments, the *Story of Jupiter and Callisto*, and for the Ulysses Gallery, which was destroyed in 1697. Here he depicted *The Story of Ulysses* in fifty-eight episodes, with the help of Niccolo dell'Abbate and other Italian artists. During the reign of Henry II, he undertook the decoration of the Ballroom. This consisted of a number of representations of Olympian gods and goddesses, but unfortunately this work has been ruined by later restoration, as is the case of everything else that Primaticcio did for Fontainebleau. He became a favourite of the Guises, and was employed on decorating buildings of the Grotto which Charles, Cardinal of Lorraine, had built at Meudon. In 1559 Catharine de Medici, who had become regent, put him in charge of the royal buildings in succession to Philibert Delorme. Thereafter, Primaticcio divided his time between architectural work and organizing the arrangement of sculptures.

Quesnel the Elder, François (1543-1619)

Born in Edinburgh, died in Paris. François Quesnel the Elder was the elder son and pupil of Pierre Quesnel, and the father of Augustin I. He was most successful as a portrait-painter. Portraits by him include the *Portrait of a Lady in her Bath*, the *Duc de La Force*, *Gabrielle d'Estrées* and the *Festivities of Henry III*. Work which we know from engravings includes *The Entry of Henry IV and Marie de Medici*, *The Coronation of Louis XIII*, *Henry IV on his Death-bed*, and the portraits of *Henry IV*, *Marie de Medici*, *Henriette de Balzac* and *Louise de Lorraine*.

Rosso, Giovanni Battista ('Rosso Fiorentino') (1494-1591)

Born in Florence, died at Fontainebleau. Nothing is known for certain about Rosso's early life. His first important work was the fresco of the *Assumption of the Virgin* in the Chiostro dei Voti in the Annunziata, which Andrea del Sarto had previously been commissioned to paint. The most important of his Florentine works is the *Descent from the Cross* in the Pinacoteca, Volterra, painted in 1521. Mention should also be made of *Moses Defending the Daughters of Jethro* (1523). In the same year the painter left for

Rome in order to study at first hand the works of Michelangelo. He led a dissipated life with a group of companions which included Benvenuto Cellini. Works of this period include two frescoes, *The Creation of Eve* and *Original Sin* in the Cesi chapel in Santa Maria della Pace, and a small easel-painting, *The Challenge of the Muses*. In 1527, when the troops of the Constable of Bourbon entered Rome, Rosso was taken prisoner by the Germans. He succeeded in fleeing and thereafter led a wandering life for a while. From this period dates a striking work, *The Lamentation of Christ*, which adorns the altar of the Orfanella in Borgo San Sepolcro. While staying with the poet Aretino in Venice in 1530, Rosso received an invitation from Francis I to go to Fontainebleau. He was welcomed by the king and entrusted with the stucco-work and paintings in the Francis I Gallery, where he did his most famous work. Besides his salary, the king gave him a canonry in the Sainte-Chapelle in Paris. The first work that Rosso painted in France was a *Leda* after Michelangelo. He also produced some easel-paintings, including a *Pietà* for the Constable of Montmorency.

'St Luke Painting the Virgin' by Martin Heemskerck

Among the unusual details which make this such a remarkable composition are the crystal sphere on which the Child is sitting; the allegorical figure, either an angel or the genius of painting, holding a torch in front of the Virgin; St Luke's Phrygian bonnet and pince-nez; the brightly coloured parrot; and the dedicatory letter stuck to the wall with wax. Donald King has written of this picture and other works such as the *Ecce Homo* (Ghent) and *Judas and Thamar* (Potsdam): ' While the artist strictly adheres to the Romanist style of Scorel, he tries to surpass it by means of dramatic lighting and plastic and trompe-l'œil effects which help to create an impression of surprise but do not succeed in hiding a certain spiritual emptiness which remains one of the characteristics of Heemskerck's painting.'

Sandart, Joachim von (1606-83)

Born in Frankfurt, died in Nuremberg. Joachim von Sandart was a German painter and writer descended from an old family from Artois. Early in life he began to devote himself to engraving. At Utrecht he became the pupil of the painter Gerhardt von Honthorst, who took him to England where he had been invited by Charles I. In 1627 he went to Italy where he visited Venice, Bologna and Florence, and then settled in Rome. Here he made numerous friends, including Poussin and Claude Lorrain. He acquired such a great reputation that Velasquez commissioned a picture from him on behalf of Philip IV, King of Spain, considering him one of the twelve most skilled painters in Rome. After staying seven years, Sandart returned to

Martin Schongauer
Male Bust
Lehman Collection, New York

Germany in 1635, while the country was being ravaged by the Thirty Years' War. Hardly had he arrived in Frankfurt, where he married, than the terrible conditions in Germany forced him to retire to Amsterdam. He married for a second time in Augsburg in 1672, and in 1673 he finally settled in Nuremberg. It was here that he published his various books for which he is more famous than for his mediocre paintings. The most important is the *Accademia dell'architettura, scoltura e pittura, oder Teutsche Academie der elden Bau, Bild und Malerey-Künste* (Nuremberg, 1675-9), which contains important information about the early German painters.

Schongauer, Martin (1440/1445-91)

Born probably at Augsburg, died at Breisach. Martin Schongauer was the son of a goldsmith from Bavaria who became a citizen of Colmar in 1445. It was here that the artist carried out all his important work. In 1472 he painted a *Virgin in the Rose-Garden* for the church of Saint-Martin. The Dominicans in Colmar then commissioned him to paint a *Passion* cycle for their new church. The sixteen pictures were actually painted by Schongauer's pupils from designs which he prepared himself. He also worked on the more delicate parts of the paintings. In 1466 he was invited to Isenheim to paint the volets to be placed on either side of a statue of the Madonna. It is Schongauer's engravings, however, that enable us to gain a just appreciation of his abilities. One hundred and sixty-three of these, consisting almost exclusively of religious and mystical subjects, have survived due to the large number of copies which were sold in France, Italy and Germany. These engravings had a considerable influence on Dürer and even Michelangelo took an interest in them. Schongauer's best-known pupil was Hans Burkmair, who worked in Germany. Dürer visited his three brothers in 1492, during his early travels.

Second School of Fontainebleau

The French artists and the Flemish Romanists who form the Second School of Fontainebleau naturally continued the traditions of Primaticcio and Niccolo dell'Abbate. They were also thoroughly familiar with the Roman artists and particularly Michelangelo, whose grand style and muscular treatment of anatomy they borrowed. They also strove to enliven the subjects of the earlier school by going beyond mythology and seeking inspiration from the epic poems of Ariosto and Tasso. The three leading figures of the Second School of Fontainebleau were Françaís Toussaint Dubreuil, Martin Fréminet and the Flemish painter Ambroise Dubois. The school had only a brief existence. Its art was transitional and prepared the ground for the French classicism of the following century.

Sfumato

This is an Italian term used to describe an extremely soft and delicate manner of painting which only vaguely distinguishes the outlines and form, but nevertheless gives the effect of objects as seen at a distance out of doors, already slightly obscured by the atmosphere. Leonardo da Vinci was the great protagonist of sfumato. In his *Treatise on Painting* he remarks: 'Apply your mind, while you are out for a stroll, to studying the faces of men and women in the evening in poor weather. What gracefulness and sweetness one can see in them! In fact, dusk, with its grey shadows, softens the face and gives it soul, just as it softens the soul and inclines it to tender and melancholy thoughts.'

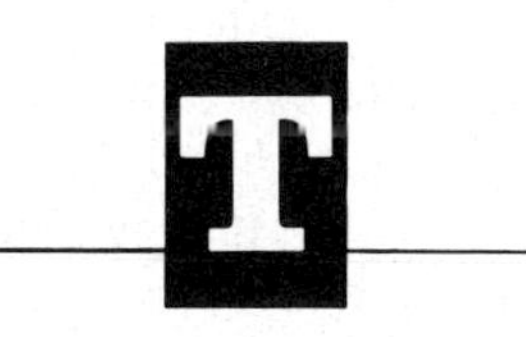

Tapestries by Jean Cousin the Elder

The tapestries which were woven after cartoons by Jean Cousin included those for Langres Cathedral. They depicted *The Life of St Mamas*. There are still three panels from the series in existence: *St Mamas Preaching the Gospel to the Wild Beasts*, *The Saint Followed by a Lion Coming before the Tribunal of the Governor of Cappadocia*, and *The Martyrdom of the Saint who is Burnt in an Oven.*

Theoretical Works of Jean Cousin the Elder

In his *Book of Perspective* (1560), Jean Cousin shows himself to have been a great mathematician. In his *Book of Portraiture* (1571), which was edited by his son and appeared only after his death, he demonstrates the techniques of drawing in perfect proportion with his own examples based on antique statues. The book also contains an account of the bones and muscles of the body and instructions for depicting the human figure in different positions. This work, which codified the new artistic ideas of Italy, had an enormous influence and popularized among artists the style of painting small heads on long slender bodies, an anatomical concept which, in the last third of the sixteenth century, became one of the basic themes of drawing lessons.

Thomassin, Philippe (1526-1622)

Born in Troyes, died in Rome, Philippe Thomassin was a pupil of Cornelis Cort in Rome, where he went and settled at the age of twenty-two. He also married in Rome. Among his pupils were Callot and Nicolas Cochin. His work includes some

Antoine Caron
Triumph of Spring (detail)
Musée des Beaux-Arts, Nancy

200 engravings, of which 52 depict ancient statues.

Triptych of the Almoners' Chapel in Antwerp by Bernard Van Orley

The central panel shows, in the foreground, some of the ' masters of the poor ' of the City of Antwerp burying those who have died destitute—one of the charitable works that they dedicated themselves to. Round about the Last Judgement is taking place. Here, Romanist concepts are clearly in evidence and are fully assimilated. The influence of Michelangelo is apparent even in the figure of the Lord meting out justice. Furthermore, the artist has attempted a novel treatment of an old theme by showing an immense crowd of people advancing across the horizon. According to Van Mander, the painter first gilded the entire panel before painting on it so that the colours would be brighter and more durable, and the sky more transparent. In fact, the tones of the picture are particularly strong and clear.

Triumphs of Antoine Caron

The *Triumph of Summer* shows Apollo, the sun god, followed by Diana with three companions, and behind her Ceres. These goddesses skipping along personify the pleasures (hunting) and work (harvesting) that fall to man during the summer. Thereafter comes the triumphal chariot bearing the charming young woman who represents the season. The chariot itself is drawn by two eagles and

the charioteer is Cupid. In the middle distance there is a landscape of copses with a lake dotted with little islands of flowers. On the lake itself, to the sound of musical instruments, a water-tournament is taking place—one of those entertainments which were laid on for court celebrations. In the sky Jupiter is flying on an eagle's back, while the three signs of the zodiac, Cancer, Leo and Virgo, again indicate that it is the summer season. *The Triumph of Winter*, which is a companion piece, is set among vast buildings covered with snow, which in many respects recall those of the Château de Fontainebleau. The mythological procession advances towards a round temple based on a design of Bramante's. In the lead is Janus, the two-faced god, who holds the key to the temple in his hand. Apollo follows him, dancing and playing the viol, a typical instrument of Renaissance concerts. Then comes Mercury, who bears on his back the tortoise-shell from which he made the seven-stringed lyre, the symbol of ancient music. Then come Minerva, three smiths with their hammers on their shoulders accompanying Vulcan, who holds a pair of pincers and a thunderbolt, and an elderly man carrying a large round vase from which smoke is pouring and who doubtless personifies cold old age. At the last comes the chariot drawn by herons, bearing along a majestic and hoary old Winter on a throne. A fleet of boats on a lake takes part in a snowball fight against a group standing on a pier—again one of the traditional entertainments that were given at Fontainebleau. 'This picture,' writes J. Ehrmann, 'summarizes the symbolism of music, architecture, painting and poetry under the domination of Minerva, patron of the arts, who personifies royalty. In these festivities there was also a religious allusion, for Catharine de Medici was in the way of making Catholic and Protestant lords fraternize in allegorical mascarades or in the opposing sides of a tourney, joust, or attack on a fortress.'

Uccello, Paolo (1397-1475)

Born and died in Florence. Paolo Uccello was apprenticed to Lorenzo Ghiberti, and worked under him on the famous bronze doors of the Baptistery. While Manetti taught him geometry, Ghiberti taught him painting. He worked in Florence, Padua and Urbino. His surname Uccello, he earned on account of his love of birds.

In 1436 Uccello painted the colossal equestrian portrait of the soldier and adventurer, *Sir John Hawkwood,* in Florence Cathedral. This is his earliest work of importance. He also painted a fresco cycle of *Scenes from Monastic Legends* in San Miniato del Monte. In 1445 he painted the fresco of *The Flood* in the Chiostro Verde of Santa Maria Novella. A few years later he produced his masterpiece, *The Rout of San Romano.* At the age of seventy-one he executed *The Profanation of the Host* for the church of Corpus Domini. His last work, *A Hunt,* is in the Ashmolean Museum, Oxford. Many of his easel-paintings have disappeared. According to Vasari, he was miserable in his old age. He was without money and his wife was sick. His friends watched him going on painting in a manner that they considered denied him the success that he deserved. 'Your perspective,' Donatello told him, 'makes you leave the certain for the uncertain. What will that lead to?' Indeed, Uccello continued to make studies of perspective. If he did not invent perspective, at least he extended the revolution that made space itself a subject of painting. He handed down to posterity an example of the technical mastery of this field.

Ulysses Gallery

For this Gallery, Primaticcio used ceiling figures after the manner of Correggio. The vaulted ceiling was covered with various arabesques of the kind that had been the fashion in Italy ever since the frescoes in the Thermae of Titus in Rome had been rediscovered. On the walls were depicted *The Adventures of Ulysses.*

Van Hemessen, Jan (*ca* 1504-before 1566)

Born in Hemixem, near Antwerp, died in Haarlem. Jan Van Hemissen, whose real name was Jan Sanders, was apprenticed to Henry Van Cleve. In 1523 he became a master painter in Antwerp. He signed his paintings ' Hemessen ', a corruption of the name of his birthplace. In 1531 he paid a brief visit to Florence. In 1548 he became dean of the Painters' Guild in Antwerp. A reversal of fortune obliged him to sell his house and, according to Van Mander, he moved to Haarlem. He was known as ' the Dutch Raphael '. One of his earliest works is *The Prodigal Son,* dated 1536. Other works include *The Calling of St Matthew* (1536), *Ecce Homo*, *Dissolute Company* and, in a different genre, a *St Jerome* as well as the important *Last Judgement* in the church of St James in Antwerp. *The Cure of Folly* is more popular in content. One of Hemessen's last works is *Tobias Healing his Father.*

Van Mander, Karel (1548-1606)

Born at Meulebeke, died in Amsterdam, Karel Van Mander was a Flemish painter and writer who was born into a rich family and received an excellent education. He spent much of his time writing poetry and drawing. He went to live with Lucas Van Herre, who was himself both a poet and a painter, and under his tuition Van Mander made great progress in both arts. He then spent a year in Pieter Vlerick's workshop. On his return to Meulebeke in 1569 he wrote six or seven plays which were performed with success, and for which he painted the scenery himself. In 1574 he left for Rome where he stayed for three years. On the journey back to his homeland he passed through Vienna, where he turned down the offer of employment in the emperor's service. On account of the unsettled times in his own country, he was forced to go abroad. He moved to Holland, where he settled in Haarlem in 1583. Here, with Hubert Goltzius and Cornelis, he founded an academy which introduced the latest Italian ideas. In 1604 he settled in Amsterdam, where he died two years later through the ignorance of a physician who turned a bout of sickness into a fatal disease. He was a representative of Mannerism. He left a number of good pictures including *The Annunciation* in Haarlem and *The Martyrdom of St Catharine* in Saint-Martin de Courtrai. But he is best known for his work *The Lives of the Most Celebrated Modern Painters*, completed in 1604, which contains important information about the painters of the Netherlands.

Van Orley, Bernard (*ca* 1488-1542)

Born and died in Brussels. Bernard Van Orley was probably born in 1488, offspring of the first marriage of his father, Valentyn, who belonged to the noble family of Van Orley. Bernard was taught painting by his father. According to one tradition, he travelled in Italy and even became a pupil of Raphael. He first visited Rome in 1509, at about the same time as Raphael arrived in the Holy City. From this moment, apparently, Van Orley attached himself to Raphael, but this has never been proved. A document dated 1602 records that ' Bernard twice visited Rome and he learnt painting from Raphael of Urbino '. It is generally agreed, however, that in 1516 Van Orley was appointed to supervise the manufacture in Brussels of Raphael's tapestries illustrating *The Acts of the Apostles* which Leo X had commissioned for the Sistine Chapel. One of the artist's earliest works is probably the *Altar-piece of the Apostles Thomas and Matthew*, painted for the Carpenters' Chapel in Brussels. In the *Triptych of the Manneton Family*, which dates from the years 1508-12, very strong Italian influences are already to be seen. In 1518 Van Orley was appointed court painter to Margaret of Austria, governor-general of the Netherlands. He was paid one sou per day, but he also received large sums for each of the pictures commissioned from him. In 1524 he received payment for eight portraits of the sovereign which he had painted. From this period dates one of his finest portraits, that of his friend *Dr George Zelle*, physician to Charles V. In 1521 Margaret of Austria commissioned him to paint a triptych known as *The Virtue of Patience*, as a gift to Antoine de Lalaing, one of her ministers. In 1525 Van Orley completed a large triptych, *The Works of Mercy*, for the chapel of the Almoners or Masters of the Poor of the City of Antwerp. Towards the end of his life Van Orley was running a large workshop where a number of assistants worked to his orders. This workshop produced a great many high-warp tapestries and also stained-glass work. For the collegiate church of St Michael and St Gudula he executed some remarkable stained-glass windows.

Bernard Van Orley married first Anne Seghers, and then again in 1539, shortly after her death, Catharine Hellinck. He had nine children, five of them boys, who all became painters. Van Orley's pupils included Michiel Coxie, Pieter Coeck, Van Aelst or Aolst, and Arnould Van der Bruggen. He died, laden with honours, at the age of fifty-four.

Van Reymerswaele, Marinus (*ca* 1493-after 1567)

Born in Zeeland, Marinus Van Reymerswaele came of a family of painters. He was first taught by his father, Nicholas Van Zierickzee. By 1509 he was ap-

Marinus Van Reymerswaele
St Jerome in his Study
Museum, Douai

prenticed to the painter and worker in stained glass Simon Van Daele of Antwerp. Some think that he then worked for Quentin Metsys, but this is unlikely for the name Van Reymerswaele is not to be found in the Guild's records. However, Metsys certainly inspired his early works, notably *St Jerome in his Study*, dated 1521. In particular, Van Reymerswaele never tired of repeating numerous versions of the theme of tax-gatherers and money-changers which Metsys had treated back in 1514. Van Reymerswaele joined in the excesses of the iconoclasts, and on 25th June 1567, he was sentenced at Middelburg to do public penance, that is to say, to take his place in a procession wearing only a shirt and bearing a candle. Thereafter he was to be banished from the town for six years for having participated in the destruction of the pictures in the Westmunsterkerk the previous month. On account of his age, this part of the sentence was not carried out. This is the last mention there is of his name.

Van Scorel, Jan (1495-1562)

Born at Alkmaar, died in Utrecht. Jan Van Scorel was the natural child of the priest in the village where he was born. He was orphaned early in life, but was sent by wealthy friends of his father to the school in Alkmaar where he remained until his fourteenth year, thus getting a firm grounding in Latin. As he showed an interest in drawing, his protectors then apprenticed him to William Cornelisz, a painter who lived in Haarlem. Three years later he moved to Amsterdam and joined the workshop of Jacob Cornelisz, who employed him as an assistant. In 1517 Van Scorel decided to travel abroad in order to visit the leading artists of his day and study their works. First he went to see Mabuse in Utrecht, and then set out for Nuremberg in order to study under Dürer. From there he went on to Venice, where he joined a group of pilgrims who were being taken on a visit to the Holy Land by a Dutch priest. He reached Jerusalem after visiting the islands of Crete and Cyprus. In 1520 he was in Rhodes, and on his way home he visited Italy. He arrived in Rome during the pontificate of Hadrian VI, but when the latter died a few months later he had to return to the Netherlands, passing this time through France. While in Italy he studied both ancient art and the art of the Renaissance. On his return, Van Scorel finally settled down in Utrecht, where he opened a workshop. He had a number of pupils to whom he taught the new ideas which he had picked up on his travels. In 1528 he was appointed canon of the church of St Mary. He died in 1562, at the age of sixty-seven.

Jan Van Scorel was not only a painter but also a musician, poet and Latin scholar. He loved good company and was a friend of the humanists, especially the writer of Latin poetry, Johannes Secundus. He behaved like a dilettante and expert patron of the arts, and he always refused to become a member of any Guild. Francis I tried to win him over and offered him the post of royal painter, but Van Scorel refused this honour and all the benefits that went with it. In 1550 he was employed together with Lancelot Blondeel on restoring the altar-piece of *The Adoration of the Lamb* by the Van Eyck brothers.
Jan Van Scorel's earliest known work is a triptych painted in 1520 for Count Frangipani. On his return from his travels he painted a number of different pictures for Herman Van Lochorst. In 1525 and 1526 he painted the *Members of the Brotherhood of Jerusalem in Utrecht*. Mention should also be made of the *Baptism of Christ*, the *Presentation in the Temple* and *The Good Samaritan*. His last works include an unfinished *Bathsheba*, *The Queen of Sheba's Visit to King Solomon*, and above all a famous *Mary Magdalen*. Van Scorel also painted portraits, including those of *Agata Van Schoonhoven*, his mistress, who bore him six children, *The Schoolboy*, *The Pilgrim* and *George Van Edmont*, who subsequently became bishop of Utrecht.

Van Veen, Otto (called Vaenius) (1558-1629)

Born in Leyden, died in Brussels. Otto Van Veen came from a noble family and was a descendant of a bastard son of John III of Brabant. In 1572 he visited Antwerp, Aix and Liège in the company of his father Cornelis Van Veen, a supporter of Philip II who had had to flee before the successes of the Prince of Orange. Otto Van Veen was a pupil of D. Lampsonius and Jean Romey. Later, in 1576, he went to Italy where he worked with Zucchero for five years. On his return to Liège after completing a mission to Rudolf II in Vienna, he was appointed page to the archbishop Ernest of Bavaria. In 1584 he returned to Leyden. In 1585 Van Veen became court painter to Alessandro Farnese, governor of the Spanish Netherlands, and went to live in Brussels. On Alessandro's death in 1592 he moved to Antwerp where he was registered as a master painter in the following year. He married Maria Loets, became dean of the guild in 1602, and subsequently court painter to Albert and Isabella. In 1612 Van Veen was appointed inspector of the mint. Among his pupils he was able to count Rubens, and this is his greatest claim to fame. He was a humanist and a man of letters who published several works, some of which are illustrated with engravings after his own drawings by his brother Gysbert, in particular the *History of the War of the Batavians* after Tacitus, *Emblems and Observations* after Horace and *Emblems of Divine Love and Profane Love*. Among his best-known paintings are *The Marriage of St Catharine*, *The Calling of St Matthew*, *Zachariah in the Fig-tree* and a series of six pictures showing *The Triumph of the Catholic Religion*.

Vos, Martin de (1532-1603)

Born and died in Antwerp. Martin de Vos was the son of the painter Pieter de Vos, and then became one of the finest pupils of Frans Floris. He went to Rome in about 1551. Subsequently he worked for a while in Venice for Tintoretto, who employed him to paint background landscapes for his pictures. The study of the Italian painters completed his training. On his return to Antwerp he was considered a painter of the first rank. He received many commissions, especially from the Medicis, for portraits and historical works. He became a member of the Painters' Guild in Antwerp in 1558, and was elected dean in 1572.
He was commissioned to paint a number of altar-pieces for the churches of Antwerp and throughout the Netherlands, but most of his works were destroyed during the wars of religion. His best-known works include the *Incredulity of St Thomas* and *Caesar's Tribute*. He also painted portraits of sturdy Flemish types, such as the *Hoffman Couple* and the *Anselm Family*.

'**View of the Region of the Danube**' by Albrecht Altdorfer

'Dürer' says Louis Réau, 'had already painted landscapes which were just as detailed and delicate among his wonderful water-colours, excellent examples of which are to be found in the Cabinet des Dessins in the Louvre; but these water-colours hastily painted were only travel sketches or studies. Never before has anyone painted an actual picture in which nature itself was the only subject. That is why this humble painting by Altdorfer marks a decisive stage in the history of the landscape.'

Wolgemut, Michael (1434-1519)

Born and died in Nuremberg. Michael Wolgemut was the pupil and assistant of Hans Pleydenwurff, whose widow he married. He appears to have held an important position in Nuremberg, where he was considered the greatest painter of his day. His masterpiece is an altar-piece painted in 1479 for the church of Our Lady in Zwickau. Albrecht Dürer was his pupil from 1486 to 1490. As a reward for decorating the Town Hall of Goslav, he was made a citizen of the town in 1501. Wolgemut was also a wood engraver, and made engravings in collaboration with his stepson. He illustrated two works which appeared between 1491 and 1494, the more famous of which is Schedel's *Universal Chronicle* (sometimes known as the *Nuremberg Chronicle*), for which he made 650 plates.
His paintings include *Scenes from the Passion*, painted for the parish church of Crailsheim; an altar-piece executed in 1480-5; the *Lamentation over Christ's Body* for the church of St Lawrence; *St Wolfgang*, *St Erhard* and a third bishop (1464); *The Massacre of St*

Gregory (1473); and a *Christ, Christ on the Cross, Virgin Mary, St John and a Donor* and *The Virgin with Apostles* in the church of Schwabach (completed in 1508).

Wood Engravings by Jean Cousin the Elder

Contemporary works which Jean Cousin illustrated with engravings include *Customs of the Bailliage of Sens and its Ancient Provinces*, printed by Gilles de Richeboys in 1556; *The Holometer*, 1555; and the so-called Jean Leclerc *Bible* of 1596. The famous wood engravings in the French edition of the *Dream of Poliphilus* published by Jacques Kerver in 1554 are also ascribed to him. Among the many beautiful individual prints which came from his hand, the most remarkable are those of *The Annunciation, The Descent from the Cross* and the *Holy Family*, the last bearing the artist's initials, I + C, and dated 1544.

Bibliography

Baldass, Ludwig: *Hieronymus Bosch*, London, n.d.

Beets, N.: *Lucas de Leyde*, Brussels and Paris, 1913.

Béguin, S.: *L'Ecole de Fontainebleau*, Paris, 1963.

Brion, Marcel: *Bruegel*, Paris, 1936.

Brion, Marcel: *Dürer*, London, n.d.

Combe, Jacques: *Hieronymus Bosch*, London, [1947].

Dimier, L.: *Le Primatice*, Paris, 1928.

Dimier, L.: *La Peinture française au XVIe siècle*, Marseilles, 1942.

Ehrmann, J.: *Antoine Caron, Peintre à la Cour des Valois*, Geneva, 1955.

Fierens, P.: *Pierre Bruegel, sa vie, son temps*, Paris, 1949.

Fourreau, A.: *Les Clouet*, Paris, 1929.

Genaille, R.: *Bruegel l'Ancien*, Paris, 1953.

Goldschneider, L.: *Leonardo da Vinci: Paintings and Drawings*, London, 1943.

Gossart, M.: *Jean Gossart de Maubeuge*, Lille, 1902.

Grossman, F.: *The Paintings of Bruegel*, London, [1955].

Haendeke: *Nikolaus Manuel Deutsch als Künstler*, Frauenfeld, 1889.

Hauser, Arnold, *Mannerism*, London, 1965.

Hoogewerff, G. J.: *Jean Van Scorel*, The Hague, 1923.

Huysman, J. K.: *Trois Eglises et Trois Primitifs*, Paris, 1908.

Knappe, Karl Adolf: *Dürer's Graphic Work*, London.

Kusenberg, K.: *Le Rosso*, Paris, 1931.

Lavalleyle, J.: *et al.: Bernard Van Orley*, Brussels, 1943.

Leroy, A.: *Hans Holbein et son Temps*, Paris, 1943.

Leymarie, Jean: *Hieronymus Bosch*, London, 1946.

Lilienfein, H.: *Lukas Cranach und seine Zeit*, Leipzig, 1942.

Major: *Urs Graf*, Strasbourg.

Marlier, G.: *Anthonis Mor Van Dashorst*, Brussels, 1934.

Moore, T. Sturge: *Altdorfer*, London, 1900.

Moore, T. Sturge: *Albert Dürer*, London, 1905.

Ninane, L.: *Van Hemessen*, Acts of the Congress of the History of Art, London, 1939.

Panofsky, Erwin: *The Life and Art of Albrecht Dürer*, Princeton, 1955.

Parker, K. T.: *Holbein: Selected Drawings at Windsor*, London.

Pevsner, Nikolaus, and Michael Meier: *Grünewald*, London.

Preibisz, L.: *Maerten Van Heemskerk*, Leipzig, 1911.

Schmid, H. A.: *Hans Holbein der Jüngere*, Basle, 1948.

Sievers, J.: *Pieter Aertsen*, Leipzig, 1906.

Terey, G. von: *Die Gemälde Hans Baldungs*, Strasbourg, 1896-1900.

Tolnay, Charles de: *Pierre Bruegel l'Ancien*, Brussels, 1935.

Venturi, Lionello: *The Sixteenth Century: From Leonardo to El Greco*, London, [1956].

Voss, H.: *Der Ursprung des Donaustils*, Leipzig, 1907.

Wölfflin, H.: *Die Kunst Albrecht Dürers*, 5th edn. Berlin, 1926.

Zervos, C.: *Les Nus de Lucas Cranach*, Paris, 1950.

List of Illustrations

Dictionary